The Digital Filmmaking Handbook
Presents

MASTERING SCREENWRITING

From Shorts to Features

Donald H. Hewitt

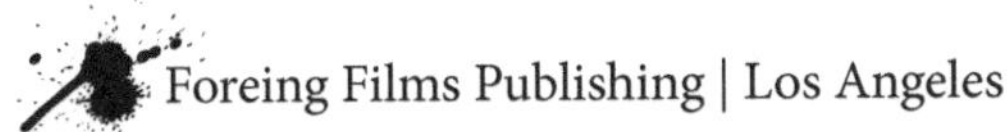
Foreing Films Publishing | Los Angeles

The Digital Filmmaking Handbook Presents (series)
Mastering Screenwriting: From Shorts to Features
Donald H. Hewitt

Foreing Films Publishing

General Manager: Rainer Plain

Project Editor: Sonja Schenk

Copy Editor: Ben Long and Sonja Schenk

Illustrator: Jianling Horton

Interior Layout Tech: FF Inc.

Library of Congress Control Number: 2024942252
ISBN-13: 978-1-7331502-4-8
ISSN 2690-0424

Foreing Films Publishing 3232 E Willow Street Signal Hill CA 90755 USA

For product information and technology assistance, contact us at:
publisher@thedigitalfilmmakinghandbook.com

For permission to use material from this text or product, submit all requests via email to publisher@thedigitalfilmmakinghandbook.com

Visit our website at **thedigitalfilmmakinghandbook.com**
and **foreingfilmspublishing.com**

Acknowledgements

To write a book like this takes a lifetime. A lifetime of watching a ridiculous number of movies and TV shows. A lifetime of struggling to write exciting, dynamic stories with intriguing, engaging characters. A lifetime of teaching screenwriting to students all over the world.

I would like to thank my former writing partner, Cindy Davis. So much of my screenwriting acumen was honed during the long hours of discussing our stories. The years we spent working together formed the foundation of my screenwriting knowledge.

I would like to thank all my talented students: their inventive writing challenges me to see story and character in a new light. I also had several wonderful students who directly helped me with this book, Martin Molpeceres, Boson Wang, and Scott Gilman from USC School of Cinematic Arts as well as Aprajita Agnihotri, an international student.

I would like to thank Mina Majstorovic, whose positive energy and undying belief in me has opened up a world of opportunities.

I would like to thank my daughter Hayley, who inspires me, puts up with me, and regularly watches movies and TV shows with me.

I especially want to thank Sonja Schenk. Our friendship started when we took our first filmmaking class together at UCSD. From bumping into each other at college parties, to working as the editor of her feature film, *The Olivia Experiment*, to this book, I consider myself lucky to know someone as incredibly smart and talented as Sonja. Her amazing work on this book continues to prove how insightful and knowledgeable she is.

About the Author

Donald H. Hewitt is a working screenwriter with over twenty-four years of experience. He is a member of the Writers Guild of America and teaches screenwriting at USC School of Cinematic Arts and UCLA Extension. His feature film credits include the English-language screenplay for the Oscar-winning film *Spirited Away*, as well as *My Neighbor Totoro*, and the Oscar-nominated *Howl's Moving Castle*. Mr. Hewitt has written for Pixar Animation Studios, Working Title Films, Miramax Films, New Line Cinema, ABC Family, Disney, Riot Games, and Fox Animation Studios. He has also had the privilege of working with some of the top producers in the industry: David Heyman, John Lasseter, Peter Chernin, Kathleen Kennedy, Frank Marshall, Eric Fellner, Tim Bevan, Viola Davis, Charles Roven, and Alex Gartner. He is currently writing the upcoming Afro-anime feature *Mfinda*.

About the Series

Mastering Screenwriting: From Shorts to Features by Donald H. Hewitt is part of the single-topic, companion-book series, *The Digital Filmmaking Handbook Presents*.

This series picks up where *The Digital Filmmaking Handbook* leaves off, tackling each topic exclusively, and as always, from the perspective of working filmmakers.

The Digital Filmmaking Handbook, 7th Ed by Ben Long & Sonja Schenk

Mastering Screenwriting: From Shorts to Features by Donald H. Hewitt

I Got You Covered by Beverly Neufeld

Premiere Pro for Filmmakers by Sonja Schenk

Table of Contents

4 Basic Story Structure   47

5 Character   65

6 Getting the Audience to Care   83

7 Character-Based Structure   91

9 Screenplay Format   119

10 Scenes   129

Introduction

Do not wait until the conditions are perfect to begin. Beginning makes the conditions perfect.

—Alan Cohen

Fade In: Becoming a Screenwriter

Screenwriting is a highly stylized form of storytelling. It has evolved over thousands of years, beginning with the Greeks and their theatrical plays. But development of the craft has accelerated over the last century as the business of film and television has grown. Now, even writers not needing to write in screenplay format use screenplay story structure and character development practices because they have been proven to yield results that audiences love. From novels to video games to reality television, people want a well-told story with compelling characters and screenplay methodology delivers that.

This book will give you a step-by-step process for writing a short screenplay. A process that also applies to writing a feature film. But wait! It will also apply to writing web series and TV pilots, whether you're crafting a sitcom, a drama, or a dramedy. But wait! These methods apply to almost any creative writing, even short stories and novels.

Embrace the Process

The only way to truly learn how to write is to do it—write. All the information in this book is necessary but you won't really *understand* it until you try to use it to write a screenplay. When you stare at the blank page (and it stares back, mocking you), you need a set of tools to approach story writing—a process.

Have you ever woken up from a dream and it felt like you had an amazing experience, but when you try to explain it to another person it falls flat— they just don't seem to understand how amazing it was? Or has someone tried to tell you their dream and it just sounds like a bunch of weird stuff?

Story ideas, when they are in your head, often seem amazing, like a complete vision. But when you begin to write them down, you will always find that there are holes, that the story is not complete.

To write a great story you must understand the whole story but to understand the whole story you need to write it down. Catch-22. Therefore, you must start writing with partial knowledge—there's no way to know everything. You have to keep working, believing in yourself and in your story. But great screenwriting requires more than perseverance and confidence. The key to successful writing is having a process to follow with clear steps and specific tools. Without the process and without the tools, you might get lucky once or even twice but it's more likely that you'll run into serious challenges.

That's what this book will give you: The process to work through writing a story.

Get Comfortable with Being Uncomfortable

At some point almost every writer hates the story they are working on. It's inevitable. The thrill of discovering a great new story gets replaced by the grind of trying to fix the problems, and there are *always* problems. The only way to solve story troubles is to work on them. There is no magic, just hard work. The writers that I know that are the most successful are not the most talented. They are the hardest working, and they have a complete set of tools. They know how to attack the story problems when they come up. They don't allow themselves to get discouraged, they just keep working, because that's the job.

To be great at writing, you must understand the entire screenwriting process (or at least a good portion of it), but you also must write to understand the different concepts that make up that process. So, you must write for a long time, each step of the way, without understanding a lot of what you are doing. This can be uncomfortable. The good news is, the more you write, the more you will understand about the act of writing.

How This Book Can Help

This book is designed to provide you with a practical guide. A step-by-step methodology that will take you from concept to a completed screenplay. Every chapter in this book contains exercises. These exercises give you a chance to practice the lessons in each chapter and to stretch your wings as a writer. Taken together, the exercises form a template for developing your story ideas into solid screenplays—short or long.

So here's your first exercise—it's a big one:

Exercise: Do All the Exercises in This Book!

Not now, of course. But as you read the book, do every single exercise. Don't skip. They will guide you through the process of creating *loglines*, determining the *major beats* of your story, developing characters, and building *outlines*. Together these exercises provide a foundation for developing your story ideas into solid screenplays that consistently deliver dynamic stories with compelling characters and you'll be able to use this process on all your future screenplays.

✔ Writing is Time

Ray Bradbury famously rented a typewriter in the basement of a UCLA library for ten cents per half hour to write his novel *Fahrenheit 451*. The evolution of *Fahrenheit 451* began with Bradbury writing a pair of short stories, "Bright Phoenix" and "The Pedestrian." That's when Bradbury went to the basement. Taking the story ideas, characters, and themes he had worked out in the shorts, he wrote the novella, *The Fireman*. The first draft for one of the most famous sci-fi novels of the twentieth century took a total investment of $9.80. Plus, the forty-nine hours to type it. Mostly it's time. Time is what you need. You need to commit to the work. (Later, he returned to the basement for another nine days to expand that draft to the full-length novel with the new title of *Fahrenheit 451*.)

Who Is This Book For?

You! If you want to learn about writing a screenplay.

You, if you have an idea for a short film and want to go out and shoot it. Making even a short film can be an enormous amount of work so you need to start with a good script. If you are going to put the necessary time and effort into a shoot, you better make sure your story is great.

You, if you are a film student. Everything starts with the screenplay, even if you want to be a producer, a director, an editor, or an actor. All these jobs are much easier if you understand screenwriting and what makes a good story.

You, if you want to apply to film school. Your writing samples will be one of the most critical aspects of the university's evaluation of your ability. Many of the acceptance rates at top film schools are only two or three percent. If you want to get into that exclusive minority then you need every advantage you can get.

What Do You Need to Get Started?

Almost nothing! That's the best thing about writing. It takes the least investment of any part of the film-making process. That said, there are some things that will help you as a writer going forward. Set aside time to write, preferably every day. Be like Ray Bradbury and make sure you have access to a ~~typewriter~~ computer and a quiet place to work. Consider purchasing screenwriting software (more on that later) or using one of the free (or cheap) browser-based apps.

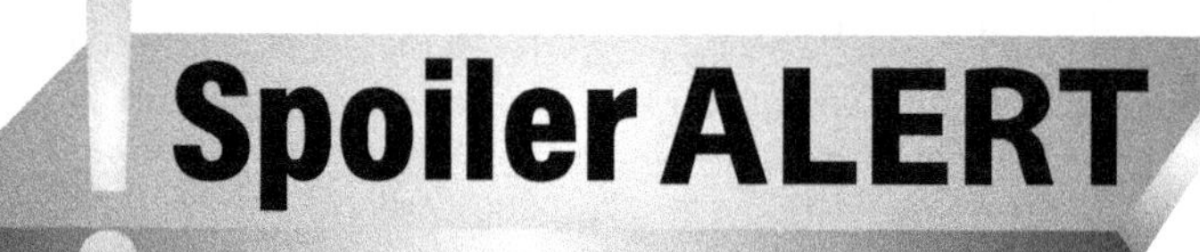

Referencing Film and Television

To properly discuss screenwriting, we will naturally be referencing a lot of films and television shows. You don't necessarily have to have watched all the referenced works, but it will help to be familiar with them. I will do my best not to reveal any great twists, but some key story elements may be revealed. If you're like me, you love to watch films and shows without any idea of where the story is going, allowing the characters to take you on a journey into the unknown.

Therefore, I've created a list of the materials that are referenced in this book, under the heading of "Spoiler Alert!" and you'll find them at the start of each corresponding chapter, when appropriate. Some films are referenced in several chapters, so they are listed in each chapter. This is not a comprehensive list that includes every movie mentioned but any movie that I use to make a point will be listed.

I've done my best to use contemporary films and shows but film is over one hundred and thirty years old. There have been some truly great films along the way. So, there are a few classic films referenced because they set the standard.

Hopefully, this will give you a great list of films to check out. You might not love every one of them, but you will learn something.

Spoiler Alert! | Chapter 1

Hearts of Darkness: A Filmmaker's Apocalypse (1991).

Burden of Dreams (1982).

Lost in La Mancha (2002).

The Disaster Artist (2017).

Six Shooter (2004).

Two Cars, One Night (2003).

Mamá (2008).

The Black Hole (2008).

Philadelphia (1993).

The Big Shave (1967).

One Day... (2001).

Short Term 12, short film version (2008).

Whiplash, short film version (2013).

Tuck Me In (2014).

1
Why Shorts?
Why Features?

I wanted to prove that I could do something, so I made a short film. That was in fact my main concern, to be able to show that I could do one.

—*Luc Besson*

Stepping Stones

Short films are not the end game. Very few people, basically no one, makes a living writing short films. So why should we study how to write a short film? There are many compelling reasons, but the main reason is that a short is the perfect stepping stone to writing longer scripts.

Writing a feature film is a herculean task. Shooting a feature film is even more challenging. If you don't believe me, check out the movies *Hearts of Darkness*, *Burden of Dreams*, *Lost in La Mancha*, and *The Disaster Artist*.

(It's worth noting that even though these movies are non-fiction documentaries, except *The Disaster Artist*, which is based on a true story, each of them has all the elements of a well-written drama. A passionate hero who stops at nothing to achieve their goal as they encounter insane obstacles.)

These films demonstrate quite clearly how challenging feature filmmaking can be. Writing a feature film can feel just as challenging. So it makes sense to start off your learning journey with something more manageable—the short film.

Skills Scale Up

The reason every film school in the world teaches writing (and shooting) short films is that the skills required to make a short scale up to features (as well as TV). All the basic screenwriting and storytelling skills transition to longer-form narratives relatively seamlessly. Nothing you learn about formatting, creating characters, or structure is wasted—it *all* applies to writing features. A feature is just longer, giving you the chance to explore the elements of your story further.

Build Confidence

When people sit down to write a feature, or even a short that they are planning to shoot themselves, they tend to tense up because they feel the script must be *really* good. That desire for greatness can be paralyzing. Trying ideas out in short form can be incredibly freeing, which is really important for creativity. Tension or pressure is constricting and limits your openness to trying ideas. You need to build confidence and comfort to write great stories; starting with a short script can give you that confidence.

Find Your Genre

You may think you know exactly what kind of writer you are, and if you do, that's amazing. In my experience, many people discover they are actually more comfortable in a different arena or genre than they imagined. For that reason, when you are starting out, it's important to try out different styles and different genres. This is one more reason the short form is so important.

ℹ️ History

In the beginning, there were only short films. As film exploded into a worldwide form of entertainment at the turn of the twentieth century, all films were one-reelers and the length of a single reel of film was twelve minutes or less. Even when films expanded to feature-length, cartoons and newsreels kept the short form alive in movie theaters for decades.

Test It Out

A short film is a great way to try out an idea. Let's say you have an intriguing idea for a feature film but you're not one-hundred percent sure. Why not try out the idea as a short first? Even if you are sure, working out the short first allows you to focus on the main character or characters and the central story idea. This way, you can test out the core of your story without having to knock out a hundred pages of a screenplay.

Shorts That Became Features

Writing (and filming) a short is an excellent path to getting the feature version of a story made. Here is just a small sample of some of the short films that became features:

Short Term 12 by Destin Daniel Cretton (2008).

Whiplash by Damien Chazelle (2013).

Proof by Kevin Reynolds (1980), which became *Fandango*.

Bottle Rocket by Wes Anderson (1994).

Mamá by Andrés Muschietti (2008).

Lights Out by David F. Sandberg (2013).

Saw by James Wan (2003).

Alive in Joburg by Neill Blomkamp (2005), which became *District 9*.

Electronic Labyrinth: THX-1138 4EB by George Lucas (1967), which became *THX-1138*.

Frankenweenie by Tim Burton (1984).

9 by Shane Acker (2005).

Peluca by Jared Hess (2002), which became *Napoleon Dynamite*.

Office Space by Mike Judge (1991), part of a series of several shorts that became the feature film *Office Space*.

The Dirk Diggler Story by Paul Thomas Anderson (1988), which became *Boogie Nights*.

Some Folks Call It a Sling Blade by George Hickenlooper and Billy Bob Thornton (1994), which became *Sling Blade*.

Calling Card Films

Short films do not have to become features to help launch your career. A well-done short film can demonstrate your ability as a storyteller. This type of short film is known as a *calling card*. It announces to the world that you are a talented filmmaker. A great short film can be your calling card to success:

Lick The Star by Sofia Coppola (1998).

Six Shooter by Martin McDonagh (2004).

Amblin' by Steven Spielberg (1968).

The Big Shave by Martin Scorsese (1967).

Eight by Stephen Daldry (1998).

Frankenweenie by Tim Burton (1984) did eventually become a feature, but it took twenty-eight years. The short more directly led to Burton getting his first feature directing job on *Pee-Wee's Big Adventure* (1985).

The Dreamer by Miguel Sapochnik (2000).

Luxo Jr by John Lasseter (1986).

Remember Me Always by Paul Feig (1983).

The Goodbye Place by Richard Kelly (1996).

The Strange Thing About the Johnsons by Ari Aster (2011).

Hansel & Gretel by Robert Eggers (2007).

Locks by Ryan Coogler (2009).

Two Cars, One Night by Taika Waititi (2003).

Challenges for Short Scripts

As a screenwriting professor at USC's School of Cinematic Arts, I read a lot of short scripts. The main issue I observe is that student writers try to do too much. If you have the time and the resources, you can tackle a complex story like the twenty-seven minute film *Six Shooter* by Martin McDonagh. It has a variety of characters, several intersecting storylines, and some very intriguing reveals and twists. This rich story led to many awards, including the Academy Award for Best Live Action Short Film.

The problem occurs when people try to put that much story into a five to ten minute short. The overwhelming majority of projects in film schools are five to ten minutes. This is also the optimum length when applying to film festivals. (Festivals group shorts for screenings and like to be able to group as many shorts as possible.) With time this limited, it is best to avoid complicated setups, too many twists, and multiple storylines.

Do your best to keep the story lean and simple. A film with a single location, like *Two Cars, One Night*, allowed Taika Waititi to focus on the characters. The single location of *Mamá* allowed Andrés Muschietti to use one continuous shot and to focus on the terrifying story. Keeping it simple allowed both filmmakers to demonstrate their skills. It doesn't have to be just one location. *The Black Hole,* by Philip Sansom and Olly Williams, is a near perfect execution of a clever idea that leads to a stunning ending. Brilliantly lean and simple.

 ## The Power of Film

Throughout history, films have influenced society. For example, D. W. Griffith's 1915 technical masterpiece, *The Birth of a Nation,* advanced filmmaking in many ways. So much so that the Directors Guild of America's Lifetime Achievement Award was originally named the D. W. Griffith Award. But the film's glorification of the Ku Klux Klan helped promote the small, dying regional clan to a national force that is still a problematic issue to this day, over one hundred years later. Conversely, the beautiful film *Philadelphia* helped to break down stereotypes and prejudices, while creating greater awareness and empathy for people suffering from HIV/AIDS.

Why Features?

For many people, the feature film is the ultimate art form. The idea that you could captivate people sitting in dark theaters across the globe for two hours is very enticing. The hundred pages of a feature screenplay give you the space to dive deeply into the characters, their relationships, and the story concepts. A powerful feature film has the ability to influence culture across the globe in both positive and negative ways.

Writing Samples

Beyond the obvious—writing a megahit movie and winning lots of Academy Awards—what are some of the motives to write a feature film?

What have you got? "Do you have a script you want to shoot?" This was the first question many famous directors were asked when they had their first Hollywood meetings. Often they got these meetings from the success of a short film they had made. But no one is talking about a short script. By script, they always mean a feature film screenplay. Hollywood is always excited to meet new talent. So if you want to be an auteur, the next great writer/director, it's critical that you have a feature screenplay ready to move that excitement into a deal.

Calling card screenplay. You're not really interested in directing; you just want to write, baby. All the working writers that I know have a go-to script: a feature screenplay that is their calling card. The one that they (or most likely their reps) send to the producers and executives who are considering hiring them. This script may not have gotten made, but it's special. When people read it, they think, "This is a writer!"

Pitch it! You've got tons of great movie ideas. You just need to get in the room to sell these suckers. Pitches seem hot these days. If you have a great idea for a movie, putting together a *pitch deck* to sell your story seems like a solid plan. And it is. But, unless you are an established writer, you will need a writing sample, and a writing sample means a complete, very well-written, feature-length screenplay. (I cover pitches more in Chapter 3, "Loglines.")

Transitioning from Shorts to Features

How do shorts and features differ? There are some differences between a feature film and a short film, but the majority are advantages that a short film offers.

My Embarrassing Secret

When I started college at UCSD, I was a computer science major and I was so terrified of writing, that I took my required writing classes pass/fail. So how did I get from there to here, a professional writer? It started with some other general ed classes in filmmaking. My fascination with the filmmaking process, and the creating of short films, drew me into the world of writing. So writing and creating short films was an incredibly important part of my development. Without the step of creating short films, I never would have gotten the confidence to become a professional writer.

Can't See the Forest Through the Trees

It's hard to lose the story thread in a short (although I've seen students do it!) But in a feature, it's easy to get lost, stepping through the plot, deepening the characters, revealing backstory… There are so many things to track in a feature, it can be a bit overwhelming.

Number of Locations and Characters

Writing a feature film with only a few characters set in a single location is extremely challenging. A short with only a few characters and one location can be exhilarating. For example, *The Big Shave*. This short, with only one location and one character, works perfectly as a short film but would be extremely difficult to expand into a feature. Often, limiting the number of characters and locations will free you up to focus on and make the most of the characters and the situation.

Distribution Potential

When writing a feature, you may want to consider if there is a market for the type of story you are writing, i.e., will anyone buy it? For example, dark comedy is very difficult to sell since these films tend to perform badly at the box office. It's important to consider this obstacle before taking the time to write a feature-length dark comedy. But a darkly comedic short is no problem. In fact, being outside of the Hollywood norms may even be considered an advantage when it comes to applying to film festivals.

Experimental or Niche Content

You can also explore unusual subject matter that may not have the huge, worldwide audience that you would need to justify a feature production. For example, in the short *One Day* by Michel Gondry (2001), Mr. Gondry exits a restroom stall only to be followed by a human-sized turd (David Cross) who pursues Gondry and harasses him. Of course, the giant feces eventually morphs into a Nazi officer. Try pitching that at your next Hollywood meeting! The idea here is that you can literally try *anything* in a short.

Expanding a Short into a Feature

Expanding a short into a feature often means going deeper with the characters and their relationships, adding levels of complexity to the story. The short film *Short Term 12* by Destin Daniel Cretton (2008) was his master's thesis film at San Diego State University and went on to win the Jury Prize in Short Filmmaking at the Sundance Film Festival. The story was based on Cretton's own experiences working at a group home for at-risk adolescents. To write the feature version of the story, Cretton interviewed employees as well as teenagers at other group homes to gather more material. He switched the gender of the lead character (which was based on himself) and made her the supervisor of the facility. The feature screenplay went on to win a Nicholl Fellowship in Screenwriting in 2010 and Cretton was able to shoot it in September of 2012.

When filmmakers create short films for the specific purpose of getting their feature screenplay produced, this type of film is often called a *proof of concept*. Damien Chazelle's *Whiplash* is a great example of this. He wrote the feature screenplay for *Whiplash* but was finding it difficult to get financing until he shot the short film *Whiplash*. But I believe that when you begin the process of writing a short screenplay, you should focus on making it the very best short you can. If you put the burden of the short being tied to a feature-length version, you may miss out on creating a terrific short like *Tuck Me In* by Ignacio Rodó. This short has played in film festivals all over the world and has millions of views online.

Exercise: Short vs. Feature

Watch a short film from the list I provided earlier in this chapter of shorts that became feature films. Then watch the feature version.

Compare and contrast the two versions. What are the key differences? How many character and story elements are similar?

Night Shift (1982).

Ataque de Pánico! (Panic Attack!) (2009).

Galaxy Quest (1999).

Go (1999).

2

Story and You

What if you mix the mayonnaise in the can, WITH the tuna fish? Or... hold it! Chuck! I got it! Take LIVE tuna fish, and FEED 'em mayonnaise! Oh this is great.

—Bill Blazejowski (Michael Keaton) in "Night Shift," written by Lowell Ganz and Babaloo Mandel

Idea File

In 1982, Bill Blaze kept his "brilliant" ideas on his portable tape recorder. That was cool back then but now we've got so many great ways to track our ideas. Phone, laptop, email. Often, I grab my phone, tap the notes app and jot down an idea. Or sometimes, when I come across a cool idea, I'll email it to myself. Sometimes I bookmark an interesting story in my web browser.

However you do it, it's critical to record your ideas. It doesn't have to be a complete movie idea. Maybe it's a funny name or a wacky conversation with someone at a diner. If you see some interesting characters at a coffee shop, jot down a description of them. Maybe you hear about a strange job that someone has—anything that tickles your imagination or makes you wonder, write it down.

Periodically, you should take all the ideas you've gathered and compile them into an *idea file*. Organize your ideas into categories: names, characters, stories, thoughts. (These are just sample categories, you can organize in whatever way makes sense to you.) All of this is potential material—seeds that can germinate into stories or fertilize an existing story. I like to think of being a writer as being someone who owns a vineyard. You want stories in all stages just like the wine in a vineyard. There are grapes growing on the vine. There are grapes that have been harvested and smashed in huge stainless-steel containers for early-stage fermentation.

Then the fermenting wine is transferred to barrels to help develop character. And finally it's bottled and ready to drink. It takes a long time to make a good wine. Often years. If the vineyard owner waited till the wine was ready to drink before growing more grapes, well obviously that wouldn't be a very smart way to run a business. You might be writing a short film today but in a couple years, you'll be mining your idea file to find inspiration for your next feature film script.

 Advanced Screenwriting

Some people seem to think that there's some sort of "advanced calculus" in screenwriting technique. Honestly, this just isn't true. Everything about screenwriting sounds simple. And really, a lot of it is. The thing is that there are thousands of these simple techniques.

Getting to the "advanced calculus"-level of screenwriting just means mastering thousands of simple little things all at once. No single aspect of it is hard. It's just really hard to do it all at the same time and in the same screenplay.

Preparing Yourself

It takes more than just desire to become a great writer. You can't just pop open your laptop and type up a masterpiece. It's like someone who decides to be a pro golfer and just shows up at Pebble Beach wanting to play in the US Open. Good luck! We know that to be a professional athlete you have to prepare—work out, study other pros, practice. We understand it's a long process. Writing a great screenplay is a long process as well. But even before you begin to study the specifics of screenwriting, there are many things you can do to prepare yourself. Much like how exercise can help prepare your body to be an athlete, these activities will help prepare your mind to be a better writer.

> **Read!** This should be pretty obvious. If you want to be a good writer, you need to read, a lot. No, X (aka Twitter) does not count! These are some of the things you should be reading:
>
> > **Screenplays.** Thirty years ago, the only places on earth you could find a screenplay were a handful of bookstores in Los Angeles. Now there are literally thousands available for free on the internet. Download the scripts from several of your favorite movies and start reading them now!

Novels. There is still nothing quite like reading a great novel. Make it a habit; I make time for novel reading every night. I'm a slow reader but it's amazing how many books I have read.

News articles. Well-written news articles are great because they get key information across quickly and economically. Stick with the reputable services like the Associated Press and Reuters, or the classic newspapers. Avoid most of the junk writing on the internet.

Do things! Go places! The more you experience life, the more you will have to draw upon when you write. Going to new places heightens our senses. We become more aware of details. You might notice that the streetlights are different and that the food in the restaurants is new. The clothes people wear might be colored differently than what you're used to. Even when you come back home and walk around your neighborhood, you will tend to notice more. As writers, we want to notice details. Train yourself to be more aware.

Meet people! This might be the most challenging one for writers because we tend to be introverts. We'd rather stand on the edge of the party and watch, or better yet, skip the party all together! But meeting people, especially people who are different from you, is critical to being able to write realistic characters. There are a lot of really interesting people out there, it's worth it to get to know some of them!

Watch everything! Well, obviously not everything. But as much as you can. Especially in the genre or area you are interested in.

Write! Journal, blog, record your thoughts and observations, write poetry—some people have been doing this since they were a kid. Good for you! The rest of us need to get ourselves into the habit of writing. It's a muscle and the more you use it, the stronger and easier it will be.

Be a Writer

If you want to write great screenplays, you need to be a writer. You can't just write whenever the mood strikes you or only on the night before an assignment is due. You need to write every day.

When I was younger, I was a surfer. It wasn't just a hobby. I didn't just surf whenever, I surfed every day. Not every day of surfing was good. Sometimes the waves were terrible. Sometimes I was sloppy. But when you do something every day, you get stronger, your skills develop. Most importantly, when the waves were good, I was there, ready and prepared to take advantage of them.

Similarly, if you write every day, not every day of writing will be good. Some days will feel like you're stuck in the mud—you'll generate no dazzling dialogue, no brilliant story ideas. But even on these days your writing "muscles" will get stronger. If you write every day, your focus will become sharper. Your ability to move thoughts and ideas from your head to the page will grow much clearer. So, when the creativity *is* there, you will be able to flow with it, knocking out great pages.

Write every day. This will improve your writing more than any technique or trick or anything you learn in this book or anywhere else. Nothing improves your writing like writing.

If you write every day, you will be a writer.

My challenge to you is to write every day.

 Writers Groups

One of the most important aspects of my development as a writer was being in a writers group. I have been in several writers groups over the years, some incredibly helpful, some less so. Meeting regularly and discussing each other's work is essential to honing your skills as a writer. Screenplays are meant to be shared. You need to know how other people react to your work.

If you are taking a screenwriting class, this is your writers group, for now. Be sure to build connections, so that when your class or classes are over, you can continue to work together.

If you are approaching screenwriting via the self-paced route, it may be a bit more challenging to create a writers group but there are definitely opportunities out there. Social media has made it infinitely easier to connect with other writers. You don't have to drive across town to meet in person, lugging a stack of printed pages like I had too! You can meet online, sharing PDFs.

Finding your core group members who are on your wavelength and share your passion might take a few tries, but I guarantee you it is worth the effort. No one makes it alone.

Finding a Story

Choosing a story may not feel like that big of a deal when writing a short. It's true you want to try a lot of styles and genres. But even a five-page story takes a lot of work, so choose wisely. As you move forward, you want to define yourself as a writer, and to develop your "voice." Your voice just means your style, your personality as a writer.

Important aspects to consider:

- Write what you love—do not chase trends.
- Be true to yourself—don't try to be something you're not.
- Pick a genre you love and would enjoy working in for years.
- If you are writing your first screenplay, do not "challenge" yourself by writing in a genre you are not familiar with. There is a time and place to challenge yourself, your first screenplay is not it.

Exercise: Writing Down the Beats of a Film

Want to get started learning story structure? Here's a great exercise.

One of the most powerful ways to learn screenplay structure is to observe it in good films. But you have to focus on it. You do that by watching one of your favorite movies and writing down each beat. A beat is anything significant. Let's first look at the beats of a dynamic short film, *Ataque de Pánico!* by Fede Álvarez.

A young boy plays with toy robots.

An "earthquake" nearly knocks the boy down.

The boy sees something: giant robots emerge from the fog.

Alien ships fly overhead.

A car skids to a stop as the giant robots pass, marching toward town.

A reporter stands before the robots.

The robots begin to attack, firing missiles.

Major buildings are destroyed.

A stroller rolls down stone stairs.

The alien ships attack people running in the streets.

Uruguayan Air Force jets counterattack.

The Uruguayan jets are no match for the invading alien forces.

A building that looks like the capital is destroyed.

Robots gather in a circle and form a protective barrier around themselves then unleash a massive explosion which seems to wipe out everything.

Even though the movie clocks in at 4:49 and the action is fairly relentless from the two-minute mark to the four-minute mark, there really aren't that many story beats.

Now, let's take a look at the start of a dense, fast-paced feature film: *Galaxy Quest* (screenplay by David Howard and Robert Gordon).

Deck of star ship, ripping off *Star Trek* (odd, non-cinematic aspect ratio.)

They are under attack, cliff-hanger ending.

Reveal: It's just an old TV show.

Reveal: We're at a fan convention.

Reveal: Actors who play the crew of the star ship, bored out of their minds backstage.

Finally, "The Commander" (Jason) shows up an hour and a half late.

Actors are introduced on stage, one by one.

The actors sit at tables, signing autographs.

Super nerd wants to ask the commander a question.

Commander hits on Gwen.

Meet very strange fans (actual aliens), they request help from the commander.

Commander overhears guys in the bathroom, calling him a loser and a laughingstock. Jason is devastated.

Super nerd returns with persistent questions; the commander blows up, it's just a show!

Other actors discuss Jason melting down, he's never done that before.

Jason drinks himself to sleep.

Jason wakes up next morning, very hungover. Aliens are there. Jason thinks it's an acting job.

Aliens are being systematically eliminated, "You are our last hope."

Riding in limo, aliens are trying to explain the situation, but Jason falls asleep. Limo transports into space, revealing to audience that these are real aliens but not to Jason since he's asleep.

Wake Jason up. Sarris, the villain, is here.

Welcome to Protector II, an exact copy of Jason's ship.

Jason sits on the command deck.

Sarris barks out his demands.

Jason, thinks this is play acting, fires all cannons on the villain.

Now he wants to leave. "Where's my limo?"

He gets coated in gel and the ship opens up, revealing to Jason that he is in outer space.

Jason is shot through a worm hole back to Earth.

This covers the first twenty minutes of the movie. By examining the beats in a film, we can begin to demystify its story. It's like an x-ray: We are looking at the bones of the story.

Watch a short and/or a feature and write out the beats.

Exercise: A Simple Writing Prompt

Here is a very simple exercise: Two people get into an elevator. That's it. That's the entire prompt. The rest is up to you. Don't worry about screenwriting format at this point, just write a scene.

Stop reading and give it a try.

How many options did you consider? Very often people go with their first or second idea. But there are literally infinite possibilities!

Let's start with the two people. They could be co-workers or maybe they live in the same apartment. Those are the obvious answers. It could be a hitman and his target. Or two people who were lovers twenty years ago and just bump into each other. It could be a person and a demon. Maybe it's a person and her doppelganger.

What about the elevator? Does it have to be a regular elevator in an apartment building or office building? Maybe it's a space elevator that goes up to an orbiting space station and these are the last two people on earth. Maybe it goes down into a nuclear bunker and the two people are the president and the person who holds the nuclear football (the case with the launch codes). Maybe it's a multi-dimensional elevator that can take you anywhere and two people are going back in time to try and fix the world before it's too late!

Or maybe you stayed with something simple but focused on the details: a sly glance or the way her hand brushed against his. Details really bring a story to life.

The idea here is to challenge yourself, push yourself to discover interesting choices and details.

The easy way ultimately becomes the hard way because you end up paying a price. You basically just make mediocre work. When you kind of force yourself to walk into the fire a bit, and you're on your toes, and you're just trying to survive constantly, then you come up with great new ideas. And you come up with more inventive solutions to the problems.

—Taika Waititi

Being Authentic

What's the difference between a story that feels real and one that falls flat? Here are a couple of simple statements:

I went to the movies last night with a friend.

Last night I went to see the latest James Bond movie with my old college buddy, Choll.

Which one sounds more authentic? Which one sounds more interesting? The one with specific details. The right details really help sell a story. Details make a story sound authentic. One of the best sources of details is you, your own memories.

Stephen King, one of the most successful writers of all time, wrote a book called *On Writing: A Memoir of the Craft*. The book starts with a bunch of chapters recalling incidents from his childhood. Many have nothing to do with writing at all. They're fun—some of them are really hilarious, so much so he could have been a comedy writer. But why his memories? What does that have to do with writing? Mr. King demonstrates that drawing detail from experience helps to bring his stories to life. The woods near Stephen King's childhood home, which he refers to as "the jungle," show up in several of his stories, from *Stand by Me* to *It*. This "jungle" of his youth plays a key role in those stories. The details from the memories of his childhood bring the jungle to life with startling reality.

Let's look at what specific details look like in a great screenplay. Here's John August's *Go*:

```
EXT. A DITCH — NIGHT

A light rain and crickets CHIRPING.
Somewhere in the night, DANCE MUSIC is
blaring, but here it's only a whisper
with a beat.

Water trickles out of a jagged pipe.
Splashing up mud, the riverlet weaves
through hamburger wrappers and
sunbleached beer cans, spent condoms and
an old Spin magazine.

The tiny stream ripples past glass and
trash and the body of a woman. Face up,
breathing. Dead grass caught in her
braids. Her name is RONNA MARTIN. She's
eighteen and bleeding.

Bleeding a lot.
```

Each paragraph has a specific goal. The first, sets the tone and atmosphere: rain, crickets, and dance music. Excellent details that paint a picture. But this paragraph also has a great sense of style. I love the phrasing, "somewhere in the night" and "but here it's only a whisper with a beat."

Next the writer zeros in on the details of the scene: trickling water and a jagged pipe. Then mud and trash. But not just any trash. This is a film about teenagers and the trash reflects that. August lists specific items: fast food wrappers, beer cans, condoms, and a music magazine. Teenagers' lives are all about food, drinking, sex, and music. Every detail helps to paint a picture of the world that this story exists in.

The third paragraph finally gets to the main character, first revealed as "the body of a woman." The reveal of a woman's body in a ditch may lead the reader to believe she is dead, but this is quickly reversed with the next line, "Face up, breathing." The line after pushes back toward the idea of death with the phrase, "Dead grass caught in her braids." There's a push and pull between life and death. Finally, it's revealed that she is eighteen and bleeding. "Bleeding a lot."

I love how the fourth paragraph is a single three-word sentence. Powerful, stylish writing. The key to this opening is the specific details that paint a realistic, intriguing picture.

(Notice that the above scene is written in the present tense. Screenplays are *always* written in present tense.)

Exercise: Memory Writing

One of the best ways to learn how to focus on details is memory writing exercises. Pick one of the prompts below, think through your life, and try to come up with a memory. Write out a page, recounting the story. Be sure to punctuate the story with key specific details.

- Favorite childhood object.
- That time at school when…
- Memorable relative.
- Scary night.
- On our family vacation…
- We were really lost…

You may want to start by creating a list of details, then build it into a story. It's fine to write in prose at this point (unless you're dying to try out your screenwriting software.) We're not looking for a long list of random details. The key here is recalling specific details that bring your story to life.

Being Creative

What does it mean to be creative? To me it's being open to new ideas and having the willingness to spend time exploring those ideas. A deep sense of curiosity is critical as well. Curiosity about life, people, places, ideas, everything. However, having such openness and curiosity doesn't mean that, when you sit down to write a story, you won't tense up or pressure yourself that, "This has to be good! It has to be important!" This desire to do great work is admirable and necessary if we are ever going to achieve true greatness but it can be paralyzing to creativity. Seriously, it's a curiosity killer. So how can we stay relaxed, open, and creative while we work on our masterpiece?

Fortunately, there are some wonderful ways to keep that creativity flowing!

> **Start by putting it down.** As soon as you start writing your ideas down, you are beginning the process of creating a story. If it stays in your head, it remains only an idea.

> **Focus on the process, not the product.** That's the whole point of this book, to give you a solid process. Don't worry about the results, you'll get there when you get there.

> **Perfection is the enemy**. Trying to be perfect is impossible and the drive for perfection is completely paralyzing. *Nothing* is perfect. Let go of that silly notion. If your goal in writing is perfection, you will be miserable.

> **It doesn't even have to be good!** Now we're getting somewhere. Relax, don't worry about quality at all. Just get the story on the page. Even if you try to write the *bad* version of your story, some of it will be good.

> **You want to be open to the happy accident.** When you are relaxed and not trying to be perfect, you are open to something unexpected. You are much more likely to stumble across some cool detail—a funny line, an unexpected twist. Now you are being creative!

> **Surprise yourself, surprise your reader.** When you surprise yourself with these happy accidents, guess what? You will most likely surprise the reader as well!

> **The key to all this relaxing** is that, by not filtering yourself, you begin to develop your voice. The real you is free to come out and play!

One of the keys to good writing is to discover who you are as a writer. You may think you know who you are as a writer but that may change and it's important to explore.

Lie Detector

To a degree, we are all human lie detectors. Most of the time, we can tell when someone is making up a story. What is it that tips us off that a story is false? We sense when the details don't add up or when the description is too generic—it doesn't feel real.

Also, the inverse is true, when a story has excellent details, it makes the story seem genuine and authentic.

Scientists have studied this concept and developed a method for detecting liars called Asymmetric Information Management (AIM.) This technique has been developed for law enforcement officers to help determine whether someone they are questioning is telling the truth or not. AIM has been tested and proven to be a reliable form of lie detection.

The key to AIM is to keep asking questions, insisting upon *more detail*. Someone who is telling the truth, can provide more details and often wants to tell more. The person who is lying will struggle to come up with more detail, often repeating simple generic information. So, it has been scientifically proven: details make a story seem more truthful, more authentic.

With screenwriting, too much detail can leave the audience overwhelmed and frustrated. It's critical to get the right amount of the right detail because you don't have unlimited space and you don't want to frustrate the reader. So, when it comes to detail, be concise and vivid.

Exercise: True Story vs. Made-Up Story

Write two single-page stories, one true and one that you make up.

- Consult with a friend or writing group colleague: Can your fellow writers tell which is which?

- Have a discussion regarding the details of your story. Which details added the most to the story? Which felt false? What's a detail that could have made that story even richer? Are there details that are unnecessary that you can cut?

Spoiler Alert! | Chapter 3

The Revenant (2015).

Rudy (1993).

Up (2009).

Taken (2008).

Finding Nemo (2003).

Erin Brockovich (2000).

The Breakfast Club (1985).

School of Rock (2003).

Armageddon (1998).

Deep Impact (1998).

Don't Look Up (2021).

Melancholia (2011).

Limitless (2011).

Charly (1968).

Whiplash (2014).

The Lives of Others (2006).

Dope (2015).

Spies In Disguise (2019).

1917 (2019).

Get Out (2017).

Pigeon: Impossible (2009).

The Strange Thing About the Johnsons (2011).

La Jetée (1962).

3

Loglines

Perhaps the best test of a man's intelligence is his capacity for making a summary.

—Lytton Strachey

The Secret Weapon

A *logline* is a powerful tool for developing a story.

Imagine: You have written a film. It was beautifully shot, acted, and edited. Now it has been accepted into the Sundance Film Festival. Many of the most important film people in the world are flying to Park City, Utah. They hop online, excited to check out the emerging talent that is featured in this year's festival line up. They scan the list of films playing, reading the titles and loglines. Which ones grab their attention? Which film will become the hot ticket that everyone wants to see? If it turns out to be yours, that might be due to the quality of your logline.

The logline is a crucial first step in creating a great film, whether short or feature-length. But it is also the first impression of your movie for others, often long after the film has been completed. On IMDb (Internet Movie Database) or Rotten Tomatoes or even on Netflix, the one- or two-sentence logline might be the most important source of information about your story. Does it grab people's attention? Is it intriguing? Does it compel people to watch your movie or read your script?

? History of the Logline

The term *logline* comes from old Hollywood. Studios often owned the rights to hundreds of screenplays. To keep track of them all, there would be a massive log book with each title and a short one-line description. This short summary eventually ended up being referred to as a logline.

I realized the importance of loglines early in my professional writing career. If you get lucky enough to gain some notoriety, people in *the business* (film and television business) will want to meet with you. These are called general meetings or *meet and greets*. Meetings are a critical part of the filmmaking process. Filmmaking is a collaborative business so people want to know what you are like. How are you in a room? If they think you're interesting or cool or have "something," they may ask you, "So, what are you working on?" This is Hollywood-speak for, "Tell me your new movie ideas." (Not the one they already read.) This is where you need to have a good logline or two at the ready. A strong logline will hopefully lead to a conversation about your new story.

When I began writing loglines, I discovered that they are actually a powerful secret weapon—*the process of writing a well-constructed logline can help you find your story.* In other words, it can help bring into focus the key elements of your story. It can even help identify whether or not you have a story. You may be thinking, "I don't need to *find* my story, I already know it. I just need to write it down." A good story, even a five-minute short, is far more complex than most people realize and "just writing it down" is actually very challenging.

In this chapter, I'll go through all the elements of a great story and show you how to build them together to create a compelling logline. The preparatory work you do in this chapter will provide an invaluable start to writing your screenplay.

What is Your Story?

The basic concept of a logline is that it answers the question, "What is your story?" A logline is designed to give a reader or listener an idea of your story without having to tell an entire synopsis. It's a mini summary—only one or two lines. This is the first road map of your story.

I know people who consider themselves screenwriters and spend a great deal of time writing but cannot tell you their story without talking for at least five minutes, often much longer. So, what happens if you're one of these people and you step into an elevator with Steven Spielberg? He pushes the button for his floor, the doors start to close. You know he would love your story, but you only have thirty seconds to tell it to him. What do you say? If you're one of those five-minute people, you're dead. The key to a quick summary is to be able to focus on what's important. Get to the heart of the story right away. That's the idea behind a logline.

Key Storytelling Terms

Before we dive into loglines, we need to establish some basic terms:

Main character or protagonist. This is the character that the story centers on. We will venture on a journey with the *protagonist*.

The Revenant Hugh Glass is a fur trader in the 1820s.

Rudy Rudy Ruettiger is a short, average, high school kid.

Up Carl Fredricksen is a grumpy old man living alone in his home.

(Note: I'm using character names to help you identify and learn the terms. When writing a logline, it's best to refrain from using character names.)

Goal. This is the task the protagonist must complete. It could be a lifelong dream or a task that has been foisted upon the protagonist. The *goal* will be the main action of the story.

The Revenant After he is mauled by a bear and his son is murdered, Hugh must find a way to survive to avenge his son's death.

Rudy is desperately trying to find a way to play football at Notre Dame.

Up Carl Fredricksen ties thousands of balloons to his house in an attempt to fulfill a lifelong dream of traveling to South America.

Stakes and/or consequences. What is the main character fighting for? It should be important, at least to them. What will happen if the main character succeeds? Or more importantly, what will happen if they fail? Often the consequences are implied by the stakes.

The Revenant Hugh Glass's brutal struggles will be for nothing if he cannot get the justice he seeks.

Rudy If Rudy doesn't get to play football at Notre Dame, he will feel like a failure.

Up Carl Fredricksen's house may seem like the answer but what is really at stake is the memory of his late wife. If Carl fails, he will have let his late wife down and he will have to live with regret for the rest of his life.

Exercise: Protagonist, Goal, and Stakes

Pick three or more of your favorite movies. Name the *protagonist*, state the protagonist's *goal* as well as the *stakes* and/or *consequences*. By identifying the key elements—protagonist, goal, and stakes in stories—this exercise helps to demystify the creative process. Identifying and understanding how these key elements work will begin to give you a foundation for understanding how screenplays work.

Focus on the Key Elements

To construct a logline, begin by identifying the most important aspects of the story and character. This sounds simple but can actually be quite challenging.

Main Character

A short description, usually with only one or two adjectives that describe key characteristics. The *main character* will have many qualities but the one or two that you identify in the logline are the characteristics that are most connected to the story/journey they will be going on. This is who the main character is when the story starts. The journey of the story will most likely change the main character. It can be useful to list many of the character's key traits or important aspects of the character's situation.

Taken:

- A divorced father struggling to connect with his daughter.
- Former black ops operative.
- Embarrassed by his ex-wife's successful new husband.

These descriptions all fit but for the logline, we want to find the one that best sets up the story. *Taken* is an action-oriented movie so the character description that is most important to the story is…

- Former black ops operative.

Let's look at some more examples.

Finding Nemo:

- Nervous, annoying clownfish.
- Overprotective dad.
- Devastated husband.

These all fit but what works best with the story? Marlin is devastated but that is not the most important aspect for the story. Marlin is nervous maybe even annoying, but it is important not to use negative descriptions when setting up our story. "Overprotective" fits best for the story. It's slightly negative but nowhere near as much as "nervous and annoying." Also, after the opening scene, we completely understand why Marlin is overprotective. It's important to know the character is a clownfish as well, so we'll add that in too.

Erin Brockovich:

- Very attractive.
- Dresses in very provocative clothes.
- Bad at relationships.
- Broke, single mom.
- Swears like a trucker.
- Very intelligent.
- No legal training.

Erin is a strong character with lots of dynamic characteristics that will all play a role in her story. But which ones are the most important? Many new writers rely on physical descriptions, often the generic "very attractive." When writing a story, we want to go beyond simple, one-dimensional physical descriptions—we want to know *who* the character is. So, for the logline, the best description would be, "broke, single mom." But "no legal training" is also important, since it acts as an important story element, so we'll use that as well.

 **Don't Name Names**

It's generally better to not use names unless it's a biopic. A *biopic* is a movie about a real person, living or dead. *Erin Brockovich* is an example of a biopic based on a real person.

Inciting Incident

Something happens, forcing our character into action. This event, or *inciting incident*, is something that changes the main character's life.

> *Taken* Bryan's daughter is kidnapped by human traffickers.
>
> *Finding Nemo* Marlin's son is captured by scuba divers.

Erin Brockovich Erin loses court case, begs for a job at the law firm.

Goal

In response to the inciting incident, the main character decides to pursue a *goal*. This should be something active and challenging. We want an active goal so that we can see the main character take physical steps to achieve it.

Taken Bryan decides to use his special skills to get his daughter back.

Finding Nemo Marlin decides to set out across the ocean to find his son.

Erin Brockovich Erin decides to help the families of Hinkley to take on the powerful public utility, PG&E, who they believe has been polluting the ground water.

(Note: In *Finding Nemo*, Marlin has a very strong emotional transformation which could be described as, "Comes to realize he was being overprotective and needs to let his son do things, experience life, and grow up." Although this is an extremely important part of the story, "Comes to realize" is not a good active goal for a logline.)

Stakes or Consequences

Often, the *stakes* or *consequences* are implied by the goal of the story:

Taken The inciting incident tells us that the kidnappers are human traffickers. That implies that if Bryan Mills fails to rescue his daughter, she will be forced into a life of prostitution.

Finding Nemo The inciting incident tells us that scuba divers have taken Marlin's son. That implies that if Marlin fails to find his son, his son will be forced to live in a fish tank.
Erin Brockovich Many of the families of Hinkley have crushing medical bills from ill or dying family members. If Erin fails, what will happen to the families in Hinkley?

Complete Loglines

Now put it all together. It's important to put the key elements together in a way that creates intrigue so that the reader or listener will want to know the whole story.

> ***Taken*** After his daughter is kidnapped by human traffickers, a former black ops operative must use all his special skills to rescue her.

We've rearranged the elements a bit. You always want to create flow and arrange the elements to make the most captivating story.

> ***Finding Nemo*** Marlin, an overprotective clownfish, sets out to cross the ocean with dingy Dory in search of his son who was taken by scuba divers.

The story is comedic so the logline should reflect that. By adding the character, "dingy Dory" we insert a bit of comedy.

> ***Erin Brockovich*** The true story of a broke, single mother with no legal training who helps sick families take on a giant public utility that has been secretly polluting the ground water.

By adding "true story," this logline becomes more believable. A single, broke mom with no legal training winning a huge legal case sounds almost ridiculous. You need to inform the reader that this is a true story, not a wacky Hollywood contrivance.

High-Concept vs. Execution-Dependent

You may have noticed that the stories we have been discussing so far are mostly *high-concept*. With high-concept stories, it is easy to understand the idea of the story and that story is intriguing and naturally dramatic. High-concept stories grab your attention. You can see the drama. You can imagine interesting scenes. The poster may even be clear to you.

Stories that are not high-concept are often referred to as *low-concept* but are more accurately described as *execution-dependent*. These stories are often character-based and tend to be a bit more difficult to describe in a logline. What execution-dependent means is that the story may be intriguing but whether or not the story is any good will depend entirely upon how well the story is written. (You may be thinking all movies depend upon how well they are written, and this is indeed true, but execution-dependent stories are even more reliant on skilled writing.)

An excellent example of an execution-dependent story would be the movie *The Breakfast Club* by John Hughes. The basic story is that five high school students are stuck in detention on a Saturday. I don't want to go to detention, why on earth would I want to watch a movie about kids stuck in detention? The plot of the story is *not* intriguing. The real story is how five very different kids breakdown stereotypes and get to actually know and like each other. As an idea, this concept could be an intriguing story, but it completely depends on how well the screenplay is written. Luckily, John Hughes did an amazing job, and *The Breakfast Club* is a classic.

Despite the challenges of an execution-dependent story, it is still critical to construct as strong a logline as possible. One big advantage of the short screenplay is that it is much easier to pull off an execution-dependent story!

Two Types of Story Ideas

I believe that there is another important division in story ideas—*the complete package* and *the setup*.

The Complete Package

Or as I like to call it, *the whole enchilada*—this type of story usually has a dynamic starting point, but the key is that an *ending* is built-in. A complete package story has a natural end point.

> ***School of Rock*** Once Dewey lies, saying he is a substitute teacher, we know at some point the lie will be discovered and he will be exposed. This is the natural conclusion to the lie and a natural conclusion to the story. (Note: This is a classic story form called the *creative lie*.)
>
> ***Armageddon, Deep Impact, Don't Look Up, Melancholia*** An asteroid (or rogue planet) is going to hit Earth. This story obviously has a clear ending, either it hits and ends the world or someone stops it. A natural ending point does not imply that there is only one story, just that the ending is built into the idea. There are incredibly different stories that can emerge from a complete package.

The Setup

This type of story idea has a dynamic starting point, but there is no implied ending—in essence it can go anywhere. You may have a clear idea of where you want the story to go but the options are endless and therefore, it can be challenging even for a short story.

For example, "A pill or medical treatment that can massively boost a person's intelligence." What will the character do with this amazing intelligence—run for president? Invent amazing new products? Win a chess championship? There are literally limitless options to where the story could go.

> ***Limitless*** An unemployed writer takes a pill that makes him super smart. He becomes a financial wizard but attracts the attention of some really bad guys.

> ***Charly*** A medical treatment gives super intelligence to Charly, a man with a fairly severe intellectual disability. Using his incredible intelligence, Charly continues the research behind his "cure," only to discover that it will reverse and there is no way to stop it.

It's important to recognize the type of story you are crafting. If your story is a setup type, you need to be sure that the logline goes past the setup and includes the action the main character(s) will take.

Determining which story type you are writing can also help you decide if a story is better suited to TV or film. Since complete package story ideas have a built-in end point, they make for good movies but don't make good stories for an ongoing TV series (although they may work for a limited TV series). Stories with a great setup tend to make the best TV series since an ongoing series can take the time to explore the multiple options available.

Other Important Aspects of Loglines

Sometimes it's important to set the stage—where and when the story is happening. Many stories can happen anywhere, but some stories are about a specific place or a specific time or both. When this is the case, it is critical to mention the location and/or time in the logline.

> ***Whiplash*** A promising young drummer enrolls at a cut-throat music conservatory, pushing himself to the limit to impress a ruthless band leader.

The "cut-throat music conservatory" is the specific place. Music schools are known for being very competitive. Including this specific location adds a strong dynamic detail to the logline.

> ***The Lives of Others*** In 1984 East Berlin, an agent of the secret police is assigned the task of spying on

a famous playwright. What he discovers leads him
to question everything he believes.

In this logline, both the time and the location are very specific. 1984 was the height of the cold war. East Berlin was the capital of the German Democratic Republic, an extremely repressive government that was infamous for spying on its own people. By specifying the time and place, the logline draws on the audience's awareness of the era and location to create a natural sense of tension.

Also, the year 1984 has a strong literary connection. George Orwell's classic dystopian novel about a ruthless government that relentlessly spies on its citizens is set in and titled *1984*.

 ## Everyone will Love It!

Unfortunately, this is never the case. There is no "universal" logline that every person will love. You could have an amazing horror idea but if someone doesn't like horror movies, they probably aren't going to like your logline. You must write your logline and your story for the audience of that story.

 ## Language Matters

Loglines are not just factual accounts of your story. The words you use must evoke the right mood and tone. Take this example of an accurate logline of a famous movie:

> *A girl goes to a strange land where she kills the first person she meets, then joins up with three strangers to kill again.*

Do you know what movie this is? (Answer is on the next page.)

It is an accurate description of the movie, but it feels wrong. This logline tells you what happens but *not* in the spirit of the story. The language doesn't evoke the mood or tone of the story but it is crucial to use language that reflects the style and mood of your story. Also, you may notice that it does not conform to our logline format. There is a protagonist and a statement of her actions but there is no goal, no stakes, and no consequences.

Answer: *The Wizard of Oz*

> ## Exercise: Write a Better Logline
>
> What would be a good logline for *The Wizard of Oz?* Construct a simple one- or two-sentence summary of the story using the key elements: protagonist, the inciting incident, the protagonist's goal. If you do it properly, the stakes and consequences should be implied.

Pitch vs. Function

There are two types of loglines: functional and pitching. Both are important. The *functional logline* is for you, the writer. It's about finding the story and defining the key elements of the story. The *pitching logline* is for selling your story. The key elements are still critical, but the emphasis is on grabbing the reader or listener's attention. Sometimes those are one and the same but for our process, we will focus on the functional logline.

ℹ️ The Truth About Pitching

Don't worry about pitching your story until you have a well-written, completed screenplay. Producers and executives will not buy a pitch from you until they have read a strong writing sample—and a "writing sample" means a *finished* screenplay.

Also, there are two versions of a pitch logline, written and oral. If you are going to speak your logline, like in the elevator with Steven Spielberg, then you need it to be lean and easy to follow. Always speak slowly and clearly. (People get nervous and tend to talk really quickly, making it hard to follow their logline.)

The written version comes into play when you are submitting your story. You may be sending a query letter to an agent or producer. Or maybe you are entering a contest and they require you to include your logline. This one can be a bit longer, a bit more complex.

Variations

An excellent step in the process of writing a great logline is to write out different versions of the logline that emphasize various aspects of your story. Here's an example of a first attempt at a logline for a potential screenplay I've been working on:

> When a Bounty Hunter finally tracks down the most dangerous fugitive of her career, he begs for his life by claiming that her father is alive, and he knows where.

This version is interesting. It sets up an intriguing main character and a mystery that calls out to be solved—is her father alive and if so, where is he?

> In 1851 San Francisco, a Bounty Hunter discovers that her father is not dead. She must team up with a devious ship captain if she has any hope of finding him.

This version has a shift in focus, adds more detail, but drops some aspects. "Dangerous fugitive," which is a bit generic, is replaced with "devious ship captain," which is more intriguing and precise. Also, the actions of "tracks down" as well as "begs for his life," are dropped. They are dynamic actions but not key elements of the story. A specific time and place, gold rush-era California, adds quite a bit since this is a vibrant time and place. This one also adds that she must team up with the devious character. Is he helping her or tricking her? This feels like a dynamic, intriguing relationship.

> Out for revenge ever since her father was murdered by a powerful wizard, a ruthless Bounty Hunter discovers that her father is alive.

This one adds a completely new element—the villain is a "wizard"—so we have a fantasy element in the story and it seems important to mention that. But several other elements have been dropped. No mention of the time and place or the other main character, the devious captain. Also, the bounty hunter is labeled "ruthless" which seems a bit harsh for our main character.

> During the California gold rush, a Bounty Hunter, who relentlessly searches for the wizard who murdered her father, is told that her father is alive. She must team up with the devious ship captain who claims to know where he is.

This one seems to get most of the key elements. Maybe it's a bit long but fantasy stories do need a lot of set up.

By writing out various loglines, emphasizing different aspects, we can begin to judge which elements are the most intriguing, which elements are the most dynamic, which elements are the most important to your story.

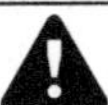 Title Troubles

So you've come up with an awesome title, you hop on IMDb and search— NO! There's another movie with the same title. It may not be a problem. Technically, titles cannot be copyrighted. If you've poked around IMDb enough, you've probably seen a Roman numeral after a title. The Roman numeral means there's more than one film (or show) with that title. Try searching for *Falling*. There's a ridiculously long list of films with this title. I've got a script with that title too. (I definitely need to change it.)

By the way, don't try naming your epic sci-fi script *Star Wars*. Some titles are so well known that they reach the trademark status. You definitely don't want to go there, unless you would like a team of lawyers calling you up.

Title

A good title can really make a logline pop. But good titles are very challenging to come up with. Nevertheless, a logline should include the title of your story. A good title is very valuable. A great title can be priceless. I have heard from multiple producers that there are projects they would buy just for the title alone. What makes a title great? Something catchy, something that stands out. Here are some examples:

> ***The Devil Wears Prada*** Great pop culture value as well as sounding cool.
>
> ***Last Tango in Paris*** Calling something "the last" almost always seems to make it dramatic.
>
> ***Raging Bull*** It has a blunt visceral quality.
>
> ***Some Like it Hot*** Playful, intriguing, and memorable.
>
> ***Cool Hand Luke*** Just sounds cool.
>
> ***Dirty Harry*** This one just sounds cool too.
>
> ***Jaws*** One of the purest titles of all time.
>
> ***The Good, the Bad and the Ugly*** Maybe the best title of all time.

The problem is that great titles are incredibly hard to find. In fact, even good titles are really challenging. A trick for finding a title is to write out all the key words, names, and places in your story. Then play with this list. Single word titles seem to be popular these days. You can try combining words, two or three, in a unique way that could create something really memorable. Avoid using common phrases, they tend to feel flat. A twist on a common phrase can be quite catchy.

You may not be able to come up with a great title, but you definitely want to avoid a bad title. A bad title can doom your story from the start. There are some things to avoid:

> ***Phffft*** Looks weird, not sure how to pronounce.
>
> ***Zyzzyx Road*** Even harder to pronounce.
>
> ***The Last Mimzy*** Sounds lame. Don't want to say it.
>
> ***Can Hieronymus Merkin Ever Forget Mercy Humppe and Find True Happiness?*** Seriously? How is this ever going to fit on a movie marquee?

Occasionally, there is some value in a title that is intentionally bad.

> ***Attack of the Killer Tomatoes*** Fun and silly.
>
> ***To Wong Foo, Thanks for Everything! Julie Newmar*** A movie about drag queens needs an over-the-top title. Done.
>
> ***Snakes on a Plane*** So stupidly simple, it just works.
>
> ***A Nymphoid Barbarian in Dinosaur Hell*** Sounds ridiculous, but in a wacky fun way.

Genre

It's important to understand what *genre* your story falls into. Identifying the genre of your story in your logline helps people understand your story more clearly. Common genres include comedy, horror, action, sci-fi, fantasy, and drama. Genres are often broken down even further into subgenres. For example, comedy can be further broken down into romantic comedy, buddy comedy, workplace comedy, black comedy, mockumentary, etc.

❓ Thinking Outside the Box

An interesting experiment is to think about changing the genre of your story. What would the comedy version of your story look like? What about making it a horror movie? It's important to question every aspect of your story, even genre.

I have often seen writers start out with a very dramatic subject but during the writing process they find the straightforward approach very challenging. It can be a great relief to add comedy to the story.

You may have noticed the similarities in the plot of *Taken* and *Finding Nemo*. In both movies the main character's child is abducted and the father will stop at nothing to get them back. The main difference is the genre. *Taken* is pretty much straight up action while *Finding Nemo* is a comedic family adventure. The completely different genres lead to completely different movies, but both are highly entertaining.

Mixing Genres

Maybe your story doesn't fit into just one genre. That's cool, mixing genres can make a story dynamic but more often it just makes it confusing. Mixing genres can even lead to disaster. For example, *Abraham Lincoln: Vampire Hunter*. Hollywood went nuts over this type of story for a short while but when the movie came out it bombed. Turns out history fans who love Honest Abe don't really want to see a vampire movie and horror fans don't want to sit through any of that boring history stuff. That's the challenge with mixing genres. Will the result be a crossover in which audiences of both genres are interested in the movie or will it be a tweener in which neither audience (i.e., no one) wants to see the movie?

Tone

In general terms, *tone* means the vibe or style of your story. But when it comes to loglines (especially pitching), the tone is often described by referencing one or two movies similar to the one you want to make. For single movie references, it usually takes the form of a well-known movie but with a twist. For example, "It's like *Raiders of the Lost Ark* but with a female lead." Or if you are crossing two movies (or shows) – "It's like *Quantum Leap* meets *CSI*." The reason these tone references are important is that there is a wide range of tones within a genre. For example, the genre of comedy is huge—there is a vast difference between intelligent comedies like *As Good as It Gets*, to broad comedies like *Dumb and Dumber*. By referencing the right movie, you tell people what sandbox your movie is going to be playing in.

(Note: If you are making a movie that is not like anything ever made, well that's a huge task. Filmmaking has existed for well over 130 years. There are a lot of films out there and just about *everything* has been tried in one way or another.)

This may seem like a cheat but in the business it is essential. Every time I've ever pitched, if I didn't identify a film that was similar to my story, the producer or executive would ask, "What touchstones do you see for your story?" In other words, "What movie is your pitch gonna be like?"

There are several important guidelines to keep in mind when referencing other movies.

- Never reference movies that were failures. Regardless of the connection, don't go there. Movies are expensive to make and mentioning anything that was not successful is death.

- It can work to reference a cult classic, but it can be a bit risky if the listener is not a fan of the movie.

- Don't reference more than two movies. It just gets too confusing. Don't turn your logline into a math problem, where people are trying to figure out how these three or four movies fit together.

- Don't reference two movies that seem completely different: "It's *Titanic* meets *Tinker Bell*." If you must explain the connection, then your references are not helping you.

(Note: Referencing other movies should not take the place of a well-written logline. Movie references only work when they are in addition to your logline.)

Put It All Together

Now it's time to finally put it all together. The order of the key pieces is important. You want to start with your title. Then comes the genre. Next is your well-constructed logline. And finally, tone, the film reference that makes it all click.

> ***Dope*** (coming of age comedic drama). Set in "The Bottoms" of Inglewood, a young black high schooler and self-professed geek finds himself stuck with a bag of drugs. He and his friends must deal with the situation or his dreams of going to Harvard will be smashed. An update of *Risky Business* set in the 'hood.

Spies In Disguise (animated spy comedy). When the world's greatest spy is turned into a pigeon, he must team up with his nerdy gadget guy to save the world. A comedic James Bond, where Mr. Bond has become a pigeon.

1917 (war action drama). Two soldiers are tasked with the nearly impossible mission of delivering a message that 1600 men are about to fall into a deadly trap. In the vein of classic war movies.

Get Out (horror). When a young African American man finally meets his white girlfriend's parents, he finds himself trapped in a bizarre world, desperately trying to survive. A twist on the classic *Guess Who's Coming to Dinner*.

 ## Heightened Genre

Get Out by Jordan Peele is a great example of what is called *heightened genre*. Sometimes also referred to as *elevated genre*, this is when you take a popular genre like horror and go beyond, adding layers of intelligence and sophistication. Horror is often a dumbed down genre, with simple plots, high body-count, and lots of scares. By adding a sophisticated plot and social commentary, *Get Out* elevates the horror genre.

Loglines for Short Films

A well-constructed logline is equally important to a short film. Let's take a look at the loglines of some very successful short films.

Pigeon: Impossible (animated spy comedy). A bumbling secret agent battles a persistent pigeon for possession of his powerful brief case to prevent the launching of a nuclear missile. A spoof of the classic Bond spy films.

The hit movie *Spies in Disguise* is very loosely based on this short.

The Strange Thing About the Johnsons (dark drama, horror). A typical suburban family devolves

> into a disturbing abusive incestuous relationship in
> this horror twist of a family drama.

This nightmare version of a family drama launched Ari Aster's career.

> ***La Jetée*** (sci-fi). After World War III, mankind has
> moved underground to survive, one man is chosen
> for a mission to go back in time in hopes of finding
> a better future.

This 1962 classic is one of the most successful and influential short films of all time. The story is told through a series of stark black and white stills and simple narration. Eventually, this powerful short became the basis for the feature film *12 Monkeys*.

(Just for fun—Try to find the one shot that is not a still.)

Test It!

One of the best ways to know if your logline works is to test it on some people. Okay, your mom loves it, that's great, now try it out on some other people. Remember film is a collaborative business. How other people react to your work is what it is all about. It's important to find the right audience. If you tell your silly friend who loves comedies about your dark drama, you might not get a positive response.

Problems

When constructing a logline there are many common problems that can trip you up. Here are just a few of them:

> **Too much information.** This is one of the most common problems with loglines: trying to cover too much. Whether it's too much character description or too many story details, too much information muddies the water and makes it very difficult for the reader or listener to understand the story. Trust your audience. Less is more.
>
> **Doesn't grab attention.** This is a tricky one. It can be difficult to determine if the problem is a poorly written logline or that your basic story idea is just not compelling enough. (Often when you are writing an execution-dependent story, the logline will not be very sexy.) You may have to try several versions to discover what

people find most intriguing about your story idea. Try adding obstacles, stakes, or consequences. Be sure the goal is challenging and that it is clear.

You've written a tagline not a logline. Taglines are great for movie posters. "Freddy was on top of the world, *until that day...*" A tagline tends to be very dramatic but only tells us a fragment of the story, sometimes even less! But when combined with images on a poster—a movie star we like, a font that gives us a vibe, some intriguing images, a good title, then we may want to know more about the movie. But a tagline by itself is a bit silly.

Self-congratulatory language. Avoid telling people how great your story is, "The most dramatic story you've ever heard!!" It's good to be confident but keep it to yourself. Your story and your writing need to be dramatic.

Telling people how they will feel. Avoid explaining the emotions of your story, "You'll laugh, you'll cry, you'll jump into the sky!" You never want to tell people how to feel. Their first reaction will almost always be "Oh yeah? I *seriously* doubt it." Your story needs to make them laugh or cry or jump or whatever.

Too mysterious. It is valuable to build in mystery but if it's so mysterious, people have no idea what you are talking about, then that's a problem. You need to give enough of the story to hook them in. You don't have to give away the ending. Whether you give the ending or not depends on the situation. If you are trying to get someone to read your script, you may want to be coy but don't make them angry.

Overall, your logline needs to be clear and specific. The language needs to reflect the tone and the intrigue needs to be there. Bottom line, your logline needs to speak for itself.

Success Story

Still not sure you need to bother writing a logline?

Let me tell you a story. Several years back when I was working with my former writing partner Cindy Davis, we went to a general meeting late one afternoon. After the normal greetings and chit-chat, the producer decided to share how hard his job was, "I listen to pitches all day long. And most of them are terrible. I hear maybe ten good pitches in a year and out of them, maybe only one is a home run."

I'm not sure why he was telling us this, maybe he just wanted us to leave so he could go out to happy hour. But to me, he had thrown down the gauntlet, I was challenged. I had to pitch him the logline for the story we had been working on. So I said, "Well, I've got one." He nodded—was he annoyed? To hell with it. I was going for it.

"It's a workplace comedy called *None of Her Business*. It's about a woman executive who gets fired from her job. So she dresses up as a man and gets her old job back. It's like *Tootsie* meets *Working Girl*."

The young producer sat up in his chair, suddenly wide-eyed and alert. "That's good. That's really good. In fact, I think that's a home run!" Then he's in high gear talking about the story and how exciting it was, wanting to hear more from us.

There were many more steps in the process, but we ended up at a meeting at New Line with different producers. We did the normal chit-chat and then they asked, "What are you working on?" I dropped the logline on them. The executives nearly jumped out of their seats. I'm thinking this is it! We've sold this pitch to a major studio, we just have to get through a twenty-minute pitch without screwing it up. I guess we didn't screw it up since we did indeed sell it. The moral of the story is that the logline was the starting point that got the ball rolling with producers and it was the big finish that sealed the deal at the studio. So, yes, I am a believer that putting in the time to construct a strong logline is time well spent!

Exercise: Write Your Loglines

Time to go to work. As I have said, there is only one way to learn how to write and that is to sit down and write.

- Write three loglines for your stories. They can be three different stories or three versions of the same story.
- Be sure to follow the proper presentation form: title, genre, logline, tone.

Helpful hint: It doesn't have to be perfect. Loglines evolve. It's impossible to know your story completely at this point. You may knock it out of the park with the logline but more likely you will tweak it for the entire process.

Spoiler Alert! | Chapter 4

The Revenant (2015).

28 Days Later (2002).

Get Out (2017).

Parasite (2019).

Jaws (1975).

Breaking Bad, pilot episode (2008).

Iron Man (2008).

Liar, Liar (1997).

The Father (2020).

Star Wars: A New Hope (1977).

Legally Blonde (2001).

School of Rock (2003).

Ataque de Pánico! (Panic Attack!) (2009).

Galaxy Quest (1999).

4

Basic Story Structure

It is necessary to build a system or a structure which will allow you to form your dream into reality.

—Sunday Adelaja

Screenwriting Rules?

What came first, story or *the rules?*

No one ever sat in a dark room and said, "I'm going to invent storytelling. Step one, make up some rules." Obviously, that's just not the way it happened. As far as we know, story "rules" first came about over 2500 years ago when the Greeks got into theater. If you've got as many as 14,000 people hanging out watching, you better put on a good show. What they discovered was that there was a *pattern* to good stories. And if you followed certain *guidelines*, your story would be more interesting.

So what we're going to be talking about here are *not* rules but guidelines that help us tell compelling stories.

So, let's fix that heading…

Screenwriting Guidelines

We've all had that friend that would start to tell a story and keep going and going and going. You're thinking, "Oh my god, are they ever going to get to the point?"

Screenwriting guidelines give us basic story markers. These story markers, or *major beats*, help ensure that you get to the point. If you don't have these major beats, your story is going to feel like that friend who just keeps talking and never gets anywhere. So, the major beats keep our story heading in the right direction.

Screenwriting guidelines are meant to help you tell a dynamic, interesting story. Even a short film will feel more complete and satisfying if you follow them. Do you have to follow these guidelines? No. Of course not. Especially when writing a short screenplay. But when you don't follow them, you are putting far more pressure on yourself to make the other elements of your story dynamic, intriguing, and entertaining.

It's important to learn the guidelines even if you want to create stories with unusual structure so that, if or when you step outside of the structural norms, you will know what kind of issues your story will face.

(In Chapter 17, "The Non-Traditional Film," we will explore some superb films that do not follow these guidelines and examine how and why they succeed.)

Okay, there is *one* rule, and it's extremely important. It's a rule that you must never break: *Do not be boring.* That's it. Everything else, well they are just suggestions to help in the quest to not be boring.

The simplest version of story structure is this: beginning, middle, and end. Or Act I, Act II, and Act III. Three-act structure. That sounds simple enough.

Will Structure Kill Originality?

Some people worry that learning story structure and other story techniques will make their screenplays cliché or formulaic. Stories are cliché or formulaic due to execution, not the story structure. Good structure is essential to allowing your great characters and dynamic scenes to shine.

Consider Vincent Van Gogh, one of the most identifiable and unique artists of all time. One aspect of Van Gogh's creative process that not many people realize is that he was obsessed with other artists. He studied most of the famous artists of the day, often imitating and incorporating aspects of their techniques. He was *always* trying to improve himself.

So if Van Gogh was always copying and imitating other artists, how is it that his paintings are so unique? Because of his brush strokes.

Vincent's brush strokes make his painting stand out. They make each of his paintings recognizably a "Van Gogh." The writer's equivalent of the brush stroke is their *voice*. For screenwriters, that means the language they use, the imagery, the characters, and the dialogue. But if you don't master story structure, your stylish voice will remain buried under clumsy technique. To be a great artist like Van Gogh, study the guidelines and learn screenwriting techniques. This will allow your "brush strokes" to shine.

The Major Beats

When filmmakers talk about story structure, they often describe it in terms of the major beats. These are the key points that make up your story. The overwhelming majority of stories out there will generally follow these story beats regardless of whether they're short films, feature films, or TV pilots. The major beats take standard three-act structure and expand upon it, identifying a specific role for each section of a story (Figure 4.1).

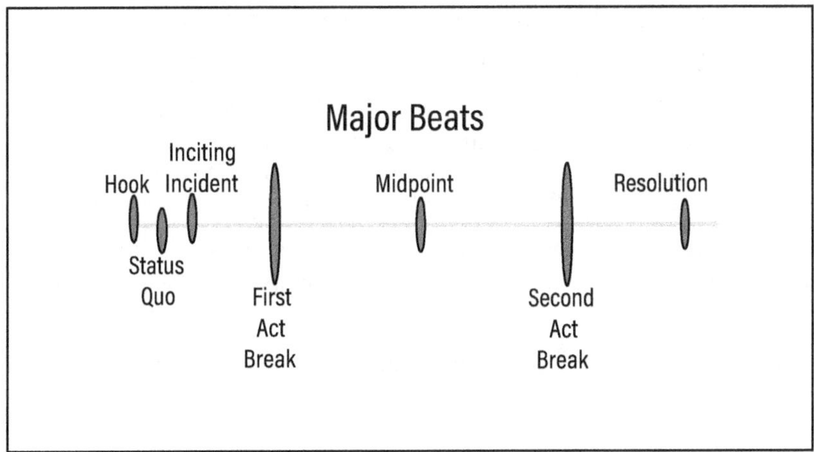

Figure 4.1

The *major beats* provide clarity and detail to traditional three-act structure.

Hook

Start off with a bang, something that will grab the audience's attention and make them want to read or watch more; that's the idea behind starting your story with a *hook*. This is especially true for short films. The hook is not always listed as one of the major beats, but it is a very effective way to jump right into the story.

Here are some great hooks:

> ***The Revenant*** The camera moves slowly over a gentle, flowing river, a man with a gun sneaks through the shallow water and some more men appear. One of the men shoots his rifle and all hell

breaks loose. Suddenly we're in the middle of an ambush. Characters crisscross in every direction. The action is intense and visceral.

28 Days Later Images of human violence on screens, a chimp forced to watch. It's a lab that is using monkeys for testing. An animal rights group breaks into the lab determined to release the animals. A scientist begs them not to, proclaiming that they are infected with rage. A woman releases a chimp and is viciously attacked. She convulses and spits blood. She has clearly been infected with something horrible! All hell breaks loose.

Get Out A short but powerful scene of a black man walking in a suburban neighborhood. He's really uncomfortable, he even says, "I stick out like a sore thumb." Then the creepiness goes through the roof when a car begins to follow the man. Terror builds until the unseen driver attacks the black man. But this is not our main character. This scene sets a tone: it tells us that this is a horror movie and race is going to play a role. Without this scene, the movie would feel totally different: A handsome interracial couple is going to meet the woman's white parents. It would take a long time to get to the horror and that would not be as dramatic.

It's important to note that a hook is not completely necessary and may not occur in all stories. But with a short film, you definitely want to think about starting fast.

In Chapter 11, "Start Fast," I will go into several powerful techniques for starting your film quickly.

Status Quo

The purpose of the *status quo* is to introduce the main character in their ordinary world. The main character's life has been going on for some time, they have hopes, dreams, and expectations. As your story starts, you want to establish who the main character is so the audience can see how they are under normal conditions. This is your main character's status quo.

Parasite The Kim family is trying to steal wifi from neighbors. This establishes that they are poor but resourceful.

Jaws Martin Brody, played by Roy Scheider, is the police chief of a small beach town who has a family and deals with all kinds of mundane things. These humdrum scenes are effective since they are in stark contrast to the opening scene (hook), where a shark rips a beautiful woman limb from limb.

> ***Breaking Bad*** After a dramatic flash forward in the cold open, where we see Walter White driving a Winnebago meth lab in his underwear, we meet him in the present day as he eats a routine breakfast with his wife and son. Next, we see him enthusiastically teaching a rude high school class that couldn't care less. Later, he moonlights at a car wash, where one of his rich students makes fun of him. Instead of being bored after watching these scenes of Walt's ordinary life, we are left wondering, "How the heck did he go from this to Underpants Man?"

The main goal of the status quo section is to get us to like your character or to find your character intriguing. In this section it is critical to get the audience onboard with your character as quickly as possible. This can be challenging if we have complex characters with negative traits.

In the opening of *Iron Man*, we meet Tony Stark riding in a Humvee in a convoy in the desert in Afghanistan. He's wearing a stylish suit, cool shades, and sipping scotch. This immediately creates an intriguing mystery: what's this cool dude doing in a military vehicle in the middle of the desert? Then he starts cracking funny jokes. We still don't know why this guy is there, but we like him. Then the convoy is attacked and Humvees blow up—oh no, what happened? We're concerned for him. Then the story flashes back, Tony is in a casino playing craps. He's supposed to be receiving an award presented by his best friend but Tony's blowing him off. Not cool. But we already like him, so we let it slide. But what if Tony being a jerk was the first scene? It would be much harder to come to like him. A screenplay is like a thousand-mile journey. If you start off in the wrong direction, you are making your journey much more difficult. And if it's a short, you have even less time to get your character back on track.

Inciting Incident

The *inciting incident* is a disruptive event. This big event changes everything for the main character. It's so big, they must stop their normal life and figure out how to address this event. It's important that the inciting incident has consequences and stakes. If the incident is small or has inconsequential effects, then it won't matter that much. We want the inciting incident to be like an asteroid hitting the main character.

> ***Parasite*** Ki-Woo's friend offers him a tutoring job with the very wealthy Park family. This seems like a huge opportunity for the Kim family.

> ***Jaws*** They discover that the woman's body found on the beach was attacked by a very large shark. The small town of Amity Island depends entirely on tourism. No one will go to a beach with a huge killer shark! This is a disaster!
>
> ***Breaking Bad*** Walter White finds out he has inoperable cancer. Finding out you're going to die of cancer is about as big as stakes and consequences get.

The inciting incident in *Jaws* and *Breaking Bad* are clearly huge problems that require action. But the inciting incident in *Parasite* seems like a positive. This could be labeled with a similar term from the hero's journey structure: the *call to adventure*. This positive opportunity leads to life-changing actions. That's the key. Whether the inciting incident is positive or negative, it must lead to action and change.

 Order of Information

One of the most critical elements of good storytelling is the order and timing in which you reveal information. A good story is going to contain a lot of information: Who the character is, what the plot is, where and when it is occurring, themes about morality, philosophy, and more. Assembled well, this information is fascinating, drawing us in and captivating us. When ordered poorly, it will feel like a bad history lesson. Choosing the order of these revelations is key to the art of storytelling. You want to create a trail of breadcrumbs (information), with each piece of story falling just far enough ahead to keep us following the story trail.

The Debate

Although it is generally not listed as a major beat, *the debate* is an important step. As the name suggests, this beat is a consideration of all the character's options. After the inciting incident there is a crisis. A decision about the course of action must be made. It is vital to consider all options and make sure the character considers them.

How many times have you been in a theater watching a movie thinking, "Why don't they just call the cops? Why don't they call the cops? This is stupid, just call the cops!"

If calling the cops is an option for the characters, as a storyteller, you *need* to address it. Maybe there's no cell reception or the police station has been overrun by zombies. Whatever the options are, you need to be sure that your characters address them all so that when they do make a decision, the audience is on board.

The movie *Liar Liar* written by Paul Guay and Stephen Mazur has an excellent debate section. Once Fletcher Reede, played brilliantly by Jim Carrey, realizes he has been cursed to tell the truth, he goes through several important steps:

- First Fletcher tries to physically defeat the curse. "It's all a matter of willpower," Fletcher proclaims. He spots a blue pen and tries to "lie" and say that the pen is r…. But no matter how hard he physically tries, he cannot say, "The pen is red." Then he tries to write the "lie." He wrestles with his arm like it's an anaconda, but he cannot write the word "red." He ends up writing "blue" all over everything including himself.

- After several embarrassing episodes, Fletcher discovers that his son's birthday wish was that Fletcher couldn't tell a lie for just one day. Fletcher buys a cake and drags Max, his son, out of school. Fletcher explains that grownups need to lie, and that Max needs to make an "unwish." Fletcher lights the candle, his son concentrates, and blows the candle out. But it doesn't work, Max really wanted his birthday wish. Doing it just because his dad asks doesn't work.

After these fantastic sequences, we know that Fletcher has no other options. He decides he must find a way to win the most important case of his life without his go-to tool, lying. It feels like an impossible task given what we've seen of the case and what we've seen of Fletcher. This is a great end to the debate and end of the first act. Now the audience is dying to see how this is going to play out.

First Act Break

At the end of the debate, the main character decides how to deal with the problem caused by the inciting incident. The key is that the main character must decide on a goal and begin to take action to achieve this goal. This shift from decision-making to action signals the end of the first act, or the *first act break*. If you have a good debate section, the audience will be on board with this choice which will be the goal for the entire second act.

Goal

The key to a working first act break is that the main character must *decide* to take *action* in an effort to achieve their *goal*. You want to be able to state your first act break like this: "The main character decides to ________."

So, let's look at our examples:

> ***Parasite*** After lying to get the job, Ki-Woo finds that working for the Parks is such a good gig, he decides to get the whole family involved in the scam.

> ***Jaws*** Martin Brody finally decides to hunt down the shark. This is after one of the longest debates in film history. Chief Brody has done just about everything to avoid going out on the water to face the shark.

> ***Breaking Bad*** Walter White decides to make meth. The story makes it clear that his family is struggling financially so we assume that he's cooking meth as a way to pay for his cancer treatment. But the expense of the treatment and whether insurance will cover the costs is never mentioned. In fact, the story is much more focused on the thrill of doing it and of breaking the law.

Obstacle

It's also important that the goal is not easy for your main character to achieve. This will keep your main character challenged and your audience interested. One of the strongest ways to make the goal challenging, is to make sure that there are clear *obstacles* to achieving the goal.

> ***Parasite*** The series of deceptions seem to get greater and the actions to get the current staff fired more extreme. We also wonder how the Kims are going to keep the Park family from finding out they are all related. This is a classic *creative lie* story. Intuitively we know the situation is doomed and at some point, the Park family will discover the deception. Creative lie stories have a great natural tension throughout the second act.

> ***Jaws*** Chief Brody is afraid of the water so going out on the water to hunt down a killer shark is definitely challenging. Plus, we've seen the shark in action and it is truly a monster.

> ***Breaking Bad*** How will nerdy, chemistry teacher Walter White make meth? Sure, he understands the chemistry, but there are clear obstacles. Making meth is illegal. This is a world of violent criminals and the police, as well as the DEA. Plus, we know from the flash forward in the cold open that things are definitely going to go sideways!

Stakes

If the main character has a challenging goal, the *stakes* will likely be clear. Take the classic *The Wizard of Oz*. Dorothy's goal is to find the Wizard, so that he can help her get back home. The stakes are clear: if Dorothy doesn't find the Wizard (and later fulfill his tasks), then she will never get back home. Clear goal, clear stakes. Also, there is a clear step for her to take: follow the yellow brick road. This is why *The Wizard of Oz* works so well—in every scene Dorothy is taking clear steps to accomplish her goal. (There is also an excellent antagonist, the Wicked Witch of the West, who creates fantastic obstacles by doing everything in her power to prevent Dorothy from succeeding.)

Let's return to our examples:

> *Parasite* The Kims go about achieving their goal through deception, so we know there will be consequences when they are found out. However, what the Park family might do when that happens is not clear. The stakes turn out to be far worse than anything we could have imagined.

> *Jaws* We have seen the deadly consequences of going head-to-head with the shark, so the stakes for Chief Brody are very strong and clear.

> *Breaking Bad* We know there are dangerous drug dealers, cops, and the DEA, all of which pose very serious threats to Mr. White. We also know, from the flash forward in the cold open, that things are definitely going to go very badly.

There are many great films with more ambiguous goals and stakes. For example, *The Father*. In this movie, an elderly man refuses help as he struggles with Alzheimer's and dementia. His goal is to remain independent. The stakes are that he will be forced to live in a retirement home if he is not able to care for himself. The goal is clear but whether or not he is succeeding is rather ambiguous. This is what makes the story so fascinating: At what point can an elderly person no longer take care of themselves? The ambiguousness makes for an extremely execution-dependent story.

Sometimes a writer may be faced with an ambiguous goal. They may find it helpful to add a more concrete goal. Take the classic *Star Wars: A New Hope*. Luke's actual goal is to join the rebels to avenge the death of his aunt and uncle and the destruction of his home. But what's at stake? It's hard to say. How do we know when he has succeeded in joining the rebels?

So George Lucas adds the much clearer goal of "rescue the princess." The stakes are also clear because the life of the princess is at risk. This goal has obvious steps and we will clearly know when Luke has succeeded. (After

❓ Different Terminology

You may have read screenwriting books, articles, or blogs that use different terms to describe the major beats in a story. The terms used in this book are those that I have encountered most often in twenty-four years of professional screenwriting. As William Shakespeare wrote, "A rose by any other name would smell as sweet." All of these terms are more or less valid. I think some screenplay analysts out there have tried to invent new terminology to give the impression that they have some innovative method of storytelling. This just isn't true. Good storytelling has been around for a long time. (Greeks!) Inventing new labels is not going to change that. Take a look at the other terms in Table 4.1. The only ones that I have an issue with are Plot Point 1 and Plot Point 2. A good short film may have five, ten, even twenty plot points. A good feature has fifty to a hundred, maybe more. But people still use these terms, so you may encounter them.

Comparing Screenwriting Terms					
Simple	**Classic**	**Major Beats**	**Other Terms**		
Beginning	Act I	Hook	Point of Attack		Opening Image
		Status Quo	Getting to Know You		
		Inciting Incident	Catalyst		
		Debate			
		First Act Break	Turning Point 1	Plot point 1	Break into 2
Middle	Act II	Attempts at Goal	Tests	Rising Action	
		Set Pieces			
		Midpoint			
		Second Act Break	Turning Point 2	Plot point 2	Break into 3
End	Act III	Resolution	Climax		Final Image

Table 4.1

The *story beats* discussed in this chapter can be referred to in different ways. Shown here are some alternate terms.

Princess Leia is rescued, the goal switches to "destroy the Death Star," again a very difficult but clear goal.)

Bigger is not always better. I think one of the big improvements in superhero movies has been the personalizing of the stakes. When the stakes are "save the Earth," we tend to check out and dismiss them. It feels obvious that the hero will win and save the Earth. That lowers the suspense and makes the story less dramatic. But if the survival of the superhero's boyfriend is at stake, then we tend to care, especially if the superhero really cares. Personal stakes are stronger than vague, overly-broad stakes.

Clear goals with clear stakes tend to fall into the high-concept category of films, while more ambiguous goals and stakes are usually execution-dependent.

Set Pieces

One of the most important aspects of film and television today is the set piece. With a set piece you try to create as much drama as you can, building as much tension as possible for the key moments in your story. Even short films can have great set pieces. (Later in this book, Chapter 16 is entirely devoted to set pieces.)

A set piece is a sequence of scenes that build up the drama and tension. It can last for a few minutes and have multiple beats. Often it will involve a setup scene and an aftermath scene. Or a set piece could start with a big moment and then follow with a series of escalating beats until boom, there is a dramatic conclusion. A set piece is often a specific event at a unique location, like a school dance, the big game, a wedding, etc.

> *Parasite* While the Kim family parties in the Park house, the doorbell rings. It's the old housekeeper and Chung-Sook lets her in. The sequence continues to escalate, including a stunning reversal and concludes with the old housekeeper being defeated with peaches. At that moment the phone rings beginning another set piece! In fact, there are three set pieces, back-to-back-to-back.

> *Jaws* The opening is a minor set piece and the final showdown with the shark is an epic set piece.

> *Breaking Bad* The cold open jumps into the middle of a set piece as Mr. White/underpants man races through the desert in an RV. Later, near the end of the pilot episode, with all the context clear to the viewers, the same set piece runs from beginning to its dramatic conclusion.

The most important aspect of creating a set piece is having an awareness that this is a key moment in your story: You want to maximize it. In fact, your entire short script could be a set piece. For example, the excellent short *Mamá*. It begins to escalate seconds into the film when the boy walks into the room and tells his sister that Mamá is back. Then the set piece builds until the terrifying conclusion.

Midpoint

The *midpoint* happens (surprise, surprise) around the middle of the story and adds a new dimension to the story. It often increases the stakes, especially for the main character. The midpoint doesn't change the main character's second act goal, but it can strengthen, clarify, or intensify that goal. There are many different types of midpoints.

> ***Parasite*** The Kim family is partying in the Park house. They have all secured jobs which was their goal, and everything is going great. They even say, "This is our house." This is the classic *false victory* midpoint. It seems like our heroes have succeeded. But this victory is fleeting. The moment they have their victory toast, the doorbell rings, and that is the beginning of a desperate struggle to hang onto those great jobs.
>
> ***Jaws*** The moment Chief Brody sees the shark, he is stunned. It is huge. He stumbles into the cabin and utters the famous line, "We're going to need a bigger boat." The problem is bigger than we thought. The characters knew the problem was big, but it turns out to be much bigger.
>
> ***Breaking Bad*** Walt and his wife are at the mall helping their son buy a new pair of jeans. The school bully, a huge football jock, makes fun of Junior. Walt knocks the bully down and stomps on his ankle. Walt towers over the jock, taunting him. Walt has changed. The script states, "Walt feels a kind of power—one brought on by an absence of fear... he likes it." This is kind of a unique midpoint. It feels like it could be a false victory and given how bad things were in the opening we're pretty sure it is. But it's actually a *character arc* moment. It's not often we witness a character arc so clear in one scene.

As you can see, each of these solid midpoints is different. There are several other strong midpoint techniques. One of my favorites is in the movie *Legally Blonde*. The second act starts when Elle enrolls in Harvard to win back her boyfriend. At the midpoint, she gets a prestigious law internship. This begins to shift her *wants* and *needs*. (We will go into wants and needs in the next chapter.) Elle is still pursuing her main goal (her want)—winning her boyfriend back—but now she begins to believe in herself (her need), that she could become a lawyer. The reason a silly, fun movie like *Legally Blonde* does so well and stands the test of time is that it really nails the basic structure (along with the other key aspects) of storytelling.

Second Act Break

The *second act break* happens when your main character fails to achieve their goal. At the beginning of the second act, the main character decides to go for a goal. The second act ends when they fail to achieve this goal. Think about the worst thing that could happen to your protagonist. This is often called the *lowest low*. The main character hits rock bottom, they are defeated, and we're afraid things are going to end badly. The more you can sell the idea that things are actually going to end badly, the stronger and more dramatic your resolution will be.

> ***Parasite*** It may seem that when the Kim's apartment is flooded, and they have to sleep in a school gym with hundreds of strangers, that they have reached the lowest low. But they still have their jobs working for the Parks so their second act goal is still intact. The true second act break comes at the impromptu party for Da-Song when Kun-Sae, the housekeeper's husband, emerges from the basement (after nearly killing Ki-Woo) and stabs Ki-Jung in the chest. There is a chain reaction of mayhem, leaving several people dead.

> ***Jaws*** Quint is killed and the boat is sinking. Brody is afraid of the water and now the boat is filling up with water. He has been relying on the shark hunter, Quint, and he is gone. Things are not looking good for Chief Brody.

> ***Breaking Bad*** Jesse, Emilio (his old cook partner), and Krazy-8 arrive at the RV. Emilio recognizes Walt from the DEA bust. Not good. The mayhem ends with Krazy-8 pointing his gun at Walt, ready to kill him.

In each of these stories, the main character seems to have completely failed in their goal, people have died or are about to die. Things seem like they are definitely going to end badly.

Resolution or End Place

After the second act ends in defeat, the third act is all about the main character finding a new way to achieve their goal, aka *the resolution.*

Parasite Amazingly, after all the death and mayhem, *Parasite* manages to have a somewhat upbeat ending. The third act starts with narration by Ki-Woo (the true main character). The dreamlike ending revolves around Ki-Woo making a grand plan to go to college, get a good job, become rich, and buy the house (freeing his father who now resides in the basement). There is clearly a theme about making plans in the story. In fact, the word "plan" is spoken twenty-four times in the screenplay. From the first line uttered to Ki-Tek, "What's your plan?" to some of the last lines Ki-Tek speaks to his son, "Don't plan at all. Have no plan." Ki-Woo has an epiphany: he goes from relying on his father's plan (which didn't really exist) to finally making a plan himself.

Jaws Chief Brody finally kills the shark. He and Hooper begin to swim back to shore. This is probably one of the shortest third acts of all time. Even though it is a very short third act, it is powerful. Throughout the movie, Chief Brody defers to others. He defers to the shark expert Hooper, who wants to close the beach, but then he defers to the mayor and leaves the beach open. Finally, he goes out to hunt the shark but defers to Quint and Hooper to lead. Brody allows others to take the lead until finally in the last moments he takes action of his own volition. So even though this is an incredibly short third act, it is true to screenwriting form: Brody solves the main story problem by acting in a new and different way.

(The short third act of *Jaws* is great news for your short film. You don't need a long drawn out third act, we just need to see the main character act in a new, dynamic way.)

Breaking Bad Walt convinces Krazy-8 not to shoot him by showing him how to cook his recipe. This leads to the climactic showdown. Walt uses chemistry to defeat the gun-toting drug dealers. We finally get back to the end of the opening sequence. Walt panics and tries to shoot himself, but the safety is on. As he fiddles with it, the gun goes off, scaring him, finally the approaching sirens arrive—they are fire trucks! They drive right by pantless Walt. Later, he's drying the cash in the clothes dryer. Finally, the episode ends with Walt powerfully making love to his wife. He is a new man.

One of the keys to a satisfying ending is seeing a character transformation, as in all three examples above. Another story that has a very satisfying transformation is *School of Rock*. Dewey, played brilliantly by Jack Black, only has one goal in life: to be a rock star. Throughout the film, we see Dewey selfishly pursue his goal until the third act, when he sees the kids he's been teaching perform at the battle of the bands. He is overwhelmed and it is incredibly satisfying. When the story started, he never could have imagined that seeing kids perform would in any way fulfill his dream of rock stardom. Over the course of the story, Dewey is transformed. Without his realizing it, he has developed a relationship with the kids and really cares about them. This transformation makes for a very satisfying ending.

Major Beats Everywhere!

Most of the examples we have looked at are feature films or one-hour pilots. But three-act structure and the major beats are extremely versatile and can strengthen almost any story. Even simple single-page children's stories can have these beats.

A great example is the work of Arnold Lobel, one of the most beloved and award-winning children's authors of all time. In his Caldecott Medal winning book *Fables*, there are twenty single-page stories. The final story is "The Mouse at the Seashore."

Here are the major beats:

> **Status Quo**: A happy mouse family (implied).
>
> **Inciting Incident**: The mouse tells his mother and father that he is going to the seashore.
>
> **The Debate**: The parents are extremely worried, the world is full of terrors.
>
> **First Act Break**: At dawn the mouse sets out on his journey.
>
> **Set Piece**: He quickly encounters trouble when a cat tries to eat him. The mouse runs for his life and narrowly escapes but loses part of his tail.
>
> **Midpoint**: He gets lost several times.
>
> **Second Act Break**: Bruised and bloodied, the mouse is tired and frightened.
>
> **End Place**: The mouse reaches the seashore. It's incredibly beautiful. He is filled with deep peace and contentment.

Even with just a one-page story, the story structure guidelines are followed and it helps make the story very satisfying. Obviously, if a single-page children's story can have three acts (and is much stronger as a result), then we can certainly fit three acts into a short screenplay and it will be stronger as well.

Exercise: Identify the Major Beats

Go back to the work you did for the exercise in Chapter 2, where you wrote out the beats for a film. Now, looking over your complete list of beats, can you identify the major ones?

Let's look at the first example from Chapter 2, the short film *Ataque de Pánico!*

Status Quo: A young boy plays with toy robots.

Inciting Incident: Giant robots emerge from the fog.

First Act Break: The robots begin to attack, firing missiles.

Midpoint: Uruguayan Air Force jets counterattack but are no match for the invading alien forces.

Second Act Break: A building that looks like the capital is destroyed.

Resolution: Robots unleash massive explosion which seems to wipe out everything.

Set Piece: The entire short is an excellent escalating set piece.

Now let's go over the major beats from the opening twenty pages of our feature film example in Chapter 2, *Galaxy Quest*.

Hook: The dramatic clip from the classic sci-fi show plays like a mini hook.

Status Quo: A group of actors from a classic sci-fi show make a living playing out their old roles and they are not too happy about it.

Inciting Incident: Unbeknownst to Jason, he agrees to help real aliens battle against a vicious villain.

That big list from Chapter 2 only contained the beats in act one, so there are just three major beats from that list.

Exercise: Major Beats for Your Story

Time to work on your own story! Start with your title and logline. You may want to rewrite your logline based on what you have learned. Now, write down the major story beats for your story:

Hook. (Not every story will have one.)

Status quo. (Could be implied in a short film.)

Inciting incident.

Debate.

> **First act break.**
>
> **A set piece.** (Could be anywhere, or entire short could be a set piece.)
>
> **Midpoint.**
>
> **Second act break.**
>
> **End place.**
>
> You can write up to several sentences for each beat. The complete document should be less than one page, with 12-point font and normal margins. I believe looking at your entire story on a single page is an incredibly powerful step.

Spoiler Alert! | Chapter 5

Forrest Gump (1994).

The Graduate (1967).

Raiders of the Lost Ark (1981).

Mad Max: Fury Road (2015).

Shrek (2001).

Sound of Metal (2019).

Locke (2013).

Fever Pitch (2005).

Her (2013).

The Fighter (2010).

Liar, Liar (1997).

Locks (2009).

The Lives of Others (2006)

Star Wars: A New Hope (1977).

Jojo Rabbit (2019).

The Godfather (1972).

Casino Royale (2006).

Manchester by the Sea (2016).

Minority Report (2002).

Saving Private Ryan (1998).

Foxcatcher (2014).

Gossip Girl, pilot episode (2007).

Fast Times at Ridgemont High (1982).

The Big Lebowski (1998).

Legally Blonde (2001).

Little Miss Sunshine (2006).

The 40-Year-Old Virgin (2005).

Breaking Bad, pilot episode (2008).

Captain Fantastic (2016).

Whiplash (2014).

The O.C., pilot episode (2003).

5

Character

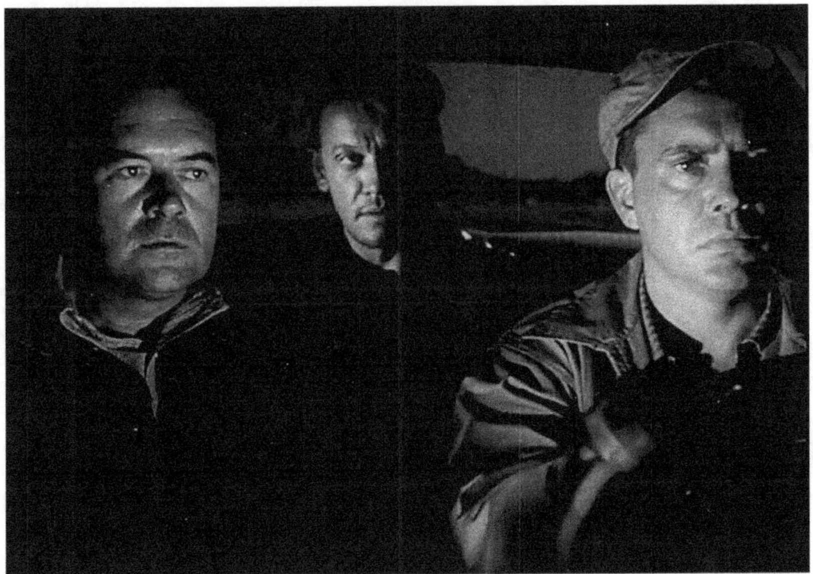

The Hitch-Hiker (1953).

Creating Great Characters

A great screenplay requires great characters. Even with a short film, you should do everything possible to create the most compelling characters you can.

There are two parts to creating great characters. The first is defining the character. Often screenwriting books and articles recommend writing long biographies to help define your characters. Where were they born? What was their favorite toy? What is their favorite color? A long list of "very important" questions. But does answering lengthy arbitrary worksheets lead you to discover a great character? I don't think so. It keeps you busy, but mostly, it's a waste of time.

Recently, at the USC School of Cinematic Arts, a group of fellow professors (all of whom are working writers) and I were discussing characters. One of the professors asked the group, "Have you ever written a character bio for a professional job?" We all laughed. Screenplays are precise and specific. When working on a deadline, you must define the character quickly and efficiently. Spending time on a rambling bio filled with random info is the last thing you need to do.

In this chapter, I will show you clear, concise steps to help define your characters.

But defining a great character is only half the answer. You still need to get those great characters down on the page in screenplay format, and that can be an epic challenge. Screenwriting is a highly evolved form of writing that is very specific. When done well, it is raised to the level of poetry. I will go over the basic tools for bringing your characters to life on the page in screenplay format. This is the first of three chapters on writing characters. In Chapter 6, we'll continue with character, discussing "How to Get the Audience to Care" and in Chapter 7, we'll look at "Character-Based Structure."

So, let's get to work on those characters!

What's in a Name?

Names matter. Take the time to choose a name that fits your character. I have read many screenplays with boring generic names. To me, this screams "lazy writer." Besides giving a bad first impression, one of the main issues when you use generic names is that characters tend to blend together. This makes reading a screenplay more difficult which is, obviously, a bad thing.

Strong names help create memorable characters. Like Forrest Gump. Now that's a name. Once you've heard that name, you never forget it.

Another common issue is when every named character in a screenplay is a first name. In *Forrest Gump,* two of the other main characters in that movie are Lieutenant Dan and Bubba. These are fantastic, distinctive names as well. If the names were first name only, they would be Forrest, Dan and Ben. It would be easy to mix up Dan and Ben while reading. Both are three letters and end with the letter "n." Way too similar. Adding the military designation, Lieutenant, makes the Dan name really pop. Similarly, using a nickname, like Bubba, makes that name clearly stand out. If you are reading the screenplay for *Forrest Gump*, you will have no trouble keeping track of who's who.

Names are the first step in creating an identity for your character. For example, if you choose the name Sebastian, that seems to imply a certain sophistication. I suspect a character named Sebastian would dress neatly and might speak with a slight foreign accent. If you choose a name like Joe, you get a character with a totally different vibe. Phrases like *average Joe* or *regular Joe* come to mind. To me "Joe" feels like a simple guy, basic. Imagine Sebastian and Joe in a scene together! There is immediate contrast and conflict. Sebastian thinks Joe is a simpleton, a bumbling commoner. Joe is immediately annoyed by Sebastian the snob. Even before there is any action, the names generate a sense of story.

How about Mrs. Robinson and Elaine? If you've seen *The Graduate*, you know exactly what I'm talking about. Even if you were just reading the story, you would never mix up Mrs. Robinson and Elaine. Mrs. Robinson is the sultry married woman who is the friend of Benjamin's parents. The "Mrs." adds tremendously to the character. It identifies her as older and married. In fact, her first name is *never* revealed in the movie!

Elaine is her daughter, the smart and stylish younger woman who also falls in love with Benjamin. What if Elaine's name were Tiffany? It wouldn't feel the same. Tiffany sounds cute, young, playful, maybe a cheerleader.

A well-chosen name can go a long way to establishing your character with identifiable characteristics. A name can also imply ethnicity, adding diversity to your story. There are lots of baby-naming websites which make it easy to look up great names from all over the world. These sites often specify country and include the meaning of the name. Picking a name with a specific meaning can bring more to your character, even if the audience doesn't know exactly what it means.

Exercise: Names from Around the World

Can you guess the country of origin of these names?

- Dikembe
- Agamemnon
- Mizuki

> Even if the country isn't apparent, what is clear is that these are not generic names.
>
> Pick three interesting names from different regions around the globe. Feel free to use various baby-naming websites for reference.

Defining Personality Trait

The *defining personality trait* is the basic idea of who your character is and how they act most of the time. A fleshed-out character will have many personality traits but which personality trait is central to the story? Which trait will we witness consistently throughout the story? This is their defining personality trait.

- Indiana Jones is a fearless treasure hunter.
- Furiosa is a relentless truck driver and the ultimate survivalist.
- Shrek is a grumpy ogre who wants to be left alone.

A well-defined, consistent main character is essential to a well told story.

A Contradiction

We want strong clear characters, but we need to avoid one-note characters. A contradiction is a personality trait that keeps your character from being cliché or falling into a stereotype. This contradiction works best when it is something that might not be expected when meeting the character.

Let's look at our earlier list of characters in terms of their contradictions:

- Indy is afraid of snakes.
- Furiosa becomes hell-bent on protecting the five wives.
- Shrek has a soft side.

Each of these characteristics seems to oppose the defining personality trait of that character. This is the first step in creating a complex character. But the contradiction needs to make sense. It can't be random. Whatever you choose, it must be believable.

Depth of Character

Complex characters should have several other key qualities that come into play in the story. These qualities help to flesh out the character, making them more human and more realistic. Riz Ahmed received an Oscar nomination for the character of Ruben in *Sound of Metal,* which is a great example:

- He's intense.
- He's a passionate musician.
- He's charming and funny.
- He's hard working and resourceful.

When we see Ruben banging on his drums like a maniac, you don't expect him to be a sweet, charming guy who is very hard working.

 ## Character Types to Avoid

Angry characters are very difficult to pull off. They tend to be unlikable and lack depth. Anger is often one dimensional. Plus, it's hard to sympathize with an angry character. Characters can get angry when it's justified but if it is their basic state of being, then that is not fun to be around.

Stoic characters are uniquely challenging. Since they have very little dialogue and they tend to not display emotions, it's very difficult to get to know these characters. The small amount of dialogue that they have must really crackle and it needs to reveal the character hidden beneath the stoicism.

Of course, there's Don Draper from *Mad Men*. This extremely well-written show is the stoic exception that proves the rule.

Their Situation

What's going on in your character's life? It's critical to make the situation as dramatic as possible. Take the movie *Locke*. Ivan Locke is the foreman for a major construction project and tomorrow morning is *the* most important step for the job he is on, the concrete pour. It's also the night of the big soccer match. He is planning to watch the game with his sons and even his wife is going to join them—a big family event. So, when Ivan decides not to go home to his family and leaves the critical job to an underling, the stakes are massive for Ivan—the situation is about as dire as it could be.

Let's look at Ruben's situation:

- He and his partner Lou are in a band together.
- He is a recovering addict. (So is she.)
- He's losing his hearing.

Notice how Ruben's entire life is wrapped up with his life partner and the band, including his recovery from addiction. If he loses his hearing, it puts every aspect of his life in jeopardy. We want to apply pressure to our characters, turn up the heat. This creates drama.

Big Problem

Characters need to have a *big problem*. Something that is keeping them from achieving what they want. (Nothing is more annoying than a flawless character.) There are several ways to approach your character's problem.

Psychology of Your Character

What makes your character tick? What drives them? What is important to them? Answering these questions will lead you to the character's big problem. Generally, the character knows about the problem, but they think it's not a problem or they tend to minimize it, thinking they have it under control.

> *Fever Pitch* Lindsay falls for Ben. He's a warm, sweet guy. But then baseball season starts and we discover that Ben is a baseball fanatic. Problem: Baseball is so important to Ben that it threatens their entire relationship.

> *Her* Theodore has become totally gun-shy about forming human relationships and is very lonely. Problem: He is so lonely that he accepts falling in love with a computer.

> *The Fighter* Dicky is so self-absorbed that he destroyed his own boxing career. Problem: He's headed toward destroying his brother's career as well.

If you understand the psychology of your character, you will be able to create an interesting problem which leads to a deep meaningful character. But this is not the only way to think about the character's big problem…

Wants vs. Needs

What your character *wants* versus what your character *needs* is another excellent way to look at the idea of a character's big problem. When a character has a conflict between their wants and their needs, it shows that they lack awareness of their big problem or how to fix it. They must discover their true need over the course of the story.

> ***Shrek*** He *wants* to be left alone. He *needs* to open up and let others in.

> ***Sound of Metal*** Ruben *wants* to get his hearing back. He *needs* to accept that he is deaf.

> ***Liar Liar*** Fletcher *wants* to make partner at his law firm and win back his wife and son. He *needs* to tell the truth and be a good father.

When a character aims for what they want, they often end up making big mistakes. By the end of the story, the character has experienced enough to realize what it is they really need. This realization is often a key step in the *character arc*.

Character Arc

The way that your main character changes over the course of the story is their *character arc*. This is where the big problem comes in. Characters need to realize what their big problem is and face up to it or they will ultimately fail. This goes beyond the main character, other characters can arc as well. But most stories focus primarily on the arc of the main character.

Having a character arc within a five- to ten-minute short may be very challenging but it is definitely worth trying. Take Ryan Coogler's *Locks*: As a young black man walks through his neighborhood in Oakland, his identity is established through a series of shots. He has a distinctive look, so when he dramatically alters his appearance, we are shocked. The powerful results of this change are revealed in the final shot. His willingness to make a visible change is the core of the character arc and it is a big part of why this short has such a powerful emotional impact.

As for *Shrek*, he *wants* to be left alone. He *needs* to open up and have friends and a relationship. The root of his big problem is that he is afraid of getting hurt. In the beginning, Shrek is extremely resistant to change, rejecting

Donkey's efforts to develop a friendship. Then at the midpoint, Shrek begins to fall for Princess Fiona and seems to begin to accept Donkey as a buddy. But by the end of the second act—the lowest low—Shrek overhears a conversation and misunderstands, which leaves him devastated. He goes back to being the grumpy ogre, proclaiming, "I live alone." In the third act, Shrek is faced with a dilemma: remain alone or change. He begins the final steps of his journey of change, his character arc, by apologizing to Donkey. Then he completes his journey by admitting his love for Princess Fiona. In the end, Shrek is completely changed. (Character arc, yay!) He has a wife and a best friend. He is no longer grumpy or alone, but truly happy.

Here are more examples of strong character arcs:

> ***The Lives of Others*** The 2006 Oscar-winner for Best Foreign Film may have one of the best character arc stories of all time. Stasi Officer Wiesler starts off as a terrifying character, brutally breaking prisoners into confessing. As he begins to observe a playwright's life, he slowly is transformed. He also begins to witness the corruption of the government he works so hard for.

> ***Star Wars: A New Hope*** Han Solo is a smuggler that is just in it for the money. He's willing to take a risk but only because there's a cash reward at the end. So, when he decides to stay and help the rebels fight the Death Star, this is a big shift in his character. This is a great example of someone who is not the main character having a strong arc.

> ***Jojo Rabbit*** Young Jojo is a gung-ho but naive Nazi youth. After developing a relationship with a young Jewish girl hiding in his home, he is completely transformed. Coming of age stories often feature a great character arc, but this one is particularly nice.

It should be clear that a good character arc is usually a journey with ups and downs, not just a single moment. But this is not always the case. In one of the all-time great movies, *The Godfather*, the character Michael Corleone goes to visit his father in the hospital after he has been shot. As Michael gets there, he realizes that something is up: many of the hospital workers have left and the ones that remain are acting really strange. He determines that there is going to be another attempt to kill his father, so he gathers some people and stops it. Over the next nine pages, Michael has one of the most famous arcs in movie history. He goes from college kid who didn't want to be involved in "the business" to a murderer: he kills a New York city police captain and the Turk. (This is also one of the greatest set pieces of all time and we'll go into set pieces in-depth in Chapter 16.)

So how do you make sure your character has a strong arc? I think it starts with the ending. You should ask yourself who your character is in the end. Then ask yourself, what big change got them there? And most importantly, who were they in the beginning? What did they lack? What did they not understand?

As you write your story, consider these questions:

- What changes will we see your character go through?
- What does your main character learn on their journey?
- What is a scene that will make your character question who they are and force them to choose?

No Character Arc

Character arcs are awesome, but do all stories feature a character who arcs?

Some screenwriting books insist that your main character must have an arc, but that is just not true. Remember, no rules! Sometimes you'll see analysis of a film that states that a secondary character is actually the main character since they arc the most. Again, this is not the case.

Let's take another look at *Forrest Gump*. Forrest is Forrest. He does not change. He's Forrest at the beginning. He's Forrest in the middle. He's Forrest in the end. No arc. Now, Lt. Dan has a pretty good arc. So, is he the main character? Of course not! The movie is titled *Forrest Gump* not Lt. Dan! Forrest is the main character and he doesn't arc. Period.

Consider Erin Brockovich. She's another powerful character that does not arc. Her situation changes dramatically, others come to see her completely differently, but she is still Erin. She has always believed in herself but because of her success now others see her the way she has always seen herself. She does not change; her situation changes.

James Bond is an interesting case. From the classic Bond films of the early 1960s all the way through to the early 2000s, Bond was a character that did not arc. This was part of his cool persona. Nothing ever got to Bond—he didn't fall in love and no matter who died, it didn't bother him. But starting with *Casino Royale* in 2006, there was a new Bond. He fell in love and could be deeply affected by the deaths of other characters. This new Bond was more human and tended to arc. It wasn't a huge arc but enough that he was affected, sometimes deeply so.

A character arc can be extremely powerful, but it is *not* essential.

Backstory

A great backstory can help you create a dynamic character. Backstory is important because your character's life does not begin at "fade in." They have been living their lives, they have hopes and dreams, and most importantly, they have psychological scars.

A mistake that writers often make is putting the backstory first. New writers often want to explain their character, dumping a bunch of backstory info on the audience like a load of wet laundry. "I know this is boring, but I have to explain..." No. Stop. You don't have to explain. In fact, when you explain, you are not storytelling. You are forcing your audience to go through a history lesson that is, most likely, really boring.

A great backstory needs to be hinted at. The writer must create a mystery. They should tease the audience, arouse their curiosity so that they can then satisfy that curiosity by finally revealing the backstory. Take *Manchester by the Sea*: Casey Affleck won an Oscar for portraying the main character, Lee Chandler. Lee must go back to his hometown, Manchester by the Sea. We can see that he is not happy to go back to the town he grew up in and we wonder why. People in Manchester by the Sea are shocked to see Lee back in town, which builds the mystery. This leads to many questions: What happened? Why is Lee uncomfortable being back home? Why are people shocked that he's here?

Around the midpoint, Lee's backstory is revealed and it's a horrific tragedy, about as bad as it could be. That's all we need to know. We understand Lee Chandler now and it's devastating.

We don't need to know what park he played in as a boy. We don't need to know whether he had a pet and what its name was. We don't need to know what kind of clothes he wore as a boy. We don't need to know any of that stuff. A backstory is not a list of stuff about a character. It is an event (or a relationship) that defines who the character is.

So how do you create a great backstory? Like obstacles and complications, a good backstory should make the task that the character must complete more difficult, if not impossible. For Lee Chandler, that task is delivered by his brother's last will and testament: he is to raise his nephew, in Manchester by the Sea. When we finally learn Lee's backstory, we understand why this seems impossible for Lee to do. Every second he is in Manchester, reminds him of the horrible tragedy he experienced.

Here are some additional examples:

Locke Ivan Locke has a great career, a loving wife, and a happy family. So why would he be willing to throw it all away? The backstory reveals the answer: his relationship with his father was so painful, and left such a psychological scar, that Ivan has lived his whole life by one motto: "Don't be like your father." That's led him to an incredibly good and successful life, but now it's become an intense obstacle that might cost Ivan everything.

Minority Report The pre-cogs predict that Chief John Anderton is going to murder Leo Crow, a man he's never met. Why would Anderton murder someone he doesn't know? Throughout the second act, Anderton's backstory that his son was abducted is revealed in three parts. This backstory solves the riddle: the one person on earth that Anderton would murder is the man who abducted his son. It also creates a huge obstacle. Anderton must find a way to alter his future, but if this is the man who killed his son… that's a problem!

Saving Private Ryan None of the guys know what Captain John Miller did before the war. It's a mystery. In fact, the guys in the company have a betting pool with everyone guessing Miller's previous job. They all figure it must have been something big, something that prepared Miller for the life and death decisions that he must make. In the end, Miller reveals that he was a high school teacher. Nothing about being a schoolteacher could prepare Miller for the horrors of war.

The key to great backstory is to create a mystery, then build on the audience's expectations and desire to know. Then you reveal the backstory when it will provide maximum value.

Exercise: Define Your Character

Continuing with the character you created from the story exercise in Chapter 4, describe your main character using all of the character tools:

- Character's Name.
- Defining Personality Trait.
- Contradiction.
- Other key character qualities or traits.
- Important aspects of their situation.
- Big problem. (Use psychology or wants vs. needs.)
- Arc.
- Backstory.

Writing Your Character

When writing a novel, you can go on at length about your character. You can pen page after page of interesting detail, and if you are a skilled enough writer, it may actually be entertaining.

Screenwriters do not have that luxury, especially when writing short films. We have a limited amount of space as well as a limited number of tools for demonstrating the main character's traits on the page in screenplay format. These limitations force the screenwriter to be extremely precise with minimal details.

Opening Description

The *opening description* of your character should only be a line or two. Since you only get a handful of lines, you need to make them really count.

A couple of basic rules apply here. The first time a character shows up in the screenplay scene description, their name must be in ALL CAPS. This tells the reader to pay attention because this is someone new. Generally, we want to include the character's age. This does not have to be an exact number. A lot of screenwriting guides state that you must include a physical description. I believe that it is only necessary if it plays a role in the story. Let's look at this example from *Foxcatcher*:

```
MARK  SCHULTZ  (27,  180  lbs.,  cauli-
flower  ears)  lifts  a  humansized,
leather WRESTLING DUMMY from the mat
to stand in front of him.
```

In this case, the description includes an exact weight which may seem odd. But Mark is an Olympic wrestler and competes at a specific weight. The addition of "cauliflower ears" informs us that Mark has paid a price for his intense competitions. So the physical description is relevant for this character.

The best character descriptions should get across some of the character's personality. Here are a few character descriptions from *Gossip Girl* that are short and stylish but still convey a lot of information. Notice how each of these character descriptions vividly portray a personality:

```
BLAIR  WALDORF,  17.  Pretty.  But  will
never  feel  beautiful  enough.
```

Here we get a physical description, wrapped in a psychology that will affect how Blair acts in almost every situation.

```
CHUCK BASS, 17.  Future Senator or
cautionary tale.
```

This dynamic description tells us that Chuck is a bold character. But will this boldness lead to greatness or a disaster?

```
DAN, 17, will be fine when he gets to
college. That is little consolation
today. JENNY, 15, isn't waiting for
college. Wants to be popular now.
```

You usually shouldn't introduce two characters in the same paragraph, but it works here since they are brother and sister, sharing the same dilemma. Dan is willing to suffer but Jenny could be a time bomb.

Clothing

The award-winning writer/director, Nancy Meyers, talks about how important choosing a character's wardrobe is to her filmmaking process. Modern film schedules leave little or no rehearsal time. So, for her, the wardrobe process becomes a multi-day discussion with the lead actors about their characters. Great directors and great actors know how critical clothing is for a character: it defines them as a person.

Here are some wardrobe classics:

- Spicoli from *Fast Times at Ridgemont High* wears checkerboard Vans. Iconic shoes, iconic character.

- In the opening of *The Big Lebowski*, The Dude wears sunglasses, a bathrobe, and slippers on a late-night excursion to Ralphs to buy a pint of half and half. His clothes tell us that this guy moves to his own drumbeat and definitely at his own pace.

- In *Legally Blonde*, Elle always wears pink. She is the ultimate sorority girl, and her clothes help her stand out even more when she attends a conservative, Ivy League college.

Transportation

Does your protagonist ride the subway, or do they get chauffeured around in a limo? Do they ride a horse, a motorcycle, or a skateboard? How your character gets around says a lot about them. Think about the broken-down VW van that the family in *Little Miss Sunshine* travels in. It seems like the perfect metaphor for their broken family—it is barely hanging on.

- James Bond always drives the latest Aston Martin, one of the most stylish cars in the world.
- In *The 40-Year-Old Virgin*, Andy rides a ten-speed bike.
- In *Breaking Bad*, Walter White drives a beat-up Pontiac Aztek. It's a car for people who want to go camping but never really do—it's actually a terrible off-road vehicle. The car is a perfect representation of Walter's life, he had dreams but never really pursued them.

Environment

The environment your character exists in has a powerful influence on how we see them. Think about the movie *Parasite*. The awful apartment the Kim family lives in has a profound effect on us. It's literally below the street, a street that people urinate in. It's also the perfect foil to the amazing house they begin to work in. Everything about the house is better, higher class. Even getting to the house, they must go up the street and up the stairs. Interesting fact: the beautiful house was not a real location. The director, Bong Joon-ho, designed and built the house for the film. That's how important the characters' environment can be. Each of these environments makes a strong statement about the main character and the world of the story:

Captain Fantastic is in the woods with his family. Their faces and arms are covered in mud. His oldest son kills a deer with his bare hands. This is not a family on a camping trip, they exist in the wild.

Sound of Metal Over black we hear sound, feedback. We're at a concert. It's loud. A building cacophony. A drummer waits to begin. Even if you don't like this type of music, it's undeniably intense.

Mad Max: Fury Road Max stands with his back to us staring out at a desert wasteland, a highly-modified muscle car nearby. He kills and eats a two-headed lizard. This world is tough.

Opening Action

We can describe our characters all day long, but it is their actions that will reveal the truth about who they are. What is your character doing when we meet them? This first impression carries a lot of weight. We want this first impression to be clear and strong.

The most critical aspect of the *opening action* is getting the audience to care about your character. (In fact, this is so important that we will devote the entire next chapter to it.) Each of these openings lets us know exactly who the main character is and what their situation is:

> ***Erin Brockovich*** In the opening scene she is interviewing for a job at a doctor's office, even though she has no medical training. You would have to be desperate to apply for a job where you have no training or experience, which is exactly Erin's situation: she's desperate.

> ***Whiplash*** Andrew is in a rehearsal studio practicing his drumming. This shows he is dedicated to his craft and working hard at it. Fletcher, the band leader, enters the studio and challenges Andrew, testing his skills. This is an amazing opening scene that demonstrates the protagonist, the antagonist, and the main conflict of the story.

> ***Her*** We start close on Theodore's face as he thoughtfully begins to compose a beautiful love letter. He's several lines in when he says, "I can't believe you married me fifty years ago." Wait. Theodore is not even fifty. How could he have been married for fifty years? Then he says, "You make me feel like the girl..." Okay. Theodore is definitely not a girl. What's going on? Then it's revealed that Theodore writes love letters for hire. It's a big company. He's alone in the office. A wonderfully intriguing opening that draws us in and gets us to care for lonely Theodore.

So what does it look like when we put it all together. Here's an amazing example of a character intro from *The O.C.* Notice how many of the elements we've been discussing come into play.

```
A banged-up Chevy NOVA pulls in.
Driving a little faster than is safe
for a parking lot. LURCHES to a halt.
DAWN ATWOOD, late 30's, opens the
door. Once an attractive woman. But
life hasn't been kind. Looks like she
just got out of bed. Not wearing
shoes. Probably drunk.
```

One note: the parking lot she is pulling into is a police station parking lot. This short paragraph uses just about every tool possible for getting character across.

Exercise: Identify Character Techniques

Explain each of the techniques that are used in the above character introduction to Dawn Atwood in *The O.C.*

Exercise: A Character in Screenplay Format

Continue developing your main character by listing their:

- Opening description
- Clothing
- Transportation
- Environment
- Opening Action

Now bring it all together: Describe a short introductory scene. (This does not have to be the opening scene of the movie.)

Alternately, you can write the introductory scene in screenplay format (one to two pages), using as many of the tools listed in this chapter as you can.

Spoiler Alert! | Chapter 6

Rudy (1993).

Jerry Maguire (1996).

School of Rock (2003).

The Shawshank Redemption (1994).

Forrest Gump (1994).

Erin Brockovich (2000).

Rocky (1976).

Howl's Moving Castle (2004).

The Devil Wears Prada (2006).

Unforgiven (1992).

As Good as It Gets (1997).

Nightcrawler (2014).

Olive Kitteridge, pilot episode (2014).

Halloween (1978).

6

Getting the Audience to Care

*I am not a bum. I'm a jerk. I once had wealth, power,
and the love of a beautiful woman. Now I only have
two things: my friends and… uh… my thermos.*

*—Navin R. Johnson (Steve Martin) in
"The Jerk," written by Steve Martin*

Why Should I Care?

"Why should I care?" is a horrible question that producers often ask. As a writer, you want to pull your hair out and scream, "Because I wrote a great story!" A great story is extremely important but the obnoxious question, "Why should I care?" is always about character. People care about characters. People fall in love with characters. Even if you have done the work to create a great character, will the audience automatically fall in love with that character? Will people find them fascinating? Will people root for them?

Why You Should Care

The best way to sell your screenplay is to have an A-list actor attached, meaning they want to play the lead in your story. But why would a top actor want to star in your story? Because your script has a dynamic, compelling character that leaps off the page—a character that people fall in love with.

Even if you are writing a short, you still should do everything possible to create compelling dynamic characters.

Techniques to Engage the Audience

So how do you get an audience to care about your characters? This may be the most important question you ask yourself as a writer/storyteller. You need to find a way to get your audience to connect with your characters. How do you build an emotional connection between your characters and the audience?

Luckily, there are some great techniques to get an audience on the side of your character.

Passion

When characters have passion, we can't help but become passionate with them.

> *Rudy* There is nothing special about Rudy. He's just a normal high school kid. No superpowers. No amazing talents. He's not that smart or handsome or tall. But he wants to play football at the University of Notre Dame. This is not a passing fancy, he spends every waking moment striving for this goal. When a character is this passionate and works this hard, we become invested in them and in their goal. The more desperate Rudy is to succeed, the more desperately we want him to succeed.

Humiliation

Seeing a person humiliated is powerful and builds strong empathy.

> *Jerry Maguire* has a moment of guilty conscience and writes a heartfelt mission statement. Although it seems to go well initially, he is quickly fired. He desperately tries to rally his clients but loses all but one. As he heads out of the office, Jerry gives a passionate speech urging others to come with him and his fish (a little comedy always helps). Crickets. Even Jerry says, "This is embarrassing." Finally, Dorothy Boyd joins Jerry and his fish. But he is clearly very humiliated.

> *School of Rock* In the opening scene, Jack Black's character Dewey, is overdoing it, people are leaving, so he takes his shirt off and does a stage dive but no one catches him! Ouch! A couple scenes later, Dewey goes to band practice and gets kicked out of the band he started! Totally embarrassing and we really feel sorry for him.

Injustice

It deeply disturbs us when we see someone treated unjustly. The quote from *The Jerk* that opened this chapter draws us in, we wonder what happened to Navin because it doesn't seem fair. Humans seem to have an innate sense of fairness. In *School of Rock*, in addition to being humiliated, Dewey is treated unfairly. How can his bandmates kick him out of the band he started? That's wrong. Treating a character unfairly is a powerful way to build empathy for that character.

> ***The Shawshank Redemption*** The opening sequence finds Andy Dufresne on trial for the murder of his wife and her lover. Even though the evidence seems quite damning, it is circumstantial, and we tend to believe Andy is innocent. He is sentenced to two life terms in the notorious Shawshank State Prison. When he arrives, he is regularly beaten and raped. This seems particularly unjust. Our faith in Andy is rewarded when he secures beer for his "coworkers" (fellow prisoners). We really want to see Andy get some justice; a redemption. This setup leads to an amazingly successful film, which is the #1 rated movie of all time on IMDb.

> ***Forrest Gump*** The neighborhood bullies throw rocks at young Forrest, hitting the poor disabled boy in the head and face. Young Jenny tells him, "Run, Forrest, run!" We feel terrible for young Forrest, with his heavy, clunky, leg braces. He can hardly hobble, let alone run. Suddenly, his braces break apart and fall away, he can run, and it feels truly rewarding.

> ***Erin Brockovich*** In an early sequence in the movie, we find Erin in court trying to sue the doctor who slammed into her car. We know it was the doctor's fault, the prior scene made that clear. But because of the way Erin dresses and talks, the jury unfairly sides with the clean-cut doctor. This is terribly frustrating and makes the audience hope that something good will happen for Erin.

The Underdog

People love to root for an underdog. There's nothing like seeing a long shot win a big horse race. Or the team from the small town beating the big town favorites. During March Madness, the NCAA college basketball tournament, when you see a 15 seed beating a 2 seed, you can't help but root for the underdog. It doesn't matter if you've never even heard of the school, you find yourself cheering them on.

Rocky One of the all-time great underdog movies: A small-time fighter with a mediocre career takes on the heavyweight champion of the world. Of course, we're going to be in Rocky's corner. Even though Rocky is very stoic and does not vocalize how he feels about winning, we see how hard he trains. These actions convince us that he is very passionate, which furthers our support of this underdog fighter.

Erin Brockovich The court room scene I mentioned earlier really is amazing because it also serves another purpose: We see how poorly Erin fares in a court of law and that's exactly where this story is headed. She is going to take on a huge public utility and their team of lawyers in court! We've just seen she can't win a case which she one-hundred percent deserved to win. Talk about an underdog.

Rudy Besides being ultra-passionate, Rudy is also one of the ultimate underdogs. Just look at his size: five feet six (1.68 meters) and 165 pounds (75 kilograms). That is small for a high school football player. Rudy walked on (no scholarship) in the years 1974 and 1975. Joe Montana was on that team—one of the greatest football players of all time. The team would go on to win the national championship in 1977, so many of the players that Rudy played with were some of the best in the game. By any measure, Rudy had no business being on the field with these great athletes. That's why Rudy is an amazing underdog.

Introduced By...

A great technique to build intrigue about a character is to have other characters talk about them. This is a fantastic way to build expectations in the audience.

Howl's Moving Castle Women at a sewing shop see Howl's moving castle emerge from the fog. They begin to chatter about the rumors they have heard. That he is a wizard and that he eats women's hearts, but only the pretty ones. This builds the tension and suspense making for a very dramatic scene when our main character meets Howl shortly after.

The Devil Wears Prada Everyone in the office is cool and hip until someone shouts, "Miranda is coming!" Suddenly total panic! The facade of cool is gone and the characters look truly terrified. This builds our expectations and heightens our anticipation. We really want to know who this Miranda is.

Unforgiven After a short opening scene, opening titles play over a long shot of a man in silhouette digging by a tree followed by a text crawl that introduces the main character:

```
She was a comely young woman and
not without prospects. Therefore
it was heartbreaking to her
mother that she would enter into
marriage with William Munny, a
known thief and murderer, a man
of notoriously vicious and
intemperate disposition. When she
died, it was not by his hands as
her mother might have expected,
but of smallpox. That was 1878.
```

This leads us to believe that the man digging is William Munny and that he is digging a grave for his wife. We feel sympathy for William before we've even met him.

When we finally do meet the notorious William Munny, he is now a farmer and he's wrestling with a pig. The pig is getting the best of William and, covered in mud, he seems pretty darn harmless. This creates a mystery in the audience's mind. Is this guy really a killer? It takes the entire length of the story to get to the answer in the climactic showdown. That's when we finally see the William Munny described in the opening text. Yes. He sure as hell is a vicious killer.

 ## Alternative Method for Hooking the Audience

A *dynamic plot* is another method for hooking the audience. But this will only work for so long. At some point, the audience *must* get on board with the characters or even the best plot will fall flat. In Chapter 11, "Start Fast," we will examine a series of various plot techniques for hooking an audience.

Unlikable Characters

How or why would an audience like an "unlikable" character? Often a character's actions on screen are reprehensible. If you knew one of these characters in real life, you would almost certainly *not* like them. And yet there is a long list of characters who behave badly but are loved by fans!

Often screenwriting guides stress *likability*: we must like the protagonist. They need to do good deeds, be heroic, be a good person. But what if the main character doesn't save the cat? What if he throws the dog down a garbage chute? That's exactly what Melvin Udall does in *As Good as It Gets*. Then he is nasty and racist. All in the opening scene. And yet Jack Nicholson won an Oscar for his portrayal of Mr. Udall. So, what's going on here?

First, this character is wickedly funny. Yes, some of it is terribly offensive but much of it is outrageously funny. Then we discover that he has OCD and dealing with it is a real struggle for him. From the very beginning, he is fascinating. A dynamic, enigmatic character. We watch him, captivated, wondering what he will do next.

Then there is Lou Bloom from *Nightcrawler*. In the opening scene, he's using bolt cutters to remove a fence and he is trespassing. When confronted by the guard, Lou wrestles him to the ground and steals his watch. These are *not* the actions of a nice guy. But Lou is intriguing, he will do anything to get ahead. We watch him wondering, how far will he go?

For both Mr. Udall and Lou Bloom, there is a certain shock value. Did they really just do that? This shock creates intrigue, what will they do next? This intrigue will keep an audience paying attention.

So, characters don't have to be likable to be interesting. But that's the key, they have to be interesting, or terrifying, or fascinating, or unpredictable. And the more dynamic qualities your character can embody, the more compelling your story will be. And then people will care.

A Character Who Takes Strong Action

Audiences love characters who take action. Even if the audience doesn't fall in love with a character, they will be deeply intrigued. It doesn't even have to be a heroic action.

> *Olive Kitteridge* is a four-hour miniseries about a less than cheerful, older woman. In the opening scene she walks out into the woods, sits down on a blanket, takes out a gun and points it at her head. Whoa. That's a strong action. The movie then jumps back twenty-five years and begins to slowly build to this scene. We're left with a mystery. Did she kill herself? What would make this woman kill herself? Now we want to watch to find out.

> *Halloween* Six-year-old Michael Myers stabs his older sister to death. That's a strong action! This clearly establishes the villain as

a true psychopath capable of doing anything. That's scary. For horror, it is often more important to establish a truly terrifying villain. This leads us to naturally develop empathy for the protagonist and fear for their safety.

Exercise: Getting the Audience to Care

Go back to any of the stories you have been working on so far. Come up with a scene that will build a connection in the audience for the main character. They could be charming or terrifying, passionate, or terribly mistreated. Something that will engage the audience.

Spoiler Alert! | Chapter 7

Star Wars: A New Hope (1977).

7

Character-Based Structure

Focus on Character

Three-act structure is incredibly versatile and works in most any type of story. But sometimes we want to look at the story structure in a different way. This shift in focus may reveal interesting new aspects of our story. It may force us to consider new options. It may expand our understanding of our characters. The more thoroughly we examine the structure of our story, the more confident we can be when we begin writing scenes in screenplay format.

In this last of three chapters on character, we will examine several character-based structures that focus on their journey.

Hero's Journey

The *hero's journey* is a very popular story structure. In fact, many people rely on this structure as their primary story structure. Your main character does not have to be a heroic knight riding off into battle and returning victorious in order for you to find this structure useful. The hero's journey is much more versatile than the name implies and it works with most character types, even anti-heroes.

The *hero's journey* is a term coined by academic Joseph Campbell in his 1949 book, *The Hero with a Thousand Faces*. Campbell describes as many as seventeen steps in this journey, which he also calls the monomyth. This format came to prominence after the phenomenal success of *Star Wars: A New Hope*. It is well-known that George Lucas used the hero's journey as a template for his epic space adventure.

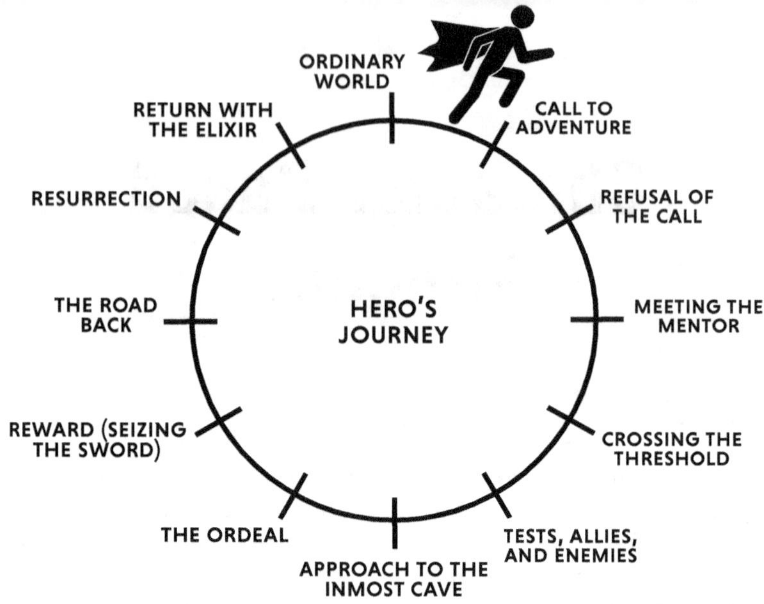

Figure 7.1
The hero's journey starts in his home and eventually returns, hitting specific beats along the way.

In *The Writer's Journey: Mythic Structure for Writers* (2007), Chris Vogler further refined the hero's journey to twelve steps, which seems to be the most common version used by screenwriters today. The journey is often visualized as a circle (Figure 7.1). The main character begins in his home, leaves on the adventure, and eventually returns.

The hero's journey is great for features, but it's a lot of plot points for a short film. However, the metaphor of a hero on a journey, encountering obstacles and returning a changed person, is valuable no matter how short your film.

Here are the twelve major steps in the hero's journey:

Ordinary World

The hero's journey begins in the *ordinary world*. This may sound familiar. It's pretty much exactly the same as the *status quo* from the *three-act structure* that I outline in Chapter 4. Establishing the main character in their everyday world is powerful. The hero is living their life. They have goals and expectations. They are not just waiting around in a castle for the villain to show up and challenge them.

Call to Adventure

The *call to adventure* is much like the *inciting incident,* but it sounds more fun, like, "Let's go on an adventure!" Just like the inciting incident, something smashes into our main character's life. It's a total disruption. Life cannot continue as it was.

Refusal of the Call

Here we cross into new territory. The main character's *refusal of the call to adventure* is powerful. This is a character-driven step. It tells us that this adventure is challenging and difficult. The hero doesn't want to be a hero, they want to stay in the safety of their *ordinary world.* This helps convince the audience that the protagonist's challenge will not be a walk in the park. It provides dramatic tension because the road ahead is hard and our hero may fail. The possibility of failure is a great source of drama for the rest of the story.

Meeting the Mentor

Now this is something completely different. Three-act structure does not specify any characters beyond the main character. (Some people insist there must always be a villain, but this just isn't the case.) The mentor is a powerful character, even when they are terribly flawed. In fact, they must have some flaws. The power of *meeting the mentor* comes from the idea that our hero is not on this journey alone. Meeting the mentor is also valuable in that it implies that the hero must learn something important if they are to succeed.

Crossing the Threshold

Crossing the threshold is a strong beat that clarifies that the hero has left home, ventured out of their ordinary world, and into the unknown. This does not mean the main character needs to physically leave home. The key here is that the character is leaving a familiar set of circumstances. They are facing an unknown situation that will challenge them.

Tests, Allies, Enemies

The obstacles, complications, and conflicts are *tests* that the hero must confront and overcome. The testing step feels similar to three-act structure, as the character attempts to achieve their goal amid many obstacles. What really stands out in this stage of the hero's journey are the *allies* and *enemies*. Here we have specific character types referenced again in the structure of the story. Sometimes the allies and enemies are obvious, but sometimes an enemy may deceive our hero or an ally may be difficult to work with. This can put a lot of dramatic pressure on our hero.

Approach to the Inmost Cave

This is a very intriguing and very personal story beat. This is not the *inmost cave* itself, which is what our hero fears the most; it is the *approach* to it. This reminds us to build up the tension. Do not just thrust the main character into their worst fear. The main character must contemplate that which they fear the most. It's not being in a dark cave; it's standing in front of the cave, peering inside, wondering and fearing, "What could be in the cave?"

The Ordeal

The hero is forced to face their greatest obstacle in *the ordeal*. The best ordeals are not just physical, but also emotional and spiritual challenges. They must confront the character's deepest fear. The ordeal forces the audience to strongly consider that the hero could lose. In fact, the more you can convince the audience that losing is the most likely outcome, the stronger and more dramatic your story will be.

Reward (Seizing the Sword)

Our hero has faced their deepest fear and now they get *the reward*, they seize the sword. The sword is not the main goal but it can be a powerful tool. We have the sense that the hero is getting more comfortable in this new world and that they are getting ready for the final battle.

The Road Back

The hero still faces major challenges before they can return to their ordinary world. Very often, *the road back* involves an epic battle, often with some sort of ticking clock or deadline and additional challenging obstacles.

Resurrection

The hero faces one final challenge. The key is that the hero has been changed by this journey. Only the new version of the hero can succeed at this challenge. We see the hero acting in a way that would not have been possible at the beginning of the story.

Return With the Elixir

The hero succeeds! They arrive back home. We want to soak this moment in. The hard-fought victory is exhilarating.

Heroine's Journey

You may have noticed that the hero's journey feels somewhat masculine. In fact, Joseph Campbell's version is very masculine. Over the years, a lot of other people noticed this as well and some of them started to consider a protagonist's journey from a feminine perspective.

Maureen Murdock, a student of Joseph Campbell and a Jungian psychotherapist, was the first to reimagine the hero's journey in her self-help book called *The Heroine's Journey: Woman's Quest for Wholeness*. Victoria Lynn Schmidt crafted another version geared toward writers in her book, *45 Master Characters*. Reframing the hero's journey with a feminine lens led to an intriguing and helpful new take on story structure: *the heroine's journey* (Figure 7.2).

These character-based story structures emerge from gender stereotypes. But I believe it is important to realize that you do not have to follow a specific journey based on your character's gender. It doesn't matter if your main character is male or female or non-binary or even non-human. You can choose the journey that creates the most interesting challenges for your character and their dilemma. As with all the information in this book, these structures are guidelines to help you, they are not meant to be adhered to rigidly. With that in mind, here are the nine steps in the heroine's journey:

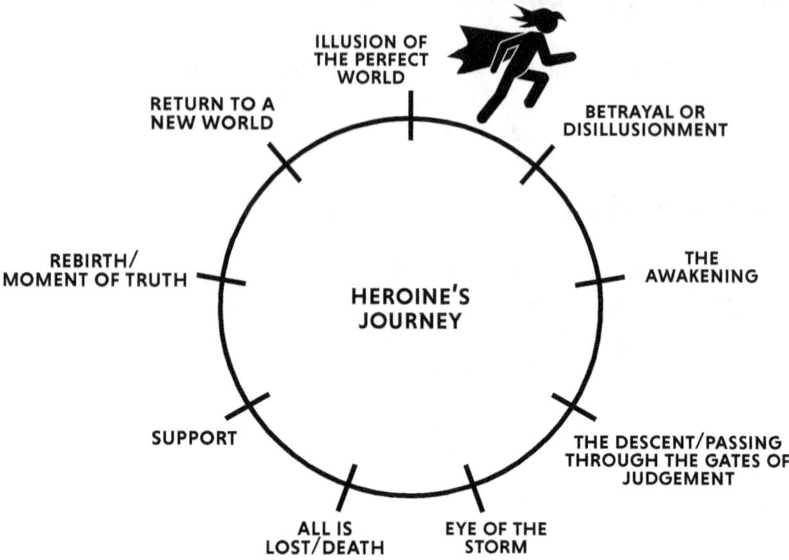

Figure 7.2

Victoria Schmidt's nine-step heroine's journey is a very powerful character-driven structure.

Illusion of the Perfect World

At the onset, our main character has convinced themselves that the world is great. This *illusion of the perfect world* is very interesting. It is the most unstable starting point of any of the structures we have looked at in this book. All the other structures imply that everything is great, but in the heroine's journey, it is the opposite. Things are not great *but* our main character doesn't know that or is actively ignoring that fact. If the character is naive and believes the illusion, then their world may feel stable to them but the audience will most likely see the self-deception from the start.

Betrayal or Disillusionment

Similar to the *inciting incident*, the main character's world is rocked by the *betrayal or disillusionment*. This may take the form of a revelation about a deception or the character's coping mechanisms may have finally ceased to work. Either way our main character's veil has been lifted and they now see clearly that their world is not perfect, far from it. Like any good inciting incident, life can no longer continue as is.

The Awakening

Similar to *refusal of the call* in the hero's journey is *the awakening*. The main character may deny what is happening, refusing to accept this new view of the imperfect world. Other characters may also discourage them from disrupting the status quo. But the character knows they must face the truth. Often, they will begin to seek help or guidance from others. Guidance from others has a familiar ring to it—perhaps the guidance would come from a mentor. It is important to note that a mentor does not have to be an old man with a beard. It could be a friend, colleague, or maybe even a group of friends.

The Descent or Passing Through the Gates of Judgment

The descent implies entering a new world or underworld, similar to *crossing the threshold* in the hero's journey. But *passing through the gates of judgment* adds a much more personal dimension.

All human beings have doubts. This beat acknowledges that when we begin a new role, enter a new world, we inevitably experience doubt. This doubt is often experienced as self-judgment.

This feels different than the hero's journey. The hero's journey makes it seem like our hero has no doubts, that they charge forward, confidently. But any story that acknowledges the true human emotions of fear and doubt is going to feel more authentic.

Eye of the Storm

The moment in the middle of an intense storm that is oddly calm is called the *eye of the storm*. This is not just metaphorical. If you look at satellite images of hurricanes, there is a clear circle of calm in the center.

As the name implies, at this point in the story, there is a calm, maybe even a *false victory*—which is a classic midpoint in three-act structure. Soon the eye of the storm passes and the chaos returns. Our heroine is challenged, undermined, and attacked.

All is Lost/Death

Our heroine is defeated. They have lost. This is a classic second act, lowest low moment when the protagonist has failed to achieve the goal that they set out for. The heroine may even consider going back to their old ways. They will often feel totally alone.

Support

The heroine realizes they are not alone. Their friends and family are there for them and they can face this together. This feels like a major shift from the macho hero facing their greatest challenge alone. Even though the heroine is facing their greatest challenge, there is a joy in facing it together with their team of supporters.

Rebirth/Moment of Truth

Facing the challenge with their supporters, our heroine is able to succeed. Doubts are finally vanquished. Again, human emotions are acknowledged. They finally overcome the main obstacle (often a villain).

Return to a New World

Our heroine returns to their world but now they are more conscious, more aware. The world is still not perfect, but they have a new strength that gives them the confidence to face it, plus they have a tighter support group.

Working Together

One of the most interesting aspects of the heroine's journey is how often it refers to characters other than the main character. This communal, social aspect to problem solving is clearly different than the lone wolf, who may get some help from others but the journey is theirs alone. The heroine's journey reflects a more social dynamic.

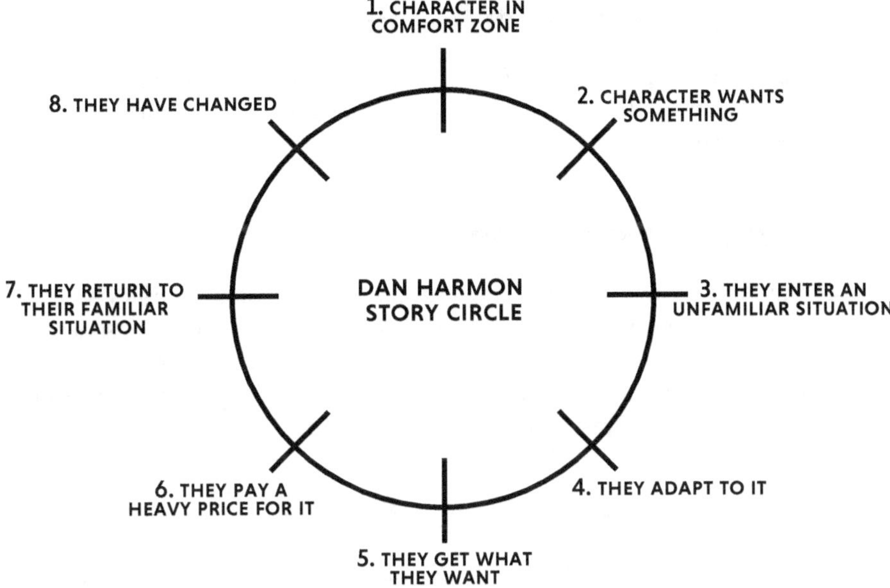

Figure 7.3

Dan Harmon's circle has eight story beats.

Dan Harmon's Story Circle

Dan Harmon is the creator of amazing shows like *Community* and *Rick and Morty*. These shows often have wild stories. Some of the plots are so outrageous and crazy, you may think that the guy responsible for these shows can't possibly be following any kind of structure, but no! Mr. Harmon is extremely strict about following his structure—his circle.

Dan Harmon's story circle is basically a simplified version of the hero's journey, but with new terms and some interesting new ideas. These new terms force us to consider even more new options for our story and allow us to examine its structure in yet another light.

It begins with the story idea, or *embryo* as Dan calls it. If the embryo does not track through all the steps in the circle, more work breaking the story needs to be done or it may not be a solid idea for a story.

Character in Zone of Comfort

The character is comfortable. This is an interesting version of *status quo*. It indicates the emotional state—we can't feel comfortable unless we're basically happy.

Character Wants Something

The usual *inciting incident* or *call to action* from the hero's journey seems to come from outside the character, but this step in the circle is instigated by the character themselves. That's an interesting shift. The motivation for change comes from within and it could be good or bad. Is it a desire to become better? Or a restlessness that wants more?

They Enter an Unfamiliar Situation

This is quite similar to *crossing the threshold* from hero's journey which in turn is similar to *entering the new world* in three-act structure. Here the character chooses to leave their comfort zone and this choice brings them to an unfamiliar place, which tends to be uncomfortable as well. This implies that the character has messed up their own *comfort zone* because *they want something*.

They Adapt to It

At first glance, this beat may seem very different from three-act structure where the main character in an unfamiliar world often fails. But in Harmon's structure, the character's early attempts to adapt may fail as well. The key is that the character adapts to the new world before the halfway point.

They Get What They Want

Now this seems genuinely counter-intuitive. We're only halfway around the circle, halfway through the story, and the character has succeeded? Is the story over? No. There will be consequences. Serious consequences. This beat plays a lot like the classic midpoint of *the false victory*.

They Pay a Heavy Price For It

Getting what you want comes at a price. A heavy price. As is often the case with a *false victory*, trouble follows directly. This heavy price is frequently very personal to the main character.

They Return to Their Familiar Situation

Paying a heavy price seems to motivate the character's desire to return home. But getting home from an unfamiliar place is not easy and they struggle to return to normal.

They Have Changed

Finally, the main character manages to get home. But they have changed. And it's not always for the better.

Perspectives on the Story Circle

As you can see, this is an extremely character-centric story structure. Every step is the character taking an action. The entire structure is based on a character's wants, leading to the character changing, and in the process suffering the consequences. Change is usually difficult and there are real stakes—even if the character does not see this when they begin.

There's an even more-simplified version of Dan Harmon's circle: You, Need, Go, Search, Find, Take, Return, Change.

Bam! Go write your story.

 **Moving Beats Around**

One important note, the sequence of actions in hero's journey, heroine's journey, and Dan Harmon's circle is flexible. Certain beats can be moved around or even repeated.

Character Roles and Narrative Function

Let's step away from story structure and examine character types and their narrative function. The concept here is that characters can't just be in your story, they must perform a role. Without a purpose, they don't belong in the story. Assigning a *narrative function* to every significant character in your story helps you clarify the role they play.

In a short screenplay, you probably won't have all of the roles listed below but thinking through the narrative function for each character can help make your characters' intentions and actions stronger and clearer.

Protagonist

Clearly, our main character, nothing new here.

Antagonist

The villain. Again, we know what this is.

Mentor

People tend to stereotype the *mentor* as the "wise old man," but it's the function of this character that is critical. The mentor could be a child, a ghost, or even an alien. The key is that this character's role is to be the conscience of the main character and the embodiment of the *theme*. They provide lessons and keep the main character on track. The best mentors are as flawed as we are.

Tempter

This character is similar to the antagonist but is not necessarily working with them. The *tempter* doesn't need to know the antagonist, but they both stand for the same thing: stopping the protagonist from achieving their goal. The tempter tries to manipulate and convince the protagonist to join the "dark side." What is interesting is that the tempter can flip sides and join our hero. This is what separates them from the true villain.

Herald

"I've got a bad feeling about this," is something a *herald* would say. They can deliver the call to adventure or ring the warning bell when there is danger. This is a great character for setting the stakes by stating the danger of a situation. Other character types can take on the role of the herald.

Ally or Sidekick

The protagonist's best friend and trusted confidant, the *ally* is always there for our hero and ready to go, sometimes even before the hero is ready themselves. The *sidekick* personifies the theme, often without consciously realizing it. The mentor can explain the theme, while the sidekick just does it without thinking.

Shapeshifter or Trickster

This is a character who could be helpful or very dangerous. In mythology, *shapeshifters* can change their physical form, but their narrative function is more metaphorical. (This is why some prefer the term *trickster*, to avoid the implication of the character changing physical form.) The shapeshifter or trickster may switch between different archetypes, sometimes acting as an ally or mentor, and other times acting as a tempter or even the villain. This character puts a lot of pressure on our hero to determine whether they are helpful or dangerous.

Skeptic

The role of the *skeptic* is to challenge the protagonist. The skeptic is the devil's advocate. The skeptic can bring up alternative actions forcing the main character to debate the moral and/or intellectual aspects of their actions. The skeptic is a free agent—not on the protagonist's side but also not on the antagonist's side. They go their own way, but the skeptic may come around and join the protagonist in the end.

Threshold Guardian

A threshold guardian is a character or situation that challenges our hero. It is a roadblock in our hero's journey. A threshold guardian will provide our hero with key tests and challenges. The hero may need help from a *mentor* or *ally* and may require great training to overcome a threshold guardian.

Other Archetypes to Consider

There are a couple other character types that can be very helpful, even if they aren't classic archetypes.

- **Emotional.** This character type acts according to their gut and lets emotions guide their decisions. They are impulsive and reactive. This character is likely to leap without looking. Sometimes *the emotional character* finds success in ways that a thinking person would never have even tried. Other times, this character gets into trouble by not thinking before they jump.

- **Logical.** This is the classic *rational thinker* who plans things out, coming up with the most logical solution. They rely on facts. Their solutions can feel cold-hearted, even brutal, reducing life to a math equation.

Star Trek is an amazing example of the effectiveness of these two archetypes. Spock is driven by pure logic while Bones, Dr. McCoy, is the emotional character. When Captain Kirk, the protagonist, faces a dilemma, Bones and Spock make their case for a solution based on emotion and logic, respectively. So, when Kirk makes a decision, it's not just choosing the best solution, but choosing between his two best friends.

Exercise: Use Character-Based Structure or Narrative Function to Expand Your Story

Go back to any of the stories you have come up with so far. Now write out the plot using one of the character-based structures. You may need to tweak some beats or even come up with some new beats. Hopefully, these new beats will make your story more dynamic, your protagonist more complex, and help you define interesting new characters.

Or

Go back to any of the stories you have come up with so far and identify and explain the narrative function for each key character. Can you come up with a new character whose role could make your story more dynamic?

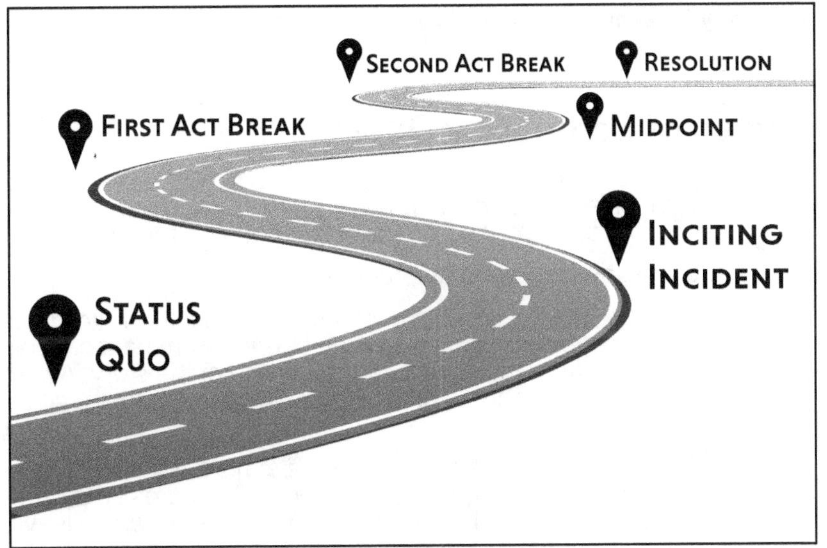

8

Outline

A Road Map

An *outline* might be the most critical step in developing a great screenplay. If you're writing a five- to ten-minute project (five to ten screenplay pages) the good news is you are basically done. The one-page synopsis of the major beats in your story that you created for the exercise at the end of Chapter 4 should be enough of an outline for a script of that duration. But if your project is any longer, you should definitely write an outline. Do you have to? No. But at some point, you will run into a wall or lose your way. The idea that seemed so complete in your head suddenly has holes, and you'll find yourself wondering how your story gets from here to there. That's why you work on an outline: it's a road map. I think of a screenplay as a thousand-mile journey. If you were going to drive one thousand miles, you wouldn't just get in your car and start driving. If you did, you'd be really lucky to get where you wanted to go. And would it be the best journey? Probably not. So, make a plan, follow a road map, and create an outline for your script.

Types of Screenplay Outlines

You may have heard various terms that sound similar: *outline, step outline, beat sheet, treatment.* In the end, they are quite similar—detailed synopses of your screenplay that act as a road map.

But there are some specific differences:

> **Outline** Basic outlines are intended for you, the writer. You do not need to outline every scene. Summarize what happens from the beginning to the end of the story. Avoid detail and dialogue. This is a bare-bones document, an X-ray of your story.

> **Beat Sheet or Step Outline** This is a more detailed outline that includes most, if not all, scenes. You are "stepping" through the story "beat by beat." But you still want to leave out scene details and dialogue.

> **Outline with Intentions** This is an outline or beat sheet that includes the reason behind each beat or sequence. This helps you understand not only what's happening but why.

> **Treatment** A treatment is an outline written with style. Treatments are primarily used to pitch your screenplay to other people. They are written in prose and should read like a story. They should have some specific details and may include a bit of dialogue, but these should both be kept to a minimum.

 **Professional Tip**

If you get hired to write a screenplay, part of the contract may include writing the outline. You're a good writer and you are planning to write an outline already, so you figure, "Sure, no problem." No. Big problem. The goal of an outline is functionality, so outlines are stripped-down, bare-bones, versions of your story. Without the detail and dialogue, the beats can sound too basic, even cliché. You will most likely end up writing something that is more like a treatment so that it goes over better with the producers and executives. And that takes a lot more work. My advice is to avoid an outline in your deal if you can.

The Basic Outline

Take your one-page synopsis from Chapter 4 and begin to flesh out what else happens. The key is to summarize the scenes or sequences. If you find yourself going into detail, that's okay. It's good to have that info, but when you are done, save the doc, create a copy, then remove the detail and summarize the action. Just be aware that you are basically writing the screenplay, and this will be a *very* slow process. Also, like writing the entire screenplay, you will get stuck. Step back and look for the key moments, fill in gaps between the key moments, and summarize. I believe an ideal outline for a feature film is four to five pages (12-point font and normal margins). If it gets to eight or more pages, you are including too much detail (or you could have too much story).

Beat Sheet or Step Outline

This form of outline includes every scene, or at least every beat, but you are leaving out detail and dialogue. It's usually not necessary to write an outline with this level of specificity, but it can give you more confidence in your story. Also, this level of detail may be necessary when pitching for a writing job.

Writing scene by scene is very difficult if you just start at the beginning. It will be much easier to write a basic outline before you write a beat sheet or step outline.

Outline with Intentions

I created this type of outline a while back, when I was hired to adapt a classic novel for an Academy Award-winning actor. There was a meeting scheduled to go over my outline with the actor and the producer. I was stressed since meetings in the past to discuss outlines had not always gone smoothly. Without the dialogue and the description of a screenplay, sometimes the beats felt thin. So, I started scribbling the purpose of each beat on my outline. Knowing the intention behind the beat seemed to make it feel more substantial. I organized the document before the meeting and the phone call was a great success! They were very happy with the outline and asked me to move on to the screenwriting phase!

Now I use this type of outline whenever I have to discuss an outline with producers and execs. I find it is a great way to keep everyone onboard as the story unfolds.

Treatment

The treatment should feel like you are telling the audience the story. The trick is to summarize the story beats, but also include just enough detail and a smidge of dialogue. The key to adding any dialogue is that it should get across the tone of the story and the voice of specific characters. It should not be simple dialogue that serves to explain the story: it needs to demonstrate the style and tone. Treatments can be challenging to write and take a lot of work to polish.

What Do They Look Like?

Let's take a look at examples of each of the different outlining techniques using a story that I wrote titled *My Prison Buddy*. We'll start with a one-page synopsis of the *major beats*. Since this is a feature, for brevity's sake, we will limit the examples to the first couple major beats—from the opening through the inciting incident which should cover the first twelve pages of a feature screenplay.

Example of Major Beats One-Page Synopsis

The one-page synopsis starts with essential, basic info about the story: title, genre, logline, tone, and even an interesting fact. The first two major beats in *My Prison Buddy* establish the main character, his flaw, and key relationships, then I explain the inciting incident that sets the story in motion.

Title: *My Prison Buddy*

Logline: Buddy comedy. A nice guy gets a call from his boss to bail him out. He goes down to the jail, pays the bail, but when the prisoner is released it's not his boss, it's this bad-ass tough guy who just happens to have the same name.

Think *Midnight Run* but the bad guy is running the show.

Interesting note: The wrong prisoner being released actually happens all the time.

Status quo: ALVIN is basically the ultimate nice guy which means a lot of people take advantage of him. Alvin has a good job but his boss, REED THOMPSON, does pretty much nothing, forcing Alvin to cover for him. Alvin has a crush on MARCI at work but can't really seem to ask her out.

Inciting incident: Alvin gets a call at five a.m. from his boss—he's been arrested. He demands that Alvin come bail him out. Reluctantly, Alvin goes down to the jail to bail out his "friend," Reed Thompson, but instead gets scary Tough Guy RAMSEY THOMPSON. Ramsey insists he's been framed and needs some time on the outside to sort things out. He needs help and he can't let Alvin go (since Ramsey's sure he would go to the cops).

As you can see, that is really a lot of information in just over two hundred words!

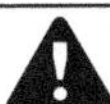 ## Always Include the Title and Logline

It's important to start any story document with the title, logline, etc. but they are omitted in the rest of the examples in this chapter for brevity.

Example of an Outline

Overall, the outline will include more detail and specifics of the major beats. Plus, we begin to add beats that happen between the major beats. (Since we're only talking about the first twelve pages of screenplay, there is not a ton more.)

I like to include the major beat headings, so readers know where they are in the story.

Title, logline, etc.

Status quo: ALVIN is done for the day but hangs around to ask Marci out. Just as he finally asks her, his boss, REED, interrupts him by giving Alvin a massive work assignment. And MARCI turns him down.

Meanwhile, Ramsey gets arrested in the jewelry district, there is blood on his hands.

Alvin's boss gets drunk and accidentally pees on a cop, which gets him arrested.

Inciting incident: Alvin gets a call at five a.m. from his boss—he's been arrested. He demands that Alvin come bail him out.

Reluctantly, Alvin goes down to the jail to bail out his boss, Reed Thompson, but instead gets scary Tough Guy Ramsey Thompson.

Ramsey insists he's been framed and needs some time on the outside to sort things out. He needs help and he can't let Alvin go since Ramsey's sure he would go to the cops. Alvin tries everything to get out of this but no luck.

For this outline, we go into more specifics about the office scene. Then there's a new location where Ramsey is introduced while getting arrested including a small detail: blood. This makes it seem like something very serious happened. The mechanics of the inciting incident hasn't changed much but the detail of how Ramsey insists that Alvin must come with him is a good addition.

Example of a Beat Sheet

The beat sheet clearly has more detail than an outline since it includes every scene in the film:

Title, logline, etc.

Status quo: In a typical office, ALVIN, 35, pretends to neaten up but is waiting for MARCI, hoping to ask her out. He finally gets his chance but his obnoxious boss, REED, yells—"Hey chipmunk!"— interrupting him and Marci turns him down.

Meanwhile, at a crime scene in the jewelry district, a cop is arresting RAMSEY THOMPSON, who has blood on his hands.

Back in the office, Alvin's boss tells Alvin he must compile the annual report which is actually Reed's job. It will take at least all weekend.

Later, it's after midnight, Alvin is still at the office working hard when his boss (who's clearly drunk) calls him from the bar, tells him not to come.

Alvin finally gets home but even his dog ignores him.

Thompson stumbles out of the bar and pees on a wall. When a cop shines a flashlight in his eyes, Thompson turns and pees on the cop. Yeah, he definitely gets arrested.

Inciting incident: Alvin gets a call at five a.m. It's a collect call from the Los Angeles Correctional Facility. His boss wants Alvin to bail him out. Of course, Alvin agrees.

Outside the L.A. Correctional Facility, Alvin, with a huge cup of coffee, crosses the parking lot. It's a scary place.

Inside the L.A. Correctional Facility, there seems to be one massive line. Alvin goes to the end of it.

> Later, Alvin finally reaches the front of the line and discovers he's in the wrong line. "You need to be over there." There's another huge line.
>
> Much later, Alvin finally gets to the window. He has to max out his credit card to pay the ten thousand-dollar bail.
>
> Much, much later, Alvin is staring at his phone when it dies. A shadow engulfs Alvin. It's Ramsey Thompson, Tough Guy. He couldn't be more intimidating.
>
> Outside, Alvin realizes that it is Ramsey Thompson that has been released, not his boss Reed Thompson. Ramsey has *no* intention of going back to jail, so Alvin must come with him to keep Thompson's release from becoming known.

Here you can see simple differences from the outline, like the scene with the boss split into two parts, separated by the scene introducing Ramsey. It also includes specifics about the task Alvin has been assigned. Plus, there are fun little details like Alvin's dog ignoring him—what dog isn't excited when their owner comes home? There are more details about the difficulties Alvin encounters trying to bail out his boss. And a key element, why Ramsey needs to keep Alvin with him.

Example of a Beat Sheet in Screenplay Format

Some people prefer to write their step outline with screenwriting software. That's fine, it saves a bit of time when you begin writing the screenplay since you will end up with your sluglines already in place. (Screenplay formatting is covered in detail in the next chapter.) This type of outline looks similar to a completed screenplay, but it lacks the standard scene description and there is no dialogue:

```
Title, logline, etc.

INT. TYPICAL OFFICE - EVENING

ALVIN, 35, pretends to neaten up but is
waiting for MARCI, hoping to ask her out.
He finally gets his chance but his
obnoxious boss yells, "Hey chipmunk!"
interrupting him, and Marci turns him
down. Meanwhile, across town --
```

```
EXT. WAREHOUSE - EVENING

A crime scene in the jewelry district. A
COP is arresting RAMSEY THOMPSON, who has
blood on his hands.

INT. CORNER OFFICE - EVENING

Alvin's boss, REED THOMPSON, tells Alvin
he has to compile the annual report which
is actually Reed's job. It will take at
least all weekend.

LATER, it's after midnight, Alvin is
still at the office working hard when his
boss calls him from the bar, tells him
not to come.

INT. ALVIN'S HOUSE

Alvin finally gets home but even his dog
ignores him.

EXT. SWANKY BAR - DOWNTOWN - 2 AM

Thompson stumbles out of the bar and pees
on a wall. When a cop shines a flashlight
in his eyes, Thompson turns and pees on
the cop. Yeah, he definitely gets
arrested.
```

You get the idea.

Personally, I find this approach a bit limiting. It's common to get locked into the simple locations that you came up with when outlining. Or you are afraid of that, so you spend too much time trying to come up with good locations during the outline phase.

Plus, I love writing dialogue and the story comes to life when I get the characters voices on the page. Without the dialogue, much of the comedy is missing. So, to me, this type of outline is a nightmare—all of the drudgery of writing without any of the fun!

Example of an Outline with Intentions

This type of outline can be stripped down, like a basic outline, or include every scene, like a beat sheet. The difference is that each beat gets an explanation that follows it. This explanation allows us to state the intention so that we understand the function of each beat. In Table 8.1, you can see the story beat in the left column and the narrative intention of each beat in the right column. As with all the outlines in this chapter, the outline with intentions should include the title, logline, etc.

You may not need to spell out every intention, some of them are pretty obvious. But still, it can be very helpful. By writing out the intention for a beat, you force yourself to answer the question, "How does this beat move the story forward?" It can also be a helpful method for coming up with scenes. If you are stuck building your outline, you could write out the intention for the next beat or even the next several beats. Stating the intention could help you come up with the next story beats.

i Creativity Within the Story vs. Creativity Outside of the Story

Don't overdo it! Some people are wildly creative. But too much so. Once you have the core story idea, you need to focus your creativity on that core. Especially when working on a short film. Too often people keep adding new elements or new characters to the story rather than developing the main story.

Here's an analogy: Let's say you are building a house. If the major beats are the frame of the house, the outline is the specific rooms—bedrooms, bathrooms, kitchen, living room, etc. Wildly creative people will sometimes want to add extra rooms, add a third floor to the house, expand the two-car garage to a five-car garage. Suddenly, the house is unmanageably large, or even collapses under the excess weight. That's what happens when you add too many elements to your story. It will become unmanageable and collapse on itself. If you are writing a short, you may have to limit yourself to a one- or two-room house. For a feature you could have a fairly large house. If your "house" is too big, the solution may be to switch the story to a TV series which needs those extra elements to sustain the drama over many episodes.

Story Beat	Intention
Status quo: ALVIN is done for the day but hangs around to ask MARCI out. He finally gets his chance but his obnoxious boss, REED, yells, "Hey chipmunk!" interrupting him and Marci turns him down.	This establishes several key characters: Alvin, Marci, and their boss, Reed Thompson. Also, their relationships are set up. Marci might be interested in Alvin, but he keeps blowing it. Alvin's boss is a jerk who keeps taking advantage of Alvin.
Meanwhile, RAMSEY gets arrested in the jewelry district, there is blood on his hands.	This establishes the second protagonist, Ramsey, and that he was arrested for what looks like a very serious crime.
Alvin's Boss gets drunk and pees on a cop, which gets him arrested.	This is a rather humorous way for the boss to get arrested (and now he needs Alvin to bail him out).
Inciting incident: Alvin gets a call at five a.m. from his boss—he's been arrested. He demands that Alvin come bail him out.	Alvin can't help but be nice and do as he is told—this clearly establishes Alvin's flaw that he is a pushover.
Reluctantly, Alvin goes down to the jail to bail out his boss, Reed Thompson, but instead gets scary Tough Guy Ramsey Thompson.	Alvin doesn't quite know what's going on and Ramsey is terrifying, so Alvin does what Ramsey says.
Ramsey insists he's been framed and needs some time on the outside to sort things out. He needs help and he can't let Alvin go since Ramsey's sure he would go to the cops. Alvin tries everything to get out of this but no luck.	This states Ramsey's goal for the story—stay out of jail while he figures out what happened and clears his name. Since Ramsey is out accidentally, he can't let Alvin go, so they are stuck together. This also establishes the basic MacGuffin of the story: Ramsey was involved in a transaction that went very wrong. The MacGuffin has basically three parts: The original deal, what went wrong, and the steps to fix it.

Table 8.1

An *outline with intentions*, shown here in two-column format, with story beats on the left and intentions on the right.

Example of a Treatment

The treatment is the most challenging and time-consuming version of an outline. A treatment should be written in a way that gets across the tone of the story, i.e. a comedy should be funny, a drama should be dramatic, etc. It should also portray the characters as they will be in the screenplay, including bits of dialogue. The main purpose of a treatment is to help sell the project.

Title, logline, etc.

Status quo: ALVIN (early 30s) neatens his already neat desk as he hangs around to ask out MARCI, a 29-year-old with attitude. But just as he starts to ask her, his boss yells—"Hey chipmunk!"—forcing Alvin to come to his office. Marci turns Alvin down implying that he seems to be dating the boss.

Meanwhile, across town, the jewelry district is lit up like a Christmas tree—at least a dozen cop cars surround a building. A police officer is arresting RAMSEY THOMPSON, who has blood on his hands.

Back in the office, Alvin's boss, REED THOMPSON, tells Alvin that he has a hot date with some alcohol, so Alvin needs to compile the annual report (which is actually Reed's job). Alvin reminds his boss that they were going to get drinks together. The boss tells Alvin he needs to focus more on work.

Later, it's after midnight, Alvin is still at the office working hard when his boss (who's clearly drunk) calls him from the bar and tells him not to come.

Alvin finally gets home but even his dog ignores him.

Thompson stumbles out of the bar but stops to pee on a wall. When a cop shines a flashlight in his eyes, Thompson turns and pees on the cop. Yeah, he definitely gets arrested.

Inciting incident: Alvin gets a call at five a.m. It's a collect call from the Los Angeles Correctional Facility. His boss wants Alvin to bail him out. Of course, Alvin, always the nice guy, agrees.

Outside the L.A. Correctional Facility, Alvin, with a huge cup of coffee, crosses the parking lot. It's a scary place, like the parking lot of a Raider game—and Alvin's got on the wrong colors.

Inside the L.A. Correctional Facility, there seems to be one massive line. Alvin politely goes to the end of it.

Later, Alvin finally reaches the front of the line and discovers he's in the wrong line. "You need to be over there." There's another huge line.

Much later, Alvin finally gets to the window. When the officer tells Alvin the bail is ten thousand dollars he freaks out. The officer reads off the charges, "Public intoxication, that means drunk. Urinating in public, took a piss. Resisting arrest, that's not good and oh, the biggie—assaulting an officer. That means he's screwed."

Alvin has to max out his credit card to pay the ten-thousand-dollar bail.

Much, much later, Alvin is staring at his phone when it dies. A shadow engulfs Alvin. It's Ramsey Thompson, the definition of a Tough Guy. He couldn't be more intimidating if he had a .44 Magnum pointed in Alvin's face. Alvin does what he is told.

Outside, Alvin realizes that it is Ramsey Thompson that has been released, not his boss Reed Thompson. Alvin says he's going back for his friend. Ramsey claims he needs twenty-four hours on the outside to clear his name and he can't have Alvin telling anyone he's out, so Alvin has to come with him.

Hopefully, this is more fun to read and gives a bit of the style and tone of the screenplay.

Overall, outlines are not fun to write. They are a lot of hard work. But they are a critical step in the screenwriting process. A solid outline will give you confidence that the screenplay journey is going to lead to a satisfying ending and that frees you up to have fun when writing scenes!

Exercise: Fleshing Out the Outline

Go back to one of the stories you have come up with so far that you believe is longer than ten pages. Start with your one-page list of the major beats (from Chapter 4) and flesh it out to a full outline. It doesn't have to include every scene. If you want to write out your intentions for each beat, that's great but it is not necessary unless it helps you.

Spoiler Alert! | Chapter 9

Alien (1979).

9

Screenplay Format

Start Off Right

The most important thing about screenplay formatting is to use screenplay formatting software. Final Draft is the industry standard, but it is a little pricey. There are a couple other apps that are used by industry professionals and there are very good, free software alternatives that are also available. Even if you are writing a short film, you should use proper screenplay formatting.

Screenwriting software is incredibly easy to use, and it makes writing in screenplay format a breeze. It's a *huge* waste of time to use a basic word processor and try to format the document to look like a screenplay. The majority of the time, it ends up looking terrible. Nothing makes you look more like an amateur than an improperly formatted screenplay. Agents and execs are looking for a reason to reject your screenplay, don't make it so obvious and easy for them.

Screenplay Formatting

Screenwriting format is unique in that there is a lot of freedom to express yourself as a writer. And yet there are many very rigid rules and if you violate them, it will be obvious you are not a professional. But don't let that intimidate you. The basic rules are simple. I will use the word "always" when stating a basic rule that needs to be rigidly adhered to.

Below are a few basics to get you started. But there's one simple rule to know right off the bat: Screenplays are *always* written in 12-point Courier font.

Sluglines

Scenes always begin with a slugline. Here is a simple example:

```
INT. HOTEL BAR - NIGHT
```

A slugline is always capitalized. If you are using Final Draft and your formatting element is set to Scene Heading, this will occur automatically. Isn't that great?

Sluglines always start with INT. or EXT. or INT/EXT.

INT. is an abbreviation for *interior*. That means the scene happens inside of a building, room, house, and so on. EXT. is for *exterior*. These scenes happen outside, in the sunlight. If you want to know why this differentiation is made, it's because of the light. Traditionally, when movies were shot on film, the difference between interiors and exteriors was vast and required different film stock, not to mention a lot of other equipment.

INT/EXT. (or I/E) stands for *interior and exterior*. I/E is used when a character is in an environment where both interior and exterior are visible in the scene. For example, if a character is standing in a doorway. They are inside the house, but we can also see outside of the house into the yard. It's the same when a character is in a car, we can see both the interior of the car and the exterior.

Next, we always have the location. In this case, HOTEL BAR. This is the physical location where the scene is taking place. This should be short and clear.

Following the location there always is <space> dash <space>.

This is always followed by time of day. It should always be in this order and punctuated this way.

Some old-school books insist that the only acceptable time of day designations are DAY, NIGHT, and CONTINUOUS. I disagree. I think variations like DAWN, SUNSET, LATE AFTERNOON, etc. add color and interesting specificity.

If you need the audience to know the exact time, you will want that to appear as a graphic on the screen. For example, there is a bomb that is going to go off in a giant warehouse. The villain has made it clear the bomb will explode at exactly nine a.m. You may want to start the scene by letting the audience know that it is 8:02 a.m.—there is less than an hour to go. To indicate this time on screen in a script, we need to show it like this.

```
SUPER: 8:02 a.m.


INT. GIANT WAREHOUSE - MORNING
```

SUPER is short for *superimposition*, meaning the text appears on screen. You can also use the term *chyron*. In this case, you would not include the time in the slugline, just the standard MORNING.

CONTINUOUS should only be used when no time passes between shots. For example, the scene is: INT. HOTEL LOBBY – NIGHT and the character races past the front desk to the open elevator. Then the next scene could be INT. HOTEL ELEVATOR – CONTINUOUS. But, unless there is a specific reason to see the character in the elevator, you may want to cut ahead to the character knocking on a door. In that situation, continuous would not be appropriate, you would use INT. HOTEL HALLWAY – NIGHT.

Lastly, your sluglines should never be longer than one line. If it is, then some of that info should be cut or possibly belongs in the next paragraph.

Scene Description

Following the slugline should be a short paragraph describing the setting. If you are using Final Draft, this element is titled Action. There must always be some scene description after a slugline, you should never go straight to character dialogue. Here is an example:

> It's like an underground cave, just
> a few late-night DRINKERS studying
> their glasses.

The scene description should be short and evocative, more than just the physical location. We want to paint a picture and set the mood. You may have noticed that the word *drinkers* is in all caps. When there is a character or characters that we have not seen before, i.e., this is the first time they appear in the screenplay, they must be identified in ALL CAPS. From that point on, in the description, characters are identified with standard capitalization.

Next should be an action line focusing on the character.

> JAMES rushes in. He desperately scans
> the patrons. She's not there.

The action is always written in the present tense. Screenplays are happening right now. We are with the character in the moment. We want to keep the action simple and powerful. Avoid too much scene description. For example, if we wrote:

> JAMES takes a half dozen steps into
> the bar. Stops. He frantically looks
> from patron to patron, searching for
> Lane. He rubs his eyes with his left
> hand. It takes him several seconds to
> realize she is clearly not there.

That's way too much detail. First, the location, the hotel bar, is stated in the slugline, so we don't need to say that James steps into the bar. If we mention the number of steps or which hand the character uses for an action, that's way too much information. With this much detail, we slow down the story while adding almost nothing of value.

Screenplays should be lean and economical. Think of it like a painting. You are *not* trying to create a realistic painting of the scene. Listing every detail and action is burdensome and boring. You want to think of your scene description like an impressionist painting—a few brush strokes of color to give the sense of the scene. Be sure to keep your scene description paragraphs to three or four lines at most.

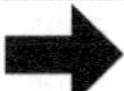 **What to Read:** *Alien*

Read the screenplay for the original *Alien* movie. It is strikingly lean. Single lines of description that read almost like poetry, yet it is incredibly powerful, and the action is amazingly clear. Not that you should emulate this style, it's actually a bit too minimalist but it can be freeing to see how little scene description you need to get the story across.

Dialogue

Next your character might want to say something.

```
     James   turns   toward   the   BARMAN   who
     nurses    a    beer    while    keeping    his
     bloodshot  eyes  glued  to  a  muted  TV.

                    JAMES
          I'm  looking  for  a  woman,  she  used
          to  come  here,  Lane.

     The Barman ignores James.
```

Character dialogue is always preceded by the character's name. The name is always in ALL CAPS and is substantially indented.

In Final Draft, hit the Tab key to go to the Character element. When the element is set to Character the text will automatically appear in all caps and be properly indented. If you hit the Enter key after the character name, Final Draft will do a standard return and change the element to Dialogue, complete with proper indentation.

Dialogue is indented on both the left and right. If you hit the Enter key after the dialogue, Final Draft will do a standard return and change the element to Action.

(Note: Barman is not a main character, so we give him a more or less generic name and we don't have to bother with a description of him. But I like to capitalize a generic name like Barman, treating it as if it is a character name.)

Other Important Aspects of Formatting

There are several other important formatting options to understand:

Camera direction. You're the writer. Let the director direct. Leave out camera direction. Jargon like *CU* (Close-Up), *pan across*, *zoom in* are boring to read and take us out of the story.

Physical wrylies. Parentheticals that are about physical aspects of the action are a necessary part of screenwriting: *into the phone*, *soto voce* (whisper voice), and *mumbles* are examples of physical actions that need to be spelled out clearly. Also, physical wrylies are necessary to direct a line to a specific a character. Let's say there's a group of characters. If the protagonist says something to one character (not the group) you may include "to" along with the character's name:

```
          RAMON
      (to Cole)
   I told you this place was off the
   hook.
```

Emotional wrylies/parentheticals. You're the writer. Let the actors act. Avoid emotional wrylies like *happily*, *angrily*, or *mopily*. If you feel like your dialogue needs this type of direction, then your dialogue isn't doing the job. Improve your dialogue and description. Sarcasm is the exception. If you don't make note of sarcasm, it may lead to confusion.

CUT TO. This transition is almost never necessary. When a scene ends, we all know it will cut to the next scene. The rare occasion to use CUT TO is for extra emphasis or irony:

```
          MALIK
   No, no. Dara does not dance.

                            CUT TO:
   INT. DISCO - NIGHT
   Dara is dancing like a wild
   woman.
```

Another example might be a scene of the hero preparing for the big showdown, CUT TO: the villain preparing for the big showdown.

FADE IN and FADE OUT. These really aren't necessary but they are fun and there's no harm in beginning the screenplay with FADE IN and ending it with FADE OUT.

Scene numbers and page numbers. You may have seen many screenplays online with *scene numbers*, found to the left and right of the slugline. Production screenplays are numbered to help coordinate the production process. Do not use scene numbers in your screenplay. (Unless you are heading into production, in which case, congrats!) Please note that screenplays must always have *page numbers* located in the upper right, starting with the first page of screenplay. (The title page is unnumbered.)

Montage. As a producer once explained to me, *montage* is French for expensive. (It's actually French for assembly.) What the producer meant is that a montage has lots of setups and locations for very little screen time. Every time a film crew moves and sets up, that costs a lot of money. So, montages cost a lot of money for very little screen time. That's not good. Basically, avoid montages whenever possible. If you need one, the way to format them is, an opening title in all caps briefly describing the montage, several lines of location and action proceeded by a dash, and finally END MONTAGE in all caps.

```
VEDA TRAINING MONTAGE

- Veda runs hard on the track.

- Veda does pull-up after pull-up.

- Veda punches a heavy bag.

- Veda doubles over exhausted, but
quickly drops and does pushups.

END VEDA TRAINING MONTAGE
```

Foreign Language There are many ways to handle foreign language dialogue. It is almost always written in italics. If there are extensive sections of foreign dialogue, you probably want to indicate how you are handling it in the scene description. For example:

```
All dialogue in italics is in Dutch.
```

Then when a character is speaking Dutch, you write their dialogue in English in italics. This way English-speaking readers can read the story and still understand how it will play out on screen. There are other situations where you may not want to make the dialogue clear. For example, an American is being held in a Russian prison. You may want to write out that dialogue in Russian using italics.

> Most readers as well as the prisoner will not understand the dialogue, increasing the feeling of unease.

There's no way to include every situation you will encounter as a writer. Sometimes you just have to make it up. The best way to get comfortable with screenplay format is to read as many professionally written screenplays as possible. That way, if you need to make up some formatting, you will feel more comfortable.

 ## Formatting Tips

Sometimes screenwriting software is a little too helpful. Final Draft has a feature called Automatic Character Continueds. If a character has a line of dialogue, followed by some scene description (Action), when the character speaks again Final Draft will add *(CONT'D)* after the character name. Sometimes this dialogue is a direct continuation of the previous dialogue but often a lot has happened and to add (CONT'D) feels totally inappropriate and wholly unnecessary. Basically, I believe it's completely unnecessary in all situations and just clutters the screenplay. Fortunately, you can turn this automatic feature off, which I do the moment I start a new screenplay.

There's another feature that's even more ridiculous, it's titled Scene Breaks. If this feature is activated, (CONTINUED) will be added in the footer of the page should a scene continue onto the next page. As if the reader would get lost when reaching the bottom of the page and not know what to do, "Is that it? Is the scene over? Oh, wait. It says CONTINUED, there must be more." I think most human beings know that when you reach the bottom of the page, you just go on to the next page. Luckily, this wacky feature defaults to off. Please don't ever turn it on.

Exercise: Using Screenplay Formatting

Go back to a story you wrote in prose (you can use one of the writing prompt exercises from Chapter 2) and rewrite it in screenplay format. Use screenwriting software. If you are still uncomfortable with the screenwriting software, there are tons of great instructional videos available online.

Nightcrawler (2014).

The Dark Knight (2008).

Up (2009).

Sound of Metal (2019).

Elf (2003).

Three Billboards Outside Ebbing, Missouri (2017).

Parasite (2019).

The Godfather (1972).

American Beauty (1999).

1917 (2019).

Swingers (1996).

Erin Brockovich (2000).

Aliens (1986).

The Big Lebowski (1998).

When Harry Met Sally (1989).

Jojo Rabbit (2019).

Baby Driver (2017).

Galaxy Quest (1999).

Out of Sight (1998).

No Country for Old Men (2007).

There's Something About Mary (1998).

10

Scenes

The Building Blocks

Scenes are the basic building blocks of a screenplay. Scenes come in all shapes and sizes, from short establishing shots to long dramatic confrontations. There is no right or wrong length for a scene; it should be as long as it needs to be and no longer. Often, the genre and pacing dictate the length of a scene. A fast-paced action or comedy screenplay will likely have short scenes, while a contemplative drama will tend to have much longer scenes.

What is a Scene?

A scene is the action that happens within a location. Scenes are always described in present tense, as if they are happening right now. We know a scene can be any length and that, as I mentioned in Chapter 9, it will have scene description and most likely dialogue, so what makes a scene good? A good scene contains two essential elements: *plot* and *emotion*. A great scene should also have three more elements: *character*, *style*, and *elements of the future*.

Plot

The first essential element for a good scene is *plot*. Something needs to be happening or there really isn't a story. In some circles, plot seems to be a dirty word. To me, plot is the main character taking action. Over the course of the story, plot is a series of interesting and dynamic actions.

A scene must have a character who wants something, has a need, or is trying to achieve a clear goal. There also needs to be an *obstacle*, something that keeps the character from achieving their *goal*. This obstacle could be anything: another character, a physical barrier, even the character themselves (self-doubt). Then there needs to be action, as the character actively tries to overcome the obstacle to achieve their goal. For each scene you should be able to answer the question, "What is the main character doing to get what they want?"

To me this is the plot—a character tries to overcome obstacles to achieve their goal. We see the character working to get what they want.

Lou Bloom, in the movie *Nightcrawler,* is an amoral character who is willing to do almost anything to get ahead. Despite this "terrible" character, people love the movie *Nightcrawler*. This is because, in almost every scene, Lou is an active character who takes bold action to get what he wants. The plot is driven by the fact that at every opportunity, Lou will do anything to get ahead. This creates great scenes in which we watch Lou, fascinated and wondering what he will do next. This is the essence of a great character-driven plot.

Conflict, Conflict, Conflict

If you've read any books or articles about screenwriting, you've definitely heard that every scene must have conflict.

Conflict is the key to dramatic stories, but so often it's done wrong or poorly. There is a very common mistake that even professional writers make: *fake conflict.*

For example, when characters argue about something pointless, this is not real conflict. Take this scene where two detectives are investigating a crime. Next to the dead body is a wedding invitation. The wedding starts in an hour. The detectives agree the killer is going to be at the wedding. "We have to go now," says Detective 1. But Detective 2 disagrees, "No, I'm hungry, let's stop and get lunch first." "The wedding is in an hour. We have to go there now." "Come on, it will only take a few minutes to get to the wedding, let's stop at a drive-thru."

I made this really obvious. They are clearly going to go straight to the wedding. Arguing about whether or not they should stop is an artificial conflict. It's just pointless arguing, and it will inevitably result in really bad dialogue. (Although, played for comedic effect, it could be hilarious because it is ridiculous.)

Real conflict happens inherently when you have an active character who wants something and an obstacle is preventing them from getting it.

There are several varieties of real conflict—physical, intellectual, and moral. Let's look at how they function:

Physical Conflict

Physical conflict occurs when a character wants something and there is a *physical obstacle* to achieving that goal. Let's go back to the murder mystery example. The detectives decide to follow the obvious clue and go to the wedding. Potential physical conflicts could be that their car is stolen or that they get shot at as they arrive at the wedding and can't go inside. These physical obstacles make it difficult for the detectives to achieve their goal of capturing the killer. (The killer also has a goal: not getting caught!)

Intellectual Conflict

Some barriers are intellectual. What if there are two clues next to the body, the wedding invitation and an invitation to an art gallery opening? Both start at the same time. The killer will be at one of them. The detectives came in the same car. Now we have an interesting dilemma: Which location should they go to? This is intellectual conflict. There can be a passionate (but short) discussion about which location makes the most sense. Each detective could quickly create a theory, listing clues to build a case for which location is the right choice. This type of argument is a real argument because it involves real dilemma. We, as an audience, can get involved. If you are watching this at home with friends, you may even hit pause to "argue" with your friends about which is the better choice. Writing the dialogue for a scene like this will be much easier and it will be a much more interesting scene because the conflict is real.

Moral Conflict

Here's another variation on the scenario: The detectives arrive at the wedding and the suspect shoots at them. The detectives want to return fire, but they are at a wedding full of innocent bystanders. But then they realize the wedding is next to a school, where there is a playground full of children!

Do they shoot back and risk a stray bullet hitting a wedding guest? But if they don't shoot back, will the suspect escape to the school playground and possibly endanger the children? Is there an alternative that doesn't require shooting? (This would be an intellectual solution to a moral conflict.) This is an authentic dilemma and real moral conflict. It inevitably leads to interesting dialogue and a truly dynamic scene.

In *The Dark Knight*, the Joker kidnaps both Harvey Dent and Batman's girlfriend Rachel Dawes. The Joker forces Batman to make a choice, he can't save both! This is another example of a real conflict, a real moral dilemma.

Batman chooses to save Rachel. Turns out the Joker lied, Harvey Dent is there. Surprise!

The thing that's really great about intellectual or moral conflict is that the audience can play along. Physical conflict is fun, like riding a roller coaster—when well done, it's thrilling. But intellectual and moral conflict engage the audience. They draw us in, and we are provoked to analyze the situation along with the characters and make decisions—either agreeing or disagreeing with the decisions of the main character.

Emotion

Why do so many people love emojis? Because people love the simple clear expressions of emotion. Life is all about emotion, and emotions are an essential part of storytelling. We tell stories to make people feel something. If you love a movie, it's probably because it made you feel something: a strong emotion, or maybe even several different emotions.

> *It's not what happens to people on the page; it's about what happens to a reader in his heart and mind.*
>
> *— Gordon Lish*

Often actors will ask, "What is this scene about?" This question is not about the plot. It is about the emotion. The plot, the action within a scene, should force the character to feel an emotion or a series of emotions. And when done right, this will make the audience feel those emotions as well.

Now by emotions, I don't just mean sad. If you Google "emotional scenes," there will invariably be lists of the saddest scenes of all time. Sad is a very strong emotion but I'm talking about all emotions. Humans have anywhere from six to twelve to twenty-seven basic emotions depending on what list you look at and hundreds of variations on them.

Let's consider an example: The opening of *Up* has a ten-minute sequence encapsulating Carl and Ellie's life. It ends with four powerful short little scenes:

- In the first scene, they are hiking up a hill for a picnic, Carl has plane tickets—they are finally going to fulfill their dream of going on an adventure but Ellie stumbles and falls: something is wrong. So, the scene starts with excitement and anticipation but ends with panic and fear.

- The next scene is Ellie in a hospital, looking at their adventure book. Carl enters with a blue balloon, and they have a sweet interaction. There are a couple emotions at play here. First is concern and fear, whatever caused Ellie to fall in the last scene is serious enough that she is staying in the hospital. It is also heartwarming since they have a sweet interaction.

- The next scene is a church. Carl sits alone with a bouquet of balloons. This scene is devastating. The fear and concern have been answered with the worst possible answer—Ellie is gone.

- Finally, Carl enters their house with a single balloon. This is the devastating conclusion of this beautiful relationship. Carl is alone.

This dynamic, emotional sequence is told entirely with visuals. No dialogue. No emotions are mentioned in the scene description and yet the emotional impact is clear and powerful.

It's not always possible to convey emotions with simple images. Sometimes we need to spell it out a bit more, especially in a screenplay. We want to avoid bluntly stating what the character is feeling, "John is sad." Flat statements like this feel disconnected and rarely generate emotion in the reader. But sometimes the character's emotions need to be indicated in the description.

In the movie *Sound of Metal*, the main character Ruben, a musician, very rapidly loses his hearing.

- Ruben first experiences a RINGING SOUND (in a screenplay, sounds are usually in ALL CAPS) while selling merch. He tilts his head, but no specific emotion is mentioned in the screenplay. We get the sense that the sound is unexpected and unwanted, which creates intrigue.

- Ruben experiences the ringing sound during a performance. Again, no specific emotion is mentioned in the scene.

- The next morning Ruben wakes up, examines his ears in the mirror, makes noise with his throat, and then coughs. His examining of his ears and testing actions clearly demonstrate that Ruben is concerned, and our concern grows as well.

- The next scene has Ruben taking a shower. The writers add, "...lost in worry." The scene description continues, adding that the sound of the water is barely audible. The action of taking a shower is rather ambiguous, even with the low water sound, so the writers wisely add the emotional description.

- A couple of short scenes of muffled sounds, including a blender. We know a blender should be very loud, so the muffled sound definitely builds the fear that something is wrong.

- In the next scene, Ruben starts their Airstream and pulls forward. He glances nervously at his partner, Lou. She asks him a question, but he doesn't hear it. The emotion is building and getting complex. Ruben is concerned that his musician partner might be able to tell something is wrong with him. If Ruben just glanced at Lou, it would be too ambiguous. Adding "nervously" makes the emotion of the scene clear. This is a rather innocuous moment for Lou, but we've seen what's happening with Ruben, so it raises our fear that this is bad.

- The next scene, they are setting up to perform. Ruben glances at Lou as she begins the sound check... increased panic... By forcing Ruben into a scene where he has to use his ears to check the sound, the writers dial up the pressure and the emotion, but the writers make sure the audience understands this by adding "increased panic." So, Ruben quickly makes an excuse and leaves.

- The next scene, Ruben frantically walks toward a pharmacy counter. Ruben's emotion has reached a peak, he's in full panic mode.

In less than two pages, Ruben has gone from his normal life to a nervous glance to increased panic to frantic. Some of the scenes work wonderfully with the images and sound, but others would be too ambiguous without the writers describing Ruben's emotional state.

As writers we want to be sure our scenes generate emotion, and that the emotion builds from scene to scene. But often a character's action can be ambiguous, so we need to include the emotion in the scene description. But beware not to overdo it with the emotion, "John cries uncontrollably." When your characters have huge emotions and act overly dramatic, that is melodrama.

Two Levels of Emotion in a Scene

What the characters are feeling, and the audience is feeling are usually in sync. But sometimes the emotion that a character experiences and the emotion that the audience experiences are different. This separation mostly comes into play in comedies. Let's take a look at the movie *Elf*:

- When "Santa" arrives at Gimbels, Buddy the Elf, played by Will Ferrell, gets ridiculously happy. His exuberance is comical and engaging. Buddy is happy and we are amused and so we are fairly aligned with the main character.

- But then Buddy realizes this guy is not the "real Santa," he becomes indignant and angry. This builds the comedy of the scene. So, Buddy's angry and we're laughing—our emotions are now going in the opposite direction of the main character.

- When Buddy rips "Santa's" beard off, he "looks at the beard in shock, like a horror movie." Also, the kids freak out, and "Santa" goes crazy. And it's totally hilarious. The emotions of the audience are definitely, completely at odds with the emotions of the characters.

If a movie is not a comedy and there is an emotional disconnect, that can be a strong indication that a scene is not working. For example, during a breakup scene where the main character is getting dumped, if the audience is laughing well, obviously that's a problem.

Revealing Character

A scene that moves the plot forward and generates emotion is good but a scene that moves the plot forward, generates emotion, and *reveals more about the characters* is great. It's amazing how information about our fellow humans fascinates us. We're drawn to it, like bugs to the light. It doesn't have to be an earth-shattering revelation. A great character is built piece by piece, like a beautiful mosaic. Like the character of Mildred Hayes in *Three Billboards Outside Ebbing, Missouri* written by Martin McDonagh:

- Mildred slows to a stop to examine three old billboards, their advertisements long faded. Reveal: Mildred is a curious woman. Why is she looking at these three old billboards? (Also, makes us curious.)

- Mildred rents the three billboards. When she hands the cards to Red, he reads them. (We don't see them.) He is stunned, looks at her sadly, and says, "You're Angela Hayes' mother." Reveal: Mildred is a mother and something bad happened to her daughter Angela.

- Later, there is a flashback that reveals what happened the night Angela was murdered. They had a fight and said horrible things to each other. Reveal: The reason why Mildred is so hell bent on solving her daughter's murder. She feels insanely guilty and needs to find someone else to blame (other than herself).

When you are adding character development to your scenes, you are really taking your script to the next level. The screenplay for *Three Billboards Outside Ebbing, Missouri* reveals something new and dynamic about a character in almost every scene. That's why this eighty-three-page screenplay is the basis for two Oscar-winning characters.

Style

Many old-school screenwriting books and teachers disregard style and actually advise you to avoid it. They insist that a screenplay is "just a blueprint." This is a *huge* mistake. Think about it. Stylish writing makes a story fun and dynamic to read. What these old-school types are saying is to make your story boring.

So many of the great contemporary screenplays are fun to read. That's because they are stylish! What producers and executives seek is for the screenplay to be "the movie on the page." To do that, you must be evocative in your writing. The story must convey emotion and not just with the dialogue but also with the scene description. Every word on the page should not just be adding to the story but also adding to the tone, enhancing the mood.

Consider the Oscar-winning movie *Parasite*:

In the opening scene, Ki-Woo is searching for wifi. His sister, mom, and dad are all lying on the floor. The fact that they don't have wifi but are trying to steal their neighbors' implies that they are poor but resourceful. Chung-Sook kicks her husband. If this were just a blueprint that would sound pretty bad, but the next line tells us—

```
She treats Ki-Tek like shit, but it
doesn't bother him.
```

Which is kind of hilarious. Next Ki-Tek removes a bag of white bread from the "sad, empty fridge." If you are writing a blueprint, then a fridge can't be sad. It would just be empty. In this case, "sad" is stylish and funny.

The opening is pretty damn funny, but it would be impossible for a reader to tell that it's funny if the screenplay description was written just as a blueprint. The stylish scene description informs the reader of the fun tone and tells us this is not some overly dramatic film about the horrors of poverty.

What's also really amazing is that this is a Korean language film and yet they took the time to write an English version of the screenplay that is fun to read. It's fun because it's stylish—stylish as hell.

Even the screenplay for *The Godfather*, written fifty years ago, has some amazingly stylish scene description. Check out the last lines of the incredible scene where Michael, the college kid, murders Sollozzo and McCluskey:

```
He looks back. He sees a frozen
tableau of the murder as though it
had been recreated in wax.
```

Wow. That is very powerful. Very stylish.

Elements of the Future

One of the key aspects of storytelling is not just moving the plot forward with each scene but each scene should make us want to read the following scene as well. This propels the story forward, keeping the audience involved. Let's go back to the scene where Mildred rents the billboards from Red in *Three Billboards Outside Ebbing, Missouri*. Mildred hands Red three index cards that say what she wants on the billboards, but we don't see them. We're very intrigued and when Red's reaction is so strong, it really dials up our desire to know what the cards say. But we have to wait until the next scene! This scene moves the plot forward (Mildred rents the billboards), plus it creates intrigue—we really want to know what's on those billboards! There is a sense of dramatic tension, since we have to wait to find out the answer.

Let's look at some great examples of directing the audience toward the future:

Parasite Min-Hyuk asks Ki-Woo to take over tutoring for a high school girl. Ki-Woo asks, "You want me to pretend to be a college student?" This simple sentence gets the audience looking forward. Will Ki-Woo, do it? Will he lie? Can he pull it off? Will he get caught? These kinds of questions keep the audience engaged and curious to see how the story will unfold.

American Beauty Lester states in the opening, "I'm 42-years-old and in less than a year I'll be dead." This is powerful and gets us paying attention. We want to keep reading/watching because we need to find out how and why Lester is going to die. Then the third act starts with Lester saying, "Remember those posters that said, "Today is the first day of the rest of your life?' Well, that's true of every day except one. The day you die." So Lester is telling us, today is the day he is going to die. That really dials up the tension and suspense.

1917 A sergeant wakes Blake and says, "Pick a man, bring your kit." It's not exactly clear what is going on, but it seems as though Blake has been chosen for some task. This brings up an interesting point. Not everything has to be explained. The action is set into motion. We will find out the details of the mission soon enough and we want to keep watching to find out what job Blake has been chosen for.

Keeping your story focused on the future is one of the keys to making your screenplay a dynamic, intriguing page-turner. In fact, elements of the future create *suspense*, which is so important that we focus an entire chapter on it, later in this book.

Scene Structure

There are several important aspects to constructing a scene. The majority of which serve to keep the scene as lean as possible. Time is money and never more so than with shooting a film. Every second of screen time costs a fortune but we want to tell meaningful stories, so the key is to say more with less. Here are several methods to keep your scenes lean...

Economy of Words

"Omit unnecessary words," is a simple rule from *The Elements of Style* by William Strunk Jr. and E. B. White. This is a general rule of thumb for all writing but even more so for screenwriting.

Screenplays do not have a lot of words, especially when compared with prose writing. Therefore, the words that are there are important. You need to make every word count. Less is more.

Come In Late

Films tend to feel like real time, but they aren't. The key is to skip the boring parts. *Coming in late* is a great way to do this. Scenes don't have to start at the beginning. You don't have to show a character enter the room and say, "Hi," and then have the other character say, "Hi." It's boring. Skip it. Start when the scene gets interesting.

Let's look at the script *Swingers,* by Jon Favreau. Below are the very first lines of dialogue:

<pre>
                MIKE
     And what if I don't want to give
     up on her?

                ROB
     You don't call.

                MIKE
     But you said I shouldn't call her
     if I wanted to give up on her.

                ROB
     Right.

                MIKE
     So I don't call either way.
</pre>

This is really jumping into the middle of things. It's clear that these guys are friends, and they are discussing what to do about Mike's girlfriend leaving him. The writer is trusting the audience. We don't need to hear them discussing where to sit and what to order. We understand what's going on. You don't have to explain everything. Trust your audience—don't bore them.

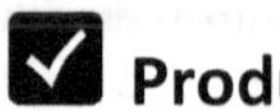 **Production Tip**

Skipping a character's entrance also has a practical purpose for shooting the scene. A character entrance adds a lot more complexity to the shot. The actor's action must be *blocked*. The doorway will have to be lit. The camera movements will have to be worked out. This is a lot of extra time and effort for something that is boring to watch. Jumping into the scene keeps the lighting and blocking to a minimum. Cutting down the extra *camera setups* allows the director (who might be you) to focus on the heart of the scene and spend more time with the actors.

 *The Digital Filmmaking Handbook*

All screenwriters should have an understanding of how production works. If you'd like to know more about blocking, camera setups, and working with actors, check out *The Digital Filmmaking Handbook* by Sonja Schenk and Ben Long.

Get Out Early

Another way to keep scenes lean is to *get out early*. Watching characters exit is just as boring as watching them enter. In the opening scene of *Erin Brockovich*, she is in a doctor's office, interviewing for a job. We all know what a job interview looks and sounds like. The writer takes advantage of that and starts the scene nice and late, in the middle of the interview. They also *get out early* as well. Erin is doing her best but at some point, the doctor looks down at her resume, then looks up at her:

```
Beat. By Erin's expression, she knows
what's coming.
```

She's not getting the job. He's going to tell her that. She knows it and so does the audience. So boom, end of scene. If she knows it and we know it, the scene is over. We don't have to sit through the doctor saying, "Erin, you seem really nice, but… blah, blah, blah." We don't have to hear Erin say, "Thank you anyways." We don't have to see her get up and leave the office. Trust your audience.

It Has to Be There

Some writers are naturally economical, but too much so. If your story is too subtle, you will be in trouble. You don't want to hit people over the head with your story but it needs to be there on the page. Here's the deal. People read screenplays quickly—very, very quickly. They are not going to stop and study your text like a college lit class studying a William Faulkner novel.

The truly great writers can do it all, have a strong clear dynamic story and have details worthy of a college lit class, yet be extremely economical.

Let's take another look at the scene where Mildred rents the billboards in *Three Billboards Outside Ebbing, Missouri*. It's a strong dynamic scene that is hilarious, intriguing, and powerful. The intention of the scene is clearly there. But there are also two short lines about Mildred and a beetle. They read like nice detail. They don't get in the way or slow down the flow. But if you were to study this screenplay in a college lit class, you probably would realize that this is a clear literary reference to Franz Kafka. The upside-down beetle is a direct reference to *The Metamorphosis*. Behind the beetle, outside the window is the police station. One of the most powerful themes of Kafka's writing is the powerlessness of people against the police and the justice system. This is a direct connection back to Mildred—she feels helpless against the police and the lack of justice. And that is why she is there, in Red's office, renting the billboards: she is desperately trying to fight injustice, but she feels more like the beetle trapped upside down. If the whole scene was about some coded message about upside-down beetles that would be a problem, but this scene has everything. It has strong action—Mildred rents the billboards. It reveals character—Mildred is Angela Hayes' mother and something really sad happened to her. We want to know what's on those cards, so it compels us forward. It's funny as hell. And it has beautiful literary references.

Some Specific Types of Scenes

There are a handful of scene types that may not conform to all the scene guidelines because they serve a very specific purpose. Let's look at a few of those:

> **Establishing shot.** Very short exterior shots that establish a specific location are called *establishing shots*. They can add scope to a movie, such as a verdant valley or a towering skyscraper. This

type of scene is becoming more rare in screenplays, but you will come across it.

Scene of preparation. This is another *element of the future*, it lets us know that an upcoming event is important. A great example is the movie *Aliens*: The Marines prepare to face the aliens. Since this is a sequel, and we've seen what one alien can do, we feel like their confidence may be a bit misplaced. This builds a great sense of dramatic tension for how the encounter will go.

Aftermath scene. Following a big scene, it's good to take a moment and assess the damage. This gives the big moment resonance. In *Aliens,* the team of Marines battles the aliens and are mostly wiped out. There is a great aftermath scene and Bill Pullman utters the classic line, "Game over, man. Game over!"

Other Important Aspects of Scenes

There are many other facets to strong scene writing. Let's look at a few more of them:

End the Scene on a Strong Line

We never want scenes to just drift off. It's important to punctuate a scene with a strong final line of dialogue. Like *The Big Lebowski*: As the Dude takes the attaché case to pay the ransom for kidnapped Bunny Lebowski, Brandt implores him —

                    BRANDT
          Her life is in your hands.

                    DUDE
          Oh, man, don't say that..

Then Brandt repeats it twice more. Technically, the last line is "And report back to us as soon as it's done." But "Her life is in your hands" directs us toward the future and sets an ominous yet hilarious tone.

If you're writing a comedy, a great last line for a scene is called a *button*. A button is a final joke that really finishes the scene off with a flourish. The classic fake orgasm scene, in *When Harry Met Sally*, ends with Estelle Reiner (director Rob Reiner's mom) delivering the hilarious line:

          I'll have what she's having.

Planting and Payoff

The theory of *Chekhov's gun* is that everything in a story must be there for a reason. What this means is that if there is a gun in the first act, someone must use it by the end of the story. We can't just throw a gun or similarly hot object into a story. When an object like this is introduced in a story, the audience pays attention. We have to reward the audience for paying attention by having a character use the gun. If the story were to be resolved without the gun ever showing up again, that would be frustrating for the audience.

The inverse is true as well. If someone uses a gun in the final act, it must have been established in an earlier act—the gun can't just appear when a character needs it. This type of setup is known as *planting and payoff.*

> ***Jojo Rabbit*** At the Nazi youth camp, Jojo and other children list the distinguishing characteristics of Jews: horns, serpent tongue, claws. This plants the idea that Jojo's conception of a Jewish person is ridiculously distorted. The payoff happens when Jojo meets, Elsa, the Jewish girl who has been hiding in his house. She has none of these features, which begins the process of breaking down Jojo's misconceptions.

> ***Baby Driver*** It is planted that Baby likes to record everything. It feels like the payoff will be that this habit is going to get him killed when Bats discovers his recording. But the real payoff happens later when he is able to listen to a recording of Doc and figure out what happened.

> ***Galaxy Quest*** At the sci-fi convention in the opening sequence, it is planted that super nerd Brandon has obsessively studied every episode. The payoff comes in the third act when Brandon's knowledge helps save the day.

Avoiding or Updating Clichéd Scenes

Sometimes we need to include a scene that we've seen before in many movies. It's important to try to put a new spin on it.

> **The meet-cute.** This is the scene where characters meet; a.k.a. where the romance starts. It is a requirement for all romantic comedies and pretty much any time the *b-story* is a romance. Having the characters literally bump into each other is probably the most common and overused *meet-cute*. In *Out of Sight*, Foley, a felon who is escaping prison, throws Karen, a federal marshal,

into the trunk of a car and gets in with her, then he proceeds to flirt with her for several minutes. Definitely not the clichéd meet-cute.

A psychopathic killer murders someone. This is definitely something we have seen at least a million times. In *No Country for Old Men*, the cold-blooded killer, Chigurh, uses an air-powered bolt gun to kill. The strange device is made to slaughter cattle. Not your typical psychopath.

A date goes terribly wrong. Bad dates scenes are pretty typical and are often just uncomfortable. In *There's Something About Mary*, Ted's prom date with Mary takes the bad date scene to an epic level. No date has ever gone this hilariously bad.

Other Options to Consider

There are several other key elements that can make your scenes more dynamic, more interesting, and more challenging for your main character, which, in turn, will make your story more dramatic.

Location. The setting can have a great effect on the characters in a scene. Too often writers just settle for office or apartment. What if that argument happened on a bike ride through a park? Now our characters need to deal with not being able to hear each other, wrangling their bikes, and potentially interacting with bystanders in the park. What happens if you move the scene to a boat? Now when one character is revealed to be a killer, the other is trapped!

Time of day. Most scenes are not that affected by the time, but it can have a profound affect. What if a character gets a text at three a.m.? "Meet me at the old barn? Now!" Someone wants to meet at three in the morning? What's up?

Weather. Snow or rain can add a great deal of complication. But there are many more options: Oppressive heat, fierce winds, bitter cold. Maybe heat and humidity make the scientist's equipment stop working. Weather is an excellent and authentic way to complicate a scene

Other characters. Teenagers could be in the living room, discussing going out, suddenly we reveal that a parent is cleaning in the kitchen. Or when a character is home alone, and they hear a noise in the next room. Other characters can dramatically shift the scene.

Props. Imagine a character is playing with a machete during a scene? Maybe that's too obvious. How about a weird doll? Or maybe something odd, like a stapler? An interesting prop can really bring a scene to life.

The key here is to question everything. Too often writers settle for the first idea that comes to their mind when writing a scene. You always want to consider every element of a scene and challenge yourself to think of interesting options.

Exercise: Making Scenes More Effective

Go back to any of the stories you have come up with so far. Pick an interesting scene and change at least one element to make it a more effective scene. Changes to try:

Conflict. Can you increase the conflict? Raise the stakes? Make the obstacle more challenging? Take a simple physical conflict and add an intellectual or moral conflict to further engage your audience?

Emotion. Identify the emotion that your character should experience. Can you find a way to increase that emotion?

Character. Can you add a revelation about your character?

Style. Can you make your descriptions more stylish? But not so much so that you lose the story.

Element of the future. Can you add an element of the future that would entice the reader to want more?

Cut in deep. Start the scene later. Don't just cut a line or two. Cut at least half a page or more. When does the scene get dynamic? Start there.

Get out early. End the scene in a more dramatic way. Cut before explaining everything. Create a mystery. What is going to happen next? But don't cut so much that you confuse your audience.

Other changes to consider:

- Change the location.
- Time of day.
- Weather.
- Add other interesting characters.
- Add a prop.

Jaws (1975).

Star Wars: A New Hope (1977).

The Dark Knight (2008).

Breaking Bad, pilot episode (2008).

The Hangover (2009).

Olive Kitteridge, pilot episode (2014).

The Matrix (1999).

The Bourne Identity (2002).

Close Encounters of the Third Kind (1977).

The Town (2010).

Raiders of the Lost Ark (1981).

*Finding Nemo (*2003).

Sunset Boulevard (1950).

American Beauty (1999).

Double Indemnity (1944).

Crazy, Stupid, Love (2011).

Mamá (2008).

11

Start Fast

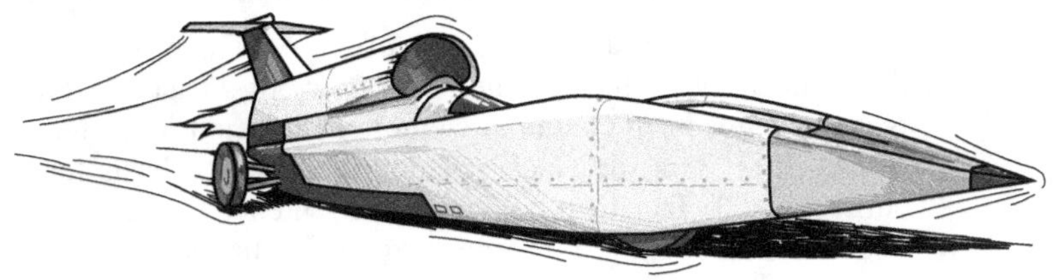

Hook the Audience

If you are writing a short film, of course you have to start fast but even if you are writing a pilot or a feature film, you must start fast as well. With so many people watching content online, it seems obvious that you need to grab their attention and hook them into the story as quickly as possible. But this idea of starting fast and hooking the audience has been around for a while.

Check out some of these opening lines from classic novels:

> *Someone must have slandered Josef K., for one morning, without having done anything truly wrong, he was arrested.*
>
> *—Franz Kafka, "The Trial"*

> *Mother died today.*
>
> *—Albert Camus, "The Stranger"*

> *It was a pleasure to burn.*
>
> *—Ray Bradbury, "Fahrenheit 451"*

These aren't short stories, these are novels! And these are the *opening* lines! Someone has been arrested, someone has died, and someone is burning something. Talk about starting fast and jumping into the action. Even *Jaws*, one of Steven Spielberg's many masterpieces, takes almost four minutes before the girl is attacked by the shark. (Although John Williams' brilliant and ominous score sets a dark tone in the first minute.)

Each of these stories begins with bold action (or statement that implies action) which is a key element of the story:

- Josef K. is arrested but does not know what he is charged with. That is the main concept of the story in *The Trial*. Josef will spend the entirety of the novel trying to defend himself from accusations that he never understands. So, the entire idea of the novel is clearly stated and set into motion in the first sentence.

- Meursault's mother dies at the start of *The Stranger*. We assume this is devastating for the main character but, in fact, it is not. Notice the line itself contains no emotion, just a simple statement of fact. It is Mersault's lack of emotion that is the basis for the entire novel. In fact, he is convicted and sentenced to death based upon his lack of emotion. So once again, this first sentence is the lynch pin upon which the entire novel turns.

- Montag is a fireman but in the dystopian world of *Fahrenheit 451*, firemen *start* fires, instead of putting them out. Montag truly believes in his government that burns books. He really enjoys what he does. Slowly this joy is stripped away as he learns about his world and evolves as a character. This leads Montag to begin to question his government. So, this statement of joy is crucial to where the story is headed.

The key here is that the bold action that kicks off each of these stories is not some random "boom" to jostle the audience, these actions are central to the story and central to the character.

Beginning with the central action is incredibly effective but there are other very powerful techniques to start fast that can kick off your story in a dramatic and dynamic way.

Open with the Villain

It may seem counter intuitive to open with the villain. We want to get to know our hero and build a connection with them so the audience will root for them. Then why show the villain first? A scene with a dramatic and dynamic villain puts the conflict that our main character must face front and center. And by demonstrating how powerful the villain is, we make it clear that our hero is in for one tough journey.

Jaws Young people enjoy a beach party. A beautiful woman wants to go for a swim and runs toward the water, stripping as she goes. A guy tries to follow but is drunk, terribly out of shape, or both. The playful, sexy scene is turned on its head by John Williams' ominous score. And suddenly the woman is viciously attacked. The great white shark, one of the most brutal and efficient killing machines nature has ever come up with, is truly a frightening villain.

Star Wars: A New Hope After the opening text crawl, we see a spaceship. It's being chased by an Imperial battle cruiser which looks at least a hundred times bigger. Next, the small ship is being boarded, as stormtroopers shoot their lasers. And then Darth Vader walks in. Wow. I can tell you as a young boy, that blew me away. One of the coolest villains of all time. I, like millions of others, was hooked immediately.

The Dark Knight opens with an amazing bank robbery sequence. The Joker leads his crew on a daring and brilliant bank robbery, but also kills each robber as they complete their part. He's a genius, but he's ruthless and insane.

The Flash Forward

Sometimes we want to jump ahead in the story to a point where the story is more dramatic. This is especially true with stories that might otherwise start very slowly. By showing a dramatic scene from later in the story, we hook the audience. Then we can slow down and properly introduce the characters.

Breaking Bad opens with a man named Underpants Man, since he's only wearing his underpants and, oh yeah, a gas mask. He is driving a Winnebago meth lab like a maniac through the desert and by the way there are two dead guys rolling around like rag dolls in the back. Okay, who the heck is this guy? I want to know more!

The Hangover A high-end wedding is being prepped. The bride is trying not to freak out, but her groom is not there. The phone rings, it's Phil, the best man. He is in the desert, he looks like hell. He explains that the bachelor party got out of hand, and they lost Doug, the groom. "But the wedding is happening in five hours." "Yeah, that's not going to happen." Boom! Very dramatic setup, now we can spend the time to get to know these guys.

> *Olive Kitteridge* This four-hour limited series is slow-paced and dramatic, but it still starts with a flash forward. Olive walks out into the forest, sets down an envelope, takes out a gun, and puts it to her head. And click—cut away. What? Why is this woman going to kill herself? Did she succeed?

The flash forward is particularly effective when you have a story that may otherwise take time to set up and get going. It would be difficult if *Breaking Bad* opened with boring husband Walter White, eating breakfast with his family, teaching chemistry, and working at a car wash. It might be even harder to get behind grumpy Olive Kitteridge, reading her loving husband's valentine card and then throwing it in the trash. The guys in *The Hangover* are pretty funny but it would feel like nothing is happening for twenty minutes and even the most charming characters are going to have a hard time keeping the audience onboard for that long.

Establish a Mystery

A mystery is definitely a fantastic way to kick off your story—it creates a compelling desire to keep watching to find out the answer to that mystery.

> *The Matrix* After the opening title, the film transitions to a blinking cursor on a computer screen. We hear the sound of an old telephone dialing. As the call is answered, we see a couple lines of odd computer text. We hear voices talking. They sound slightly muffled as if over an old phone line. As numbers scroll down the screen, one-by-one locking in on a digit, we hear one voice say to the other, "We're going to kill him. You understand that?" Wait, who is going to get killed? And who are you? All this before the first frame of the first scene.

> *The Bourne Identity* A body floats in the water. The crew fishes the corpse out of the ocean and onto the deck of an old fishing boat. Suddenly, it moves! He's alive! (The writer actually uses the word "corpse" in the screenplay, even though indeed, he is not dead.) The ship's old cook "operates," removing two bullets and an odd plastic tube. Finally, the "corpse" wakes up. "Who are you?" "I don't know." That's a great hook. Talk about a mystery— a body is fished out of the sea, with two bullets and a plastic tube in his back, plus he doesn't know who he is.

> *Close Encounters of the Third Kind* A sandstorm blows in the Mexican desert, a team of scientists arrive. They find several WWII-era fighter planes in near perfect condition. The numbers on the engine blocks are checked. These are the planes from

Flight 19 that disappeared in the Bermuda Triangle forty years ago! One of the most famous mysteries of all time.

Opening Set Piece

Opening with a set piece is a classic way to kick a story off. (We'll go into detail about how to build a set piece in Chapter 16, "The Set Piece.") Almost every superhero movie, every James Bond film, and any action movie, like *Mission Impossible,* starts with a great action sequence. There are other types of set pieces, but we're focusing on the action type here.

> *The Matrix* After that great mysterious opening, *The Matrix* kicks it into high gear. Cops arrive at a broken-down, old hotel to arrest Trinity. She stands, hands in the air, back to the squad of cops with guns drawn. Below, on the street, the agents arrive. The lieutenant says two units of men are bringing her down. "No lieutenant, your men are already dead." Then boom! Trinity kicks into action and takes the cops out. The agents arrive and there's an epic chase with superhuman feats that define the world as something other than normal. Wow. If the mystery didn't grab you, this amazing action sequence sure will.

> *The Town* It's a bank robbery movie, so it starts off with a great bank robbery sequence. It opens with the crew going over the plan, describing the guards and their routines. The two main characters disagree about whether or not to hurt the guards—creating conflict. Then it kicks into action. The robbery is shockingly violent and intense, very visceral. There are several complications, increasing the drama. It's a fantastic sequence that definitely opens the movie with a bang and sets a dangerous tone for the rest of the story.

> *Raiders of the Lost Ark* From the moment Indy enters the cave, the tension begins to build: spiders, booby trap spears with skeletons, a deep pit. Then in the idol room, Indy dodges tiles on the floor that trigger poison darts. Indy seems to make the switch for the idol perfectly but then it sinks down, triggering total chaos. Indy dashes through a barrage of darts, as the room seems to collapse. Indy gets to the pit right after his partner has crossed. Indy tosses him the idol but his partner double crosses him. Indy manages to jump across the pit before it really gets crazy. After this amazing opening the audience is totally onboard for the ride!

Defining Moment

Some stories explore how a single moment can affect a character for the rest of their life. As storytellers, it's crucial to put this defining moment in just the right place in your story. Kicking the story off with such an intense scene can be very powerful.

> ***Finding Nemo*** Marlin and his wife have found a great home to start their family. They have hundreds of healthy little eggs getting ready to hatch. It all seems perfect until a barracuda shows up. Marlin tries to defend his wife but is knocked out. When he comes to, all is gone except for a lone egg. Very dramatic opening. Definitely gets your attention.

The brain trust at Pixar did not originally plan to open their story with such a dark scene. But without it, Marlin's character is so overprotective of Nemo that he comes off as super annoying. So, by shifting this defining moment to the opening, it creates sympathy and empathy for Marlin, and drama for the audience.

Already Dead

If you have a dark story that ends with the hero dying, you may want to prepare your audience for it. A great way to do that is to make it the opening scene. So, you start with a bang and you prep your audience for the inevitable. This is a very specific form of flash forward. Several all-time greats do exactly that.

> ***Sunset Boulevard*** Opens with police racing down Sunset Blvd. at five in the morning. There's been a murder, a narrator tells us. There's a body floating in the pool, two bullets in the back, one in the stomach. The narrator refers to the body as a nobody and a poor dope. As the narrator transitions back to the beginning of the story, we realize the narrator is the poor dope, the dead guy in the pool. Now we're paying attention. What happens? How does this struggling writer end up dead in a pool?
>
> ***American Beauty*** Opens with a strange handheld video of a girl complaining about what a dork her father is and the cameraman offers to kill him. Then we're flying above a suburban neighborhood. A narrator tells us he is Lester Burnham and that, "In less than a year, I'll be dead." That's pretty shocking. Is the daughter going to kill her father? The video is actually a remnant of the original framework, the daughter was on trial for killing her

father. That story line was cut, but the video along with Lester's narration really kicks the film off with a bang.

Confession

Another way to deal with a dark story, where a hero acts less than heroically, is to open with a confession. This is powerful evidence that the story we are going to witness is going to be dark and is not going to end well. You've been warned.

Double Indemnity opens with a car racing through downtown L.A. late at night. An injured man, Walter Neff, gets out of the car and goes up to his office. He lights a cigarette and begins a Dictaphone recording:

```
                NEFF
Office memorandum, Walter Neff to
Barton Keyes, Claims Manager.
Los Angeles, July 16th, 1938. Dear
Keyes: I suppose you'll call this a
confession when you hear it. I
don't like the word confession. I
just want to set you right about
one thing you couldn't see, because
it was smack up against your nose.
You think you're such a hot potato
as a claims manager, such a wolf on
a phony claim. Well, maybe you are,
Keyes, but let's take a look at
this Dietrichson claim, Accident
and Double Indemnity. You were
pretty good in there for a while,
all right. You said it wasn't an
accident. Check. You said it wasn't
suicide. Check. You said it was
murder. Check and double check. You
thought you had it cold, all
wrapped up in tissue paper, with
pink ribbons around it. It was
perfect, except that it wasn't,
because you made a mistake, just
one tiny little mistake. When it
```

> came to picking the killer, you
> picked the wrong guy, if you know
> what I mean. Want to know who
> killed Dietrichson? Hold tight to
> that cheap cigar of yours, Keyes. I
> killed Dietrichson. Me, Walter
> Neff, insurance agent, 35 years
> old, unmarried, no visible scars --
>
> (He glances down at his
> wounded shoulder)
>
> Until a little while ago, that is.
> Yes, I killed him. I killed him for
> money -- and a woman -- and I
> didn't get the money and I didn't
> get the woman. Pretty, isn't it?

Screenwriting books and guides are always telling you not to write long monologues and for the most part they are right. Except if you can write like this. Neff's monologue is the definition of *film noir*. The good guy gets pulled into a dark world for money and sex, but life is cruel and he gets screwed. This brilliant monologue kicks the story off with style and prepares us for the dark narrative to come. Neff, the main character, was so powerful that Fred MacMurray, the fantastic actor who portrayed him, vowed to never play a bad guy again.

Drop the Bomb

When a character reveals a big piece of information, that's called *dropping the bomb.* It's often a big shock to the other primary characters and it's definitely a shock to the audience. It's a great way to start fast and kick the story into high gear. Here's the opening page to *Crazy, Stupid, Love* by Dan Fogelman.

> FADE IN:
>
> INT. FRENCH RESTAURANT (PASADENA, CA) -
> EVENING
>
> Soft music. A classy joint. Below the
> tables, WE PAN well-heeled feet nuzzling.
> Finally we SETTLE ON:

A PAIR OF FEET WHITE SNEAKERS sitting
opposite FANCY HIGH HEELS. These feet
aren't nuzzling. There's distance here.

PULL UP, REVEALING CAL WEAVER (42) and
his wife, TRACY (41). A handsome couple.
He'd be JFK to her Jackie O... if he gave
a shit. Unfortunately, he doesn't (i.e.:
white sneakers in fancy French
restaurant).

Cal pulls out READING GLASSES, looks at
the menu.

> CAL
>
> Well, I'm full. You were right,
> hon. I shouldn't have eaten all
> that bread.
>
> (then)
>
> Want to just share a dessert?

Tracy is lost in thought, gazing at a
menu.

> CAL
>
> You okay, babe? You seem out of
> it.
>
> TRACY
>
> Yeah, I'm just thinking about
> what I want.
>
> CAL
>
> Me too. Okay, let's say it at the
> same time. One. Two. Three...
>
> TRACY   CAL
>
> I want a divorce. Crème brulee.

Boom! That is dropping the bomb. Cal is totally clueless. He has no idea
this is coming. As for the audience, there are some small clues that he is not
trying at all, wearing white sneakers in a fancy restaurant. But for the most
part it is shocking and dramatic. It definitely grabs our attention.

(Note: I'm not a big fan of *dual dialogue*. It's overused and most of the time completely unnecessary. But this is a prime example of when to use it. It perfectly captures how the characters are completely out of sync.)

Grab the Audience's Attention

All these methods of starting fast are very effective ways to kick your story off with a bang and grab the audience's attention. But really, the start of a film can be anything that grabs attention, like the opening cheer in *Bring it On*—it's obnoxiously funny.

The bottom line is that whatever opening you choose, you want to captivate your audience and set a tone. Like Bette Davis in *All About Eve*, downing her martini and announcing to the party, "Fasten your seat belts; it's going to be a bumpy night." You want to let people know your story is going to rock.

 Homage to Greatness

Something you may have noticed is that some of the opening scenes I've discussed in this chapter are very similar. There is a reason: Great writers and directors study all the great writers and directors that have come before them. So, when Tony Gilroy wrote the opening for *The Bourne Identity* with a body floating in the water, it's not a coincidence that he started with basically the identical shot to the opening of *Sunset Boulevard*. He knew what he was doing and made a conscious choice. It's an homage to the great filmmakers that have come before him and it's also a really cool opening shot!

Satisfying Conclusion

It's difficult, if not impossible, to have a good ending if you don't get your story going extremely quickly. It might seem strange to be talking about endings in a chapter about beginnings, but one of the biggest challenges of writing the short film is coming up with a satisfying conclusion. If you are writing a five- to ten-page story (a common length in film school), then you don't have a lot of space to develop the story. You will need to start with a bang. I believe the key is this: You have to start in the middle, when the story is up and running already.

For a conclusion to be satisfying, it must answer the question that the dramatic opening raises. The fantastic short film *Mamá* opens with a girl sleeping. In the background, the door opens and a boy enters walking backwards, which is very odd. He wakes his sister and tells her they have to go, Mamá is back. So thirty seconds into the story, the main characters are both frantic and trying to escape their home. That is a very fast start and it creates a great mystery. Why are these kids terrified of their mother? The second you see Mamá, you understand why the children are terrified. This all leads to a dramatic and intense conclusion. For a film that clocks in at just over two minutes and thirty seconds, it really packs a punch.

Exercise: Open with a Hook

Go back to any of the stories you have come up with so far. Now try to think of a way to start the story fast. Can you come up with a powerful hook? Write the new opening scene.

Spoiler Alert! | Chapter 12

The Departed (2006).

Hacksaw Ridge (2016).

Galaxy Quest (1999).

Baby Driver (2017).

Manchester by the Sea (2016).

Body Heat (1981).

Swingers (1996).

The Big Lebowski (1998).

Ozark, pilot episode (2017).

Crazy, Stupid, Love (2011).

Lady Bird (2017).

12

The Role of Dialogue

Nothing teaches you as much about writing dialogue as listening to it.

—Judy Blume

What Are We Talking About?

Well-crafted dialogue sells scripts and it sells the writer. Dialogue is the heart and soul of your screenplay. It is where we get to know your characters. It's where you stretch your wings and express yourself as a writer. Great dialogue brings characters to life. And when paired with dynamic action, it's how you get people to love your characters.

```
Toto, I've got a feeling we're not in
Kansas anymore.

May the Force be with you.

I'll have what she's having.

I see dead people.

I'm going to make him an offer he
can't refuse.

Hello, my name is Inigo Montoya, you
killed my father, prepare to die.

I feel the need — the need for speed.
```

You probably recognize most, if not all, of these classic lines of dialogue. You may even be able to repeat hundreds of famous lines from your favorite films. There are great lines in every genre from the heroes to the villains or, in the case of "I'll have what she's having," a character who is only on the screen for a few seconds!

These lines connect you to these movies. They connect us to these characters. They connect us to each other. People say the eyes are the window into a person's soul—for a writer, dialogue is the window into the soul of their characters.

The Job of Dialogue

Before you start writing all those clever lines, dialogue needs to fulfill some basic functions for your story. It's one of the main tools for getting the idea of your story across to the audience, as well as being one of the most important tools for helping them understand each character.

Information and Exposition

Characters need to share information about themselves and about the story. This is called *exposition*. Done well, it is stylish and entertaining. It creates mysteries or answers questions for the audience. Done poorly, exposition will ruin even the cleverest plot. So how do we write good exposition?

First, the character must have a reason to talk: a need, a desire, or a goal. If your character is talking just to tell the audience information, then that's a problem.

Information must arise naturally in the flow of a conversation and within the context of a situation. The character wants something, so they must speak to get it. Take this scene from *The Departed*. The screenplay, written by William Monahan, won the Academy Award for Best Writing, Adapted Screenplay in 2007.

```
INT. AN APARTMENT OVER THE HARBOR - NIGHT

A BUILDING MANAGER switches on lights. An
empty, flash apartment. More than you'd
think a cop could afford. It has a modern
sterility. Colin looks at it.

                  BUILDING MANAGER
          You can see the commuter boats.
             (uneasy)
          You're a policeman?
```

```
                    COLIN
          State police detective.

                BUILDING MANAGER
          Married?

                    COLIN
          No.

                BUILDING MANAGER
          You intend to have a housemate?

                    COLIN
          Let's say I have a co-signer.
          Give me the papers.
```

This fantastic half-page scene gives us lots of great information that arises naturally from the situation. State Police Detective Colin has a clear goal: he wants to rent an apartment. The building manager also has a clear goal: he wants to rent out this expensive apartment, but he has a strong need to be sure that the person renting the apartment can actually afford it. This creates a natural conflict: the building manager needs to know more about Colin, but Colin doesn't want to say any more than is necessary.

The drama of the scene is set up by the scene description, even before the dialogue begins, by explaining that the apartment is, *"More than you'd think a cop could afford."* The film is set in Boston, where apartments are expensive. This apartment is overlooking the harbor which probably makes it one of the most expensive apartments in an expensive city. How could a cop afford this place? All the dialogue furthers this mystery—how will this state police detective pay for an apartment that is priced far beyond his means? The building manager doesn't get an answer and neither does the audience.

The audience is left with the mystery: Where is Colin getting all this extra money? The withholding of information is one of the keys to great storytelling. Imagine if Colin said, "I can afford this place, I'm a dirty cop. I work for the local mafia. They pay me a ton of money." When a character starts explaining things, it's almost always considered bad dialogue. (There are obvious exceptions, like towards the end of a story when we want the truth to finally come out.)

The secret of being a bore is to tell everything.

—Voltaire

Revealing Conflict

One of the best ways to reveal conflict is through dialogue like in the wonderful screenplay for *Hacksaw Ridge,* written by Robert Schenkkan and Andrew Knight.

```
EXT. PARADE GROUND - DAY

Howell double-time marches the men over
to a rack of rifles.

            SGT. HOWELL
      Grab a gun and fall in!

Everybody around him is grabbing a gun
but Desmond just stares at the rack, some
powerful emotion working on him.

Irritated, Howell storms up behind
Desmond.

            SGT. HOWELL
      Do we not have one in your size,
      soldier?!

            DESMOND
        (quietly)
      No, Sergeant. I can't...won't
      touch a gun.
```

The dialogue in this fantastic little scene reveals a major conflict, the key conflict of the story. This is, in fact, the first act break. Desmond refuses to use a gun—he won't even touch it. That is a big problem. Desmond enlisted in the army. They are training to go to war (World War II). Everyone is going to have a gun. The enemy will be shooting at them. Guns are a really big part of being in the army. But Desmond won't grab a gun. And he doesn't explain his rationale, he just refuses to pick up a gun. The result is a major conflict. The entire story turns on these three simple lines of dialogue. The dialogue works in concert with the scene description, which reveals the physical action. But it's the spoken words, as Desmond refuses the order of his superior, that reveals the conflict.

It's important to be careful when trying to create conflict using dialogue. Arguing can be a form of *fake conflict*, which I discussed in Chapter 10. But arguing can result in authentic conflict when there is a real dilemma to debate. In the above example, the dialogue *reveals* that Desmond's core values are in conflict with the mission of the U.S. Army. The dialogue doesn't create the situation, it just brings it to light.

Revealing Relationships to a Character

"We need to talk." If you've ever heard that phrase uttered by your partner, you know it means you're going to be talking about your relationship. Talking is one of the most important aspects of human relationships. It's also a crucial aspect of dialogue in story. A well-written scene with authentic dialogue is how we reveal character relationships in screenplays.

Let's take a look at an example of dialogue that reveals protagonist Jason Nesmith's relationship to his coworkers in this powerful scene from *Galaxy Quest*.

```
INT. MEN'S ROOM

Jason enters to witness the incongruous
sight of four MANK'NAR beasts at the
urinals taking a MANK'NAR piss.

Jason enters a stall and sits on the lid,
trying to get a moment to think. But two
CYNICAL 20-SOMETHINGS enter, laughing
their assess off. He can hear their
voices echo from the other side.

          CYNICAL GUY 1
     You're right. What a FREAK SHOW.
     This is fricking HILARIOUS.

          CYNICAL GUY 2
     Yeah, what a bunch of losers. And
     those poor actors. They've done,
     like, WHAT for twenty years? I
```

              think Fred Kwan did a dog food
              commercial... Sad.

                    CYNICAL GUY 1
              Did you hear Nesmith up there?
              That's the saddest. I think he
              actually gets off on these nerds
              thinking he's a space Commander.
              It's pathetic. And his friends...

                    CYNICAL GUY 2
              ... they HATE him. I know, did
              you hear them ragging on him?!!
              "Commander furry!..."

                    CYNICAL GUY 1
              He has no idea that he's a
              laughingstock... Even to his
              buddies.

          They exit, their laughter ringing in
          Jason's ears.

Wow. Devastating. This is a powerful moment. Imagine if you heard people calling you "pathetic," a "laughingstock," and saying that your friends hate you! Jason's relationship with his coworkers is revealed with this brutal verbal exchange. Earlier scenes in the story made their relationship clear to the audience, but Jason doesn't know how they feel. He seems blissfully unaware or at least he's pushed the truth so far down he doesn't feel it. This section of dialogue makes Jason face the truth—he's a fake and his friends hate him. This will be his flaw that he will desperately try to overcome throughout the rest of the story.

Revealing Relationships to the Audience

Sometimes characters already have a clearly established relationship between them. Then the goal of the scene, and specifically the dialogue, is to reveal this existing relationship to the audience. Since the characters know the situation, they tend to *not* talk about it. It is critical to avoid clunky exposition when explaining a relationship to the audience. This type of scene requires some finesse since the relationship must be implied and not clearly spelled out.

In the movie *Baby Driver*, Baby (worst character name ever) is the driver during a bad ass getaway after a bank robbery. He's amazing. Afterwards, the gang meets up at their headquarters and the boss, Doc, divides up the money. Everyone, including Baby, gets a full share—an entire duffel bag of money. Then everyone takes the elevator to the parking garage. The last two are Baby and Doc.

```
INT. UNDERGROUND PARKING P3 - CONTINUOUS

PING. Baby and Doc exit into a cavernous
parking lot. They walk over to Doc's
shiny Black Merc. Doc opens the trunk.

                DOC
      Now you know I don't like taking
      candy from Baby, but…

Doc holds out his hand. Baby gives him
his holdall. Doc takes out one stack of
bills and throws both bags in the trunk.

                DOC
      Didn't want to embarrass you in
      front of the gang. When we're
      square we'll work out a new deal.
      Deal?

                BABY
      Uh. Yeah.

Doc gives Baby the one stack of bills.
Gets into his car.

                DOC
      Don't go crazy with that. I want
      you back behind the wheel and
      soon. I'll call you.

Doc pulls out. Leaves Baby all alone.
```

In the scene with the whole gang, Doc insists that Baby gets a full share, but alone in the garage, he takes Baby's share. So, Baby owes Doc, big time. We don't know why but it's clear that whatever Baby owes Doc, it's a lot. Enough that an entire duffle bag of cash does not pay off the debt. The dialogue (and action) clearly establishes their relationship.

Advancing the Story

Moving the story forward is one of the key roles that dialogue plays. We often learn valuable information that motivates the character to take action. Let's take a look at a very simple scene from *Manchester by the Sea* by Kenneth Lonergan.

```
EXT. LEE'S BUILDING - WINTER - DAY

Lee is shoveling snow. The air is clear
and cold. The whole street is beautified
by the recent snow storm. His iPhone
rings. He takes off his gloves. Digs out
the phone.

                LEE
      Hello... This is Lee... Oh...
      When did that happen?... Well,
      how is he?... OK. Uh...No. Don't
      do that. I'll come up right
      now... OK. Thank you.

He hangs up and goes inside with the
shovel, leaving the snow before the
building only partially cleared and
salted down.

I./E. LEE'S CAR - DAY

Lee sits behind the wheel, trying to get
out of Boston and onto Rt 1 North. He's
talking on his iPhone.

                LEE
            (Into his iPhone)
      Mr Emery, it's Lee again. I
      contacted Jose, who says he can
      cover for me til Friday night at
      least, and then Gene MacAdavey
      can take over till I get back.
```

> I'll be in Manchester at least a
> week or two. I'll call again when
> I have more information. Goodbye.

He hangs up and drives into increasingly
heavy traffic.

>   LEE
> Come on, come on.

The traffic slows. He becomes increasingly
anxious.

Two short simple scenes. Lee Chandler receives a phone call. Something has happened. "How is he?" tells us they are talking about a person and that they are probably unwell. We learn that it is an urgent situation since Lee says, "I'll come up right now." The action confirms the dialogue since Lee leaves immediately: he doesn't finish shoveling the snow.

Next the story cuts ahead to another phone conversation and we learn more. We don't need to see Lee pack his bag or get into his car, or the first phone call to his boss. We know there have been other phone calls since it starts with, "It's Lee again." We know it's something serious since it will take, "At least a week or two." Whatever it is, it is upsetting to Lee.

Again, we don't need every piece of information explained to the audience. By leaving out key pieces of information the audience is anxious to find out what is happening. We always want to leave the audience wanting more information. What is happening? Why is Lee upset? This simple dialogue exchange advances the story by forcing Lee to return to his hometown, a place he does not want to go. And the need to know why Lee feels this way compels the reader or viewer to continue. Finally, there is additional, physical conflict—Lee wants to get there quickly but gets stuck in traffic.

Building Expectations

This is one of the most potent aspects of the dialogue toolbox: building expectations. Most heroes tend to be reckless; they want to rush in and save the day. By having another character state what *could* go wrong, the audience will start to worry and get tense. This might not go well for the hero. Check out this scene from *Body Heat* by Lawrence Kasdan. Teddy, the "rock'n roll arsonist" is showing Racine how to set up an incendiary device. Teddy gets offended when Racine asks, "Is that all there is to it?"

                    TEDDY
No. No-no-no-no. That ain't all
there is to it. You gotta get in,
you gotta get out. You gotta pick
the right spot and the right
time. And you gotta try not to
get famous while you're in the
act.

     (gestures at the device)

If that was all there was to it,
any idiot could do it.

                  RACINE
Sorry.

                  TEDDY
Hey, now I want to ask you
something, Are you listening,
asshole, because I like you?

     (Racine nods)

I got a serious question for you.
What the fuck are you doing? This
is not shit for you to be messing
with. Are you ready to hear
something? See if this sounds
familiar. Anytime you try a
decent crime, there is fifty ways
to fuck up. If you think of
twenty-five of them you're a
genius. And you're no genius.

Racine may not be a genius, but this scene is genius! Having Racine think the task is simple, forces Teddy to clearly explain all the complications. If Racine's casual attitude toward committing a serious crime isn't enough of a red flag to get the audience nervous, having Teddy state everything that could go wrong certainly will. You may think this is violating our "give less info" guideline but then Teddy speaks some of the greatest lines ever: "Anytime you try a decent crime, there is fifty ways to fuck up. If you think of twenty-five of them you're a genius. And you're no genius." This should set the audience on red alert. Building expectations this way results in dynamic scenes that compel the audience to continue watching.

Emotional State of Your Characters

Another key purpose of dialogue is to fill us in on how each character is feeling. Recall the opening scene from *Swingers* that we looked at in Chapter 10. Mike and Rob are talking. We start in the middle. Information is implied: Mike's girl dumped him; Rob wants to help him. We understand this all from the context of the dialogue.

From the dialogue we come to realize Mike's emotional state—he is desperate to find a way to get his girlfriend back. Mike's good buddy, Rob, is trying to keep his friend from getting hurt further. The dialogue is stylish yet authentic. It implies much more than is on the page.

Personality and Attitude of Your Characters

Another important role of dialogue is giving us an idea of the character's personality and attitude. Few characters have ever graced the screen with more personality and attitude than John Goodman as Walter Sobchak in *The Big Lebowski*. Early in the story, at a league bowling match, Walter is calmly discussing why he is taking care of his ex-wife's dog when he sees Smokey's toe slip over the line, which is a foul. Walter insists that the score be marked zero, Smokey disagrees. Then Walter pulls out a gun and says:

```
Smokey my friend, you're entering a
world of pain.
```

Walter's personality swings wildly from calmly discussing a dog to violently protesting Smokey's score.

Smokey refuses to mark the score zero. Walter cocks the gun and points it at Smokey's head.

```
HAS THE WORLD GONE CRAZY? AM I THE
ONLY ONE HERE WHO GIVES A SHIT ABOUT
THE RULES? MARK IT ZERO!
```

I'm not a fan of all caps, it's usually too much. But Walter is such an over-the-top character that it works here. This intense rant indicates that Walter presents himself as a man of extreme principles that wants to follow the rules at all costs.

(Note: Walter Sobchak can be a very angry character, which can be problematic, but in this film it's always handled with humor. His anger is almost always wildly inappropriate, to the point that it's comic.)

Later, Walter asks Dude to ride along for the ransom drop, then forces Dude to follow along with his crazy plan. When Walter completely messes up the ransom exchange, he simply responds—

```
        Ah fuck it, let's go bowling.
```

Here Walter's attitude completely changes. Despite the fact that it was entirely his plan, and it went completely wrong, he takes no responsibility.

Later, at the bowling alley, Dude is ranting that they're going to kill that poor woman, which Walter completely dismisses. Then Walter is told that their next bowling match is on Saturday and he has a complete meltdown.

```
        Saturday is shabbat. Jewish day of
        rest. Means I don't work, I don't
        drive a car, I don't ride in a car,
        I don't handle money, I don't turn on
        the oven, and I sure as shit don't
        fucking roll!
```

Now we're back to crazy, rule-following Walter. This intense rant is hilarious especially in contrast to his lackadaisical response to the failed ransom drop.

The comedically paradoxical attitude of Walter Sobchak is revealed through his wildly different lines of dialogue.

Philosophy of Your Characters

A character's philosophy can be a cornerstone upon which an entire story is built. That is exactly the case for Marty Byrde in the show *Ozark*. In the opening scene of the pilot episode, we see him slogging through a mucky forest with a pair of coolers. During this mysterious action, we hear a voiceover from Marty.

```
              MARTY (V.O.)
        Scratch. Wampum, dough, sugar,
        clams, loot, Dead Presidents -
        though technically incorrect as
```

```
neither Hamilton nor Franklin
were ever president -- bills,
bones, bread, bucks. Money. That
which separates the "haves" from
the "have-nots." But what is
money, really? Everything if you
don't have it, right?
```

This voice over continues and eventually transitions to Marty's accounting office. This monologue is his investment speech to potential new clients. Marty's outward goal in the scene is to get a young couple to invest. But actually, it is a statement of Marty's philosophy: Money. Marty values money. He thinks about money, a lot. It's important to him. Very important. This philosophy serves as a justification for him laundering money for a drug cartel.

Show Don't Tell

This familiar adage is often a subject of confusion. We want to see the story happen, not have a character sit there and tell us a story. (Of course, there are always exceptions to the rule like in the case of movies like *My Dinner with Andre* and *Swimming to Cambodia*—very good movies where characters just tell us stories.)

The big confusion comes from the misunderstanding that dialogue is not action. But dialogue can be action. For example, if a character says, "I want a divorce," like in the *Crazy, Stupid, Love* example from Chapter 11. That's a strong action. How about a character who says to another character, "I believe in you." That's a powerful statement, an act of faith. Words have power and they can definitely represent strong action at times.

Actions Speak Louder than Words?

A question you always want to ask about dialogue is, "Can that emotion be demonstrated with an action?" Let's go back to the powerful line, "I want a divorce." The other character could scream, "NOOO!!" But that is a bit obvious. The other character could punch a wall. Or they could start sobbing. Or maybe they say nothing, like the Cal character in *Crazy, Stupid, Love*. He refuses to talk or engage in any way with his wife until he finally opens the door and rolls out of the moving SUV! That's a powerful action! (Note: *Crazy, Stupid, Love* came before *Lady Bird*, both are great movies, and in both of them, when the character opens the car door and rolls out of a moving vehicle, it is awesome.) Choosing whether your character speaks or acts or some combination of both can go a long way to establishing who your character is.

Exercise: Dialogue Skills

Test your dialogue skills. Write a scene that accomplishes one of the following:

- Revealing conflict.
- Revealing a relationship.
- Reveals an ongoing relationship.
- Providing information/exposition in an interesting way.
- Advancing the story.
- Building expectations.
- Revealing the emotional state of each character.
- Revealing the personality and attitude of each character.

Spoiler Alert! | Chapter 13

Lady Bird (2017).

Apocalypse Now (1979).

Erin Brockovich (2000).

Midnight Run (1988).

Little Miss Sunshine (2006).

The Big Lebowski (1998).

Fargo (1996).

True Romance (1993).

Reservoir Dogs (1992).

Five Easy Pieces (1970).

Dirty Harry (1971).

Tonight, He Comes screenplay (1996).

Howl's Moving Castle (2004).

13

Dialogue Techniques

It's not enough simply to record the way people actually talk. The dialogue must be concentrated, shaped, dramatically moving, in a way that real-life conversation seldom is.

—Philip Gerard

How to Make It Great

Now we know that all dialogue in your screenplay must serve a purpose, perform a role, or fulfill a specific task. But how do we make that dialogue great? First, you must become a great listener. Train your ear to identify interesting speakers. Become a connoisseur of language. (It's more difficult these days since the majority of people have grown up with the homogenized language of television.) Another source of dialogue stylings is the well-written novel. I say well-written since there are mountains of mediocre to poorly written novels. But there are more than enough great novels to fill several lifetimes of daily reading. Which is what you should be doing—reading, every day. So beyond listening and reading, what are the tricks of the trade?

Less is More

Whatever dialogue is on the page must be great. That's it.

Oh, you want more? Okay, well how about this, one of the surest ways to make your screenplay boring is by having too much dialogue. Have you ever wondered why the portions in most fancy restaurants are so small? You get a few delicious bites and then it's over. You want more. This is the idea with great dialogue. Leave them wanting more.

There are some basic keys to writing less. One of the keys is no chit-chat. What is chit-chat? It's the filler. The boring stuff.

Check out this exciting exchange:

<pre>
                    JOE
     Hey.

                    BOB
     Hey.

                    JOE
     How are you?

                    BOB
     I'm good. How you doing?

                    JOE
     Oh, you know, same old, same old.

                    BOB
     I hear ya.

                    JOE
     Can I ask you something?

                    BOB
     Sure.
</pre>

If you have dialogue like this in your screenplay, just highlight it and hit the Delete key right now. It does not make your screenplay sound more authentic, it just makes it really boring. Yes, there are people who actually talk like this, but who is going to pay twenty dollars or more to listen to them?

The key to determining if your dialogue is chit-chat or filler is to ask yourself, "What do I learn from these lines of dialogue?" In the above example, you learn *nothing*. It might be about to get interesting, *if* Joe asks an interesting question, such as:

<pre>
     If you were going to murder someone,
     how would you do it?
</pre>

Now we are getting somewhere. Now I want to keep reading. But the scene could *start* with that line. That would be starting the scene with a bang!

Naturalistic Dialogue

Often, we want our characters to seem like real people. The best way to do that is through *naturalistic dialogue*. Naturalistic means it sounds authentic. When dialogue sounds authentic, we tend to believe the characters are real people. The problem is that if you write down an actual conversation exactly as you heard it in real life, it will almost certainly sound clunky. So, what's going on here?

The trick to naturalistic dialogue is to cut it down. The key is learning how to edit a "normal" conversation so that it still sounds authentic but has that flow we've come to expect from movies. For an excellent example, let's look at the opening lines of dialogue from the first scene of *Lady Bird,* written by Greta Gerwig.

```
                LADY BIRD (V.O.)
           Do you think I look like I'm from
           Sacramento?

                                    CUT TO:

           Lady Bird stares at Marion as she makes
           the bed.

                     MARION
                You are from Sacramento.

                     LADY BIRD
                   (re: making the bed)
                You don't have to do that.

                     MARION
                Well it's nice to make things
                neat and clean.
```

This fantastic little scene sounds very authentic due to the excellent use of naturalistic dialogue. Something we do as humans is to blurt out thoughts that pop into our head. Lady Bird has one of those typical teenage thoughts, worrying about how she looks. She's worried that being from Sacramento is not cool and suddenly she's concerned that maybe people can tell she's from Sacramento just by looking at her—which would make her uncool. This rich thought process is brought to light perfectly with nine words. But her mom isn't worried about all this and states the obvious, that Lady Bird *is* from Sacramento.

Then the conversation quickly jumps to Lady Bird giving her mom advice. We get a lot of character from this exchange. Lady Bird is a typical teen, living by the motto, "Don't do anything you don't have to." We also come to realize a lot about her mom, Marion. She likes order and is willing to do more than is necessary to get it. In fact, she is making hospital corners, just as they are about to leave the room. They are not coming back. So that could be considered seriously OCD.

A ton of personality and information about the characters in four simple lines. The topics are everyday life, where the character is from and making a bed. A beginning writer might make this exchange into a page or more of back-and-forth dialogue, which would kill the magic.

Heightened Dialogue

The opposite of naturalistic dialogue is *heightened dialogue*. This type of dialogue highlights larger-than-life characters who seem to act and react outside of what we might call normal. In *Apocalypse Now*, written by John Milius and Francis Ford Coppola, Lieutenant Colonel Bill Kilgore (Robert Duvall) walks around shirtless on the beach in the middle of a battle. He's seemingly unaffected by bullets and bombs whizzing by as he pontificates about napalm.

```
I love the smell of napalm in the
morning.

...it smells like... Victory.
```

Does this sound like natural dialogue from a "normal" person? This is extremely heightened dialogue. This is a larger-than-life character. He is not reacting to the situation like we would. All of the other soldiers are hiding in fox holes trying to not get their heads blown off. In fact, Colonel Bill Kilgore insists that several soldiers head out into the water and *surf* in the middle of the firefight! A larger-than-life character seems much more brave than we are—completely unaffected by fear. They say way cooler things than we do too. This cool dialogue is "heightened" dialogue.

More Techniques

There are several additional techniques, ranging from basic to advanced, that you can use to improve your dialogue writing. It's important that the style of dialogue you choose for a character is *not* random: the quirks or uniqueness of a character's dialogue must emerge from *who the character is*. For example, if you have a high energy character, they most likely would speak in short fast bursts. Whereas a mellow character would speak slowly and use far less words.

Vocabulary

Varying the level of vocabulary between the characters is a great way to make them stand out. Well-educated characters tend to use more sophisticated words and concepts, while a young character or uneducated character may use less-polished verbiage. But you can change that up. What if a blue-collar woman spent every free minute reading? She could have a sophisticated vocabulary. But the twist might be that she occasionally mispronounces or misuses the words.

Big Talker vs. The Silent Type

Big talkers and *silent types* are classic character types. For example, Erin Brokovich is a big talker. It's clear from the first scene in the movie that she loves to talk. It's a big part of who she is and it's part of the story. In fact, over the length of the scene, Erin has 257 words to the doctor's 17. That's a big difference! This is a great way to emphasize what a big talker a character is, by placing them in a scene with a character who is more of the silent type.

Taken to the extreme, the differences between these character types can be the basis for a great comedy, like *Midnight Run*. The hilarious script by George Gallo, has Jonathan Mardukas, played by Charles Grodin, as a mob accountant on the run up against Jack Walsh, played by the master of the minimalist dialogue, Robert DeNiro. Walsh is a bounty hunter tasked with capturing and transporting Mardukas across the country. "The Duke" chats non-stop, driving the quiet Walsh nuts until he finally utters the infamous line, "I've got two words for you, Shut, the fuck, up."

Little Miss Sunshine takes the quiet character to a new level. Dwayne refuses to speak entirely! Only writing short notes on his little pad some of which are outrageous, including, "I hate everyone." (Dwayne actually underlines it twice.) I had a t-shirt with that one. People seemed compelled to comment on it pretty much every time I wore it. That is powerful provocative dialogue (even if it was never actually spoken).

Contrast

There are many more types of contrasting characters beyond those I just mentioned. Take one of the all-time great characters, the Dude from the Coen brothers' *The Big Lebowski*. The Dude is introduced as quite possibly the laziest man in Los Angeles. (He isn't really, if he was, he wouldn't take action, and there wouldn't be a movie.)

The Dude meets with the "real" Lebowski to complain about his rug getting peed on. The self-proclaimed hard-working Mr. Lebowski delivers his dialogue rapid fire, cutting off the Dude's every sentence. Mr. Lebowski bellows and rants while the Dude (who gets confused about what day it is) calmly tries to make his point. This contrast in dialogue makes the Dude's laid-back persona even clearer.

Contractions, Lingo, Slang

Informal language can increase the sense of authenticity. Also, the lingo or slang of a specific region or culture can further identify you as a trustworthy writer. But it's important to use caution: don't overdo it. It's easy to make a script clunky or even difficult to read. In the movie *Fargo*, the Coen brothers strike a great balance with their use of contractions, lingo, and slang, capturing perfectly the quirks of the North Dakota dialect. It reveals the flavor of the region without overdoing it, so that the script remains very readable.

Have an Opinion

I believe one of the reasons Quentin Tarantino's dialogue stands out is that his characters have strong opinions. From Clarence's love of Elvis and Sonny Chiba movies in *True Romance,* to Mr. White's passionate argument for why he won't tip their waitress in *Reservoir Dogs*, Mr. Tarantino's characters have deeply held opinions and it comes across in how they speak.

Voice of a Generation

Tapping into something that everyone is feeling can be very powerful. This is somewhat similar to having an opinion but not just your opinion—one that a generation shares. A great example comes from a scene in the 1970 classic film, *Five Easy Pieces*, written by Carole Eastman. Bobby, played by Jack Nicholson, is ordering lunch, but not exactly what's on the menu. The waitress tells him, no substitutions. Bobby just wants a side of toast with his meal. No dice. The waitress falls back on the classic, "I don't make the rules." This is the key line. This era, the late sixties and early seventies, was the height of the counter-culture revolution. The young people of the era were incredibly frustrated. There seemed to be all these rules that didn't make sense and yet people were blindly following them.

> BOBBY
>
> Okay, I'll make it as easy for you as I can. Give me an omelette, plain, and a chicken salad sandwich on wheat toast -- no butter, no mayonnaise, no lettuce -- and a cup of coffee.

She begins writing down his order, repeating it sarcastically:

> WAITRESS
>
> One Number Two, and a chicken sal san -- hold the butter, the mayo, the lettuce -- and a cup of coffee... Anything else?

> BOBBY
>
> Now all you have to do is hold the chicken, bring me the toast, charge me for the sandwich, and you haven't broken any rules.

> WAITRESS
> (challenging him)
>
> You want me to hold the chicken?

> BOBBY
>
> Yeah. I want you to hold it between your knees.

Bobby's effort to get a simple side order of toast, from a diner that clearly makes toast but just won't allow him to buy it as a side order, illustrates the absurdity of some rules. This scene captures the generation's shared feelings of frustration about society's ridiculous rules.

No Boundaries/Extremes

You may have a friend who will say anything. Sometimes it's funny, sometimes it's embarrassing. Usually even these people have limits. But we writers can have our characters actually say *anything*. This kind of freedom can lead to outrageous characters, like Grandpa, played by Alan Arkin in *Little Miss Sunshine*, written by Michael Arndt. Warning! Hilariously bad language below.

```
          Grandpa sees the bucket of chicken on
          the dinner table.


                    GRANDPA
          What is this?! Chicken?! Every
          day it's the fucking chicken!
          Holy God almighty! Is it
          possible, just one time, we could
          have something for dinner except
          the goddamn fucking chicken?!
```

This type of character could get pretty dark if we're not too careful, but Michael Arndt has the perfect light touch to create a wickedly funny free spirit, and the result is an Oscar-winning character.

Turn a Movie Convention on Its Head

Often we have to write a scene that we've seen over and over in other movies or TV shows. You want to avoid the cliché, find a way to break from convention in your dialogue.

In the 1970s, in action movies, it became a thing to count bullets during a shootout. The hero would race over to the bad guy and say, "I counted six shots, you're out of bullets." The bad guy would pull the trigger—click. Out of bullets. So along comes *Dirty Harry*. He watches a bank robbery take place, but he doesn't rush in, he finishes his hot dog, then calmly walks across the street and starts shooting bad guys. Finally, Harry's got his big gun pointed at the last bad guy, whose gun is lying next to him. The bad guy looks like he's going to grab the gun.

```
          DIRTY HARRY
I know what you're thinking. "Did
he fire six shots or only five?"
Well, to tell you the truth, in
all this excitement I kind of
lost track myself. But being as
this is a 44 Magnum, the most
powerful handgun in the world,
and would blow your head clean
off, you've got to ask yourself
one question: Do I feel lucky?
Well, do ya, punk?
```

Instead of falling back into an over-used movie convention, the writer, John Milius, (although not a credited screenwriter on the film, this monologue is attributed to Mr. Milius) comes up with this amazing rant which completely turns the convention on its head, creating one of the most iconic movie monologues of all time.

Over the Top Monologue

As writers, we are often pushing the boundaries, trying to find that big moment. One of the ways to do this is the *monologue*—when a character gives a long speech. Tarantino has made a very good living writing epic monologues.

Most screenwriting guides will tell you to avoid these monologues. And for the most part they are right. *Unless* you can really knock it out of the park. In the mid-nineties, a script showed up on the Hollywood scene, *Tonight, He Comes* by Vy Vincent Ngo. Execs were passing it around telling their friends, you *have to* read this (even though it was a very flawed story). The writing made an impression.

```
BLACK. It's everywhere. It swallows the
screen. And so, we stare into a sea of
black.
```

```
          NARRATOR (V.O.)
I saw a severed head once. Except
for the paleness, it looked
healthy, well-fed. The end came
abruptly you could tell 'cause
the mouth froze in mid-sentence.
"Shh…," the curled lips
```

> attempted. Like it started to say
> "shucks" or "Shirley" or… "shit
> happens." Your eyes don't forget
> things like that. Like you don't
> forget the sound animals make
> when they're humping. Primal.
> Raw. They endure in you forever
> because the senses have a brain
> all their own and they recall
> long after you've succumbed to
> the la-la of forgetfulness.
>
> > (a pregnant beat)
>
> Sometimes when it's dark out, so
> dark it's black, I'll see HIM.
>
> > (a beat)
>
> And it starts all over again.

Not everyone is going to like this. Some will flat out hate it. When you write with an extremely edgy style, you are crossing a line most won't cross. Some will love you for it. But lots of people won't. One thing you can count on is that people are never neutral about a scene like this. If you're wondering what became of this screenplay, it was heavily re-written by Vince Gilligan becoming the movie, *Hancock*.

 Don't Stress Out

Feel like there's just too much to think about when writing dialogue? Well, here's a helpful hint: Don't worry about perfecting your dialogue on your first draft. You want to get an idea of who your characters are and what is happening in the scene, but their dialogue can still be clunky or even on-the-nose. The most important thing is not to stop yourself if your dialogue isn't great on your first pass. Get it down on the page. It's a process. The scene you're working on might not even end up in your final draft. So don't beat yourself up over it!

Checklist: Test Your Dialogue

Testing your dialogue is a critical aspect of writing. Filmmaking is a collaborative art. It is a business that involves many people. It should be obvious that a screenplay is a document that is meant to be shared. In the movie business often hundreds of people will read this document—your screenplay. So it's critical to test it:

> **Read it out loud.** Dialogue is meant to be spoken. You can't really tell what it sounds like until you read it out loud.

> **Try reading one character at a time.** Skip everything else, the description, the other characters, everything. This is a great way to see if the character is consistent.

> **Switch the characters.** You want to check whether your characters sound too similar. If you can switch which character is saying which line, then you don't have enough differentiation between the characters and the way they speak. Your characters are too similar. You should *not* be able to switch characters.

> **How does it look?** Just like with scene descriptions, you don't want to have big blocks of dialogue. You want a screenplay to look lean and balanced.

> **Stage a reading.** People are amazingly open to helping out. Especially if you offer some free pizza and maybe even some beer and wine. Or now you can even have a Zoom reading. People all over the country, even across the globe, can join it. You want to invite a nice blend of actors and writers. Once the RSVPs roll in, be sure to carefully cast it. Afterwards, have a brief discussion. You may want to organize the talk by asking questions. This should be the final test. You want to be pretty solid on your story and characters before you go for a reading.

 ## Tips from the Pros

Final Draft, as well as many other software programs, can "read" your screenplay out loud. You can even assign different voices to the various characters. It's really a powerful tool.

Yes. It sounds robotic and a bit stiff, but the computer will read *exactly* what you have written not what you *think* you wrote. It is an amazing way to catch typos! And if a joke sounds funny with that robotic monotone voice, then you've got a heck of a funny line!

✓ From the Trenches

No matter how much you go over a script, there can still be lines of dialogue that are clunkers. They seem to be able to hide until the worst possible moment. Like, when you're on a sound stage with a big-name actor. They deliver your line and … Clunk. Yikes! That didn't work. Everyone knows it. Everyone turns to look at you, the screenwriter. And you start rewriting as fast as you can!

It happened to me. Lauren Bacall, one of the greatest actors of all time, was performing the voice of the Witch of the Waste for the English-language version of *Howl's Moving Castle*. Everything was going very smoothly. Even her little dog sitting on her lap was well behaved!

And then it happened, Clunk!

"Something is definitely off," Ms. Bacall calmly stated.

Instantly, everyone in the room started writing new versions of the line, the producer, the director, the editor—everyone. People were calling out potential variations on the line. But it just seemed to get worse.

"Now you're just trying to justify it!"

Finally, we fixed the line. Ms. Bacall was happy, the director was happy, and the rest of the recording went off without a hitch.

A final note to the story. The world premiere of the English-language version of *Howl's Moving Castle* was at the Museum of Modern Art in New York City. Hayao Miyazaki, who is famous for *never* watching his films once they were complete, was in the audience. He was going to break his famous rule for one reason: he was a big fan of Lauren Bacall and he wanted to hear her performance. After the movie was over, the lights came up, everyone in the theater was looking in one direction, at Mr. Miyazaki. Did he like it? Yes! He loved it!

Exercise: Differentiating Characters through Dialogue

Write a scene with two very different character types. The differences should be clear from the dialogue. There should be no way you could switch names on the dialogue. Be sure the dialogue still fulfills a narrative role.

14

Scene Description

Always get to the dialogue as soon as possible. I always feel the thing to go for is speed. Nothing puts the reader off more than a big slab of prose at the start.

—P.G. Wodehouse

Style and Substance

In a screenplay, the *scene description* tells us what we'll see on the screen, as well as the action that takes place. Every scene begins with a *slugline,* which informs us of the location. After the slugline, at least one sentence of scene description is considered mandatory. I believe scene description is best when it is split into two separate parts. First, describe the location. Second, let the reader know which characters are in the location and what they are doing. Sounds simple enough. The trick is getting just the right amount of description as well as being stylish. Think Goldilocks. Too much description is boring. Not enough is confusing. The issues with style are: not enough style is boring; too much style tends to get in the way of the story. We want just the right amount of description spiced up with an appropriate dose of style.

Even if you are writing a short script, you should develop good screenwriting techniques. If you are planning to shoot it yourself, you will have other people who are going to read it, so you want it to read as strongly as possible. Good scene description is critical to that.

I have made this letter longer than usual, only because I have not had time to make it shorter.

—French philosopher, Blaise Pascal

❓ Scene Description or Action?

In some circles, people refer to the scene description as *action* or *action lines*. But scene description is meant to present the character(s) and the location, as well as describing the action. So, I believe the term *scene description* covers its function more accurately.

Location Description

The slugline gives us the basic idea of the location. The location description will explain what the location looks like. So, what does just the right amount of location description look like? Let's take a look at some examples…

```
INT. CLASSROOM - LATE AFTERNOON

The large old classroom is a mess.
```

This minimalist amount of description just feels uninspired. It's generic information and lacks style. Plus, since "classroom" is in the slugline, repeating it in the scene description is a waste. If you get feedback like this on your screenwriting, you may want to really push both the information and the style.

```
INT. CLASSROOM - LATE AFTERNOON

Sun pierces the dangling blinds, cutting
like golden blades through the dust that
hangs in the air of the cavernous room.
The long-abandoned learning space looks
like it had been left in a hurry - the
small desks disorganized, the tiny chairs
tossed aside. On the chalkboard, a lesson
cut short - The brown dog ju—. Some of
the faded artwork still hangs along the
dull walls, but most has long since slid
down to the dirty floor. Lonely books are
haphazardly piled and splayed along
broken bookshelves.
```

This writer definitely upped the style, included tons of detail, and even broke out the thesaurus, but whoa, way too much. The sentences are overly long and convoluted, plus it feels like they're trying to describe everything. They're likely to get SIFYN, which means, "Save It For Your Novel." In a properly formatted screenplay (on traditional 8.5" x 11" paper), this paragraph would be nine lines long. That's way longer than the standard three, maybe four, lines that is the maximum that a paragraph of scene description should contain.

But this isn't a terrible paragraph and it may even be a helpful step. Some people like to really visualize a scene and write out all the details. That's great, just don't make the reader sort through your mess. A screenplay should guide the reader, including *only* what is important. Are all these details important? Nope. Not even close. Let's see if we can find the Goldilocks sweet spot.

```
INT. CLASSROOM - LATE AFTERNOON

Sun pierces the dust that hangs in the
air of the long-abandoned room. It was
left in a hurry - the small desks
disorganized, the tiny chairs tossed
aside, a lesson on the chalkboard cut
short -- The brown dog ju --.
```

I've shortened several of the lines of description, cutting them down and making them more readable. There is no more mention of the classroom being large. It's just not relevant to the story. I like to ask writers about a detail like this and often their response is, "That's just the way I imagined it." That's great but if it doesn't have relevance to the story, leave it out. I've pulled out the information about the artwork since I'm saving that to be the focus of the character's action in the scene, which you'll see in a bit. I've also cut the description of the "lonely" books which was nice but doesn't play a role in the scene.

Technically, it's still on the long side—four lines in proper screenplay format on traditional-width paper. But I like the juxtaposition of the beautiful sun with the disheveled room. Also, the clear impression that the classroom was left in a hurry is unsettling—did something bad happen here?

Character and Action Description

Next, we focus on our characters and the action. A character may already be in the room when the scene begins. In that case, what are they doing? Or you may choose to have them enter and begin to do something:

> Eden rushes into the room. She takes in
> the clutter but quickly focuses on the
> faded artwork that still hangs along the
> dull walls.

Instead of something bland like, "Eden enters," we go with, "Eden rushes." This gives the scene a sense of urgent movement. She takes in the room but gets to the main objective, the children's artwork.

> As she approaches the back wall, Eden
> notices that most of the artwork had long
> ago slid down to the dirty floor.
>
> As she scans the floor, she spots it --
>
> The serial killer's logo rendered in a
> child's fingerpaint.

In the initial description of the character's action, the art is along the walls. The next paragraph of description narrows the focus to the back wall. The point is we don't have to pinpoint the location in the first mention. Also, we usually go from broad descriptions to more focused. The point of this scene is the final line. Notice that this key line is a paragraph unto itself. Separating a critical line so it is more easily seen by the reader is called *billboarding*. This is an essential tactic in great screenwriting.

Now, the description of the location, character, and action sets the tone for a gritty thriller. What would the description look like if we were writing in a different genre?

Scene Description Must Fit the Genre

We want to be stylish in our descriptions, but they have to suit the *genre* in which we are writing. That's a big part of why style is important. It sets the mood and tone for a genre.

What if you are trying to write a heartfelt drama? If we start with the same location as before, what might the scene description be for this new genre? Perhaps we keep the opening location description from earlier but add new character and action description:

> Eden leads the excited CHILDREN into the
> room. In an instant, the room is alive
> with activity. The children chat
> excitedly as they grab chairs and happily
> plop into them.

I really like the contrast of the happy children to the dreary room. So, what's going on here? The story could be about a country that was invaded a few years back. Cities were evacuated immediately, including all schools. Now the war is over, and the children are very excited to be back in school. The description is colored with a lot of positive, upbeat language. This positive style lets the reader know this is a joyous moment.

Our location easily transitioned from a gritty thriller to an upbeat drama. How about if we really switch gears and change it to a comedy? The location description will not work in that case. We could change it to this:

```
INT. CLASSROOM - LATE AFTERNOON

The long-abandoned room is a mess.

Eden stumbles in. She gags as the smell
smacks her in the face.

                EDEN
        Eugene?

There's a GRUNT from the back wall. Eden
clambers over the chair and desk obstacle
course.

She spots Eugene, flopped down along the
back wall on a bed of fallen artwork. He
holds up a finger painting.

                EUGENE
        I found it! My favorite painting!
        But it's not as good as I
        remember.
```

For a comedy, the location description is stripped down and simplified. The character and action descriptions are also simplified with classic comedic type actions like stumbling and smelling bad odors. The disorganized tables and tossed aside chairs are now fun obstacles for our main character to navigate. Comedies often rely on the dialogue for humor, but well-written scene description can add a lot of physical comedy.

Whatever genre you are working in, you need to deliver scene descriptions that are lean and stylish and that set a tone that corresponds to your chosen genre.

Exercise: Getting Description Just Right

Take a scene or series of scenes and rewrite the description so that it hits that Goldilocks sweet spot.

Did you have to cut down your scene description? Or add to it? Did you have to reduce the amount of style or dial it up?

It's critical to understand what your weaknesses as a writer are so that you can work to improve them.

Or, take one of the examples in this chapter and continue the scene for a page or two. Focus on writing just the right amount of description in the appropriate style for your genre.

Spoiler Alert! | Chapter 15

Bicycle Thieves (1948).

The Hangover (2009).

The Town (2010).

The Wrong Man (1956).

Logan (2017).

Sideways (2004).

Fever Pitch (2005).

When Harry Met Sally (1989).

Hitch (2005).

Tucker & Dale vs. Evil (2010).

Parasite (2019).

Breaking Bad, pilot episode (2008).

Toy Story (1995).

Beauty and the Beast (1991).

The Godfather (1972).

Locke (2013).

Alien (1979).

Jaws (1975).

15

Suspense

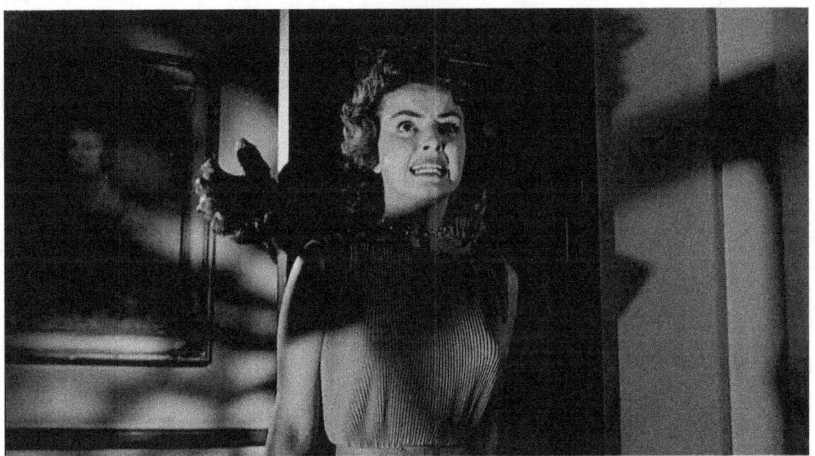

House on Haunted Hill (1959)

Not Just for Thrillers

I believe suspense is an essential element of any well-told story. When a story feels flat, the most likely culprit is a lack of suspense. If you are looking for a way to make your film really grab people's attention, focus on creating suspense.

Without suspense, you put tremendous pressure on yourself as a writer to make every scene, every moment, and every line intensely interesting. Or perhaps you want to make a movie about floating down a river, watching the nice scenery drift past? That's what watching a movie feels like without suspense.

> **suspense** (noun), a state or feeling of excited or anxious uncertainty about what may happen.
>
> —*Oxford Languages*

The key to the definition of suspense is *uncertainty*. When we know where the story is going, or that the story is not going anywhere, there is no suspense. We've all sat in the theater and felt like we knew where the story was going. It's a huge emotional letdown and we almost always check out. When an outcome becomes certain, the excitement is gone. No suspense equals no excitement.

You want to engage your audience by creating a dramatic situation and a building of expectations. You want the audience on the edge of their seat, wondering what will happen next. This audience anticipation can take several forms:

- What does the audience *think* is going to happen?
- What does the audience *hope* is going to happen?
- What does the audience *fear* might happen?
- What's something *unexpected* that could happen?

These questions reflect that the story is focused on the future and that the future is uncertain.

Creating a suspenseful, uncertain situation starts when something is at stake. The character has a goal but there are obstacles preventing them from achieving the goal. The suspense comes from building expectations or fears about the outcome. Will the character be able to achieve their goal? How will they go about it? What will happen if they fail? These kinds of questions tell us that the outcome is uncertain and that is engaging.

Start with the Concept

The basic idea of your film should have suspense built into it. A strong concept will make your story engaging and suspenseful from beginning to end.

> *Bicycle Thieves* This Italian neorealist classic is about as simple as it gets. In post-World War II Italy, unemployment is rampant. Antonio manages to get a job because he has a bicycle, but then it is stolen. The suspense is: Will Antonio be able to find his bicycle? It's gut-wrenching to watch a father and his son desperately searching Rome in what feels like a hopeless mission.
>
> *The Hangover* Right from the start, we learn that the bachelor party got a little out of hand and they have lost the groom, Doug. On top of that, they don't remember what happened last night. The suspense is: Where is Doug and what the hell happened last night?

The Town He's a bank robber and he's falling in love with a former hostage. This sets two very suspenseful questions in motion: What's going to happen when she finds out? What's going to happen when the rest of his crew finds out he's dating their former hostage? They basically wanted to kill her, so it won't be good.

Of these examples, only *The Town* would be considered a traditional thriller. But they all have great suspense, which makes them thrilling, *no matter the genre*.

 Master of Suspense

Alfred Hitchcock was known as the *Master of Suspense*. He instinctively knew that suspense was the most critical element of storytelling and was therefore drawn to stories that maximized suspense—thrillers. In 1956, Hitchcock stepped away from his normal fare with the docudrama, *The Wrong Man*, based on a true story about a man who is arrested after being falsely accused. The story is an excellent drama that is suspenseful and terrifying.

Save the World!

Bigger isn't always better. When the villain's plot will destroy the entire world, we kind of know that isn't going to happen. So, when the hero is trying to save the world, there's actually *less* suspense. One of the more interesting superhero movies is *Logan*. The aging former X-man is working in El Paso as a limo driver. He has to take care of his elderly father, Charles Xavier, who is suffering from dementia. Logan's situation is complicated by the need to get his daughter to safety. A man trying to protect his father and his daughter is far less grand than trying to save the world, but the suspense is intense because the villain, X-24, is a clone of Logan back in his prime. so he's clearly far more powerful than the real Logan. How can Logan defeat a better version of himself?

The Problem with Romantic Comedies

Great romantic comedies are rare these days. The problem is the lack of suspense. When we see two attractive, charming movie stars, we just know they are going to end up together. Finding something that is a legitimate obstacle is challenging. This is what makes romantic comedies so hard— there's no suspense since everyone knows that in the end, they are going to end up together. Let's look at how some romantic comedies generate true suspense plus one exception:

> ***Sideways*** Miles and Jack, while on a wine-tasting adventure, meet some amazing women, Maya and Stephanie. Miles, who has really been struggling to get over his divorce, seems to have a real connection with Maya. The suspense comes from the fact that Jack is getting married next weekend and the women definitely don't know this. The women are undoubtedly going to find out and it feels like it will be the end of Miles' relationship with Maya. That is an authentic and legitimate obstacle which creates genuine suspense.

> ***Fever Pitch*** Lindsey meets Ben and he seems perfect. The legitimate obstacle kicks in the moment baseball season starts. Ben is a serious baseball fanatic. Lindsey does not share his love of the game. The suspense is: Can Ben have two loves? This feels authentic and legitimate. We know how obsessed people get over sports and we completely believe that it is a real threat to the relationship.

> ***When Harry Met Sally*** is an exception to the rule. When Harry and Sally meet, it's pretty clear that they are going to end up together. I mean, come on, the title implies they are together and we're watching the story of how they ended up together. So without the aid of suspense, the story relies on great dialogue, intriguing scenes, and captivating characters. There are very few movies like *When Harry Met Sally*!

Dramatic Irony

When the audience knows something before a character does, it's referred to as *dramatic irony*. This is a great tool that creates excellent tension. For example, if it is established that a man and woman are good friends but then the audience discovers that the woman loves the man, now there's dramatic irony. This generates immediate suspense. It ups the drama and tension of any scene they are in. Will she tell him? Will he find out? Dramatic irony really turns up the juice and engages the audience.

There are many films that use dramatic irony as a major part of the premise:

> ***Hitch*** is a dating coach, but his new girlfriend doesn't know this. In fact, she is a reporter, and she is trying to track down whether the dating coach is real or an urban myth. In the b-story, Hitch is coaching the character played by Kevin James to help win over his girlfriend and, of course, she doesn't know this.

Tucker & Dale vs. Evil This hilarious horror-comedy is based on a huge misunderstanding. Some college students camping in the woods believe that Tucker and Dale are murderous kidnappers, while we know that in fact, they are a couple of sweet hillbillies who are trying to help the kids.

Parasite The Park family has no idea that all the new employees they just hired are the scamming Kim family. This generates tremendous suspense: Will the Kim family be able to keep their identity a secret?

In *Hitch* and *Parasite*, the end of the second act (the lowest low) happens when the characters who are in the dark find out the truth. The lies of the main characters collapse. Intuitively, we knew this was coming but when done right, it is still devastating. In *Tucker & Dale vs. Evil*, the comedy comes from the misunderstanding and it continues in one form or another until the end.

Relationships Built Around Dramatic Irony

Dramatic irony can play a major role in developing suspense even if the premise is not built around dramatic irony. Character relationships constructed around dramatic irony can add tremendously to the suspense:

Breaking Bad Hank Schrader is a DEA officer obsessed with finding the notorious drug kingpin, Heisenberg. We know all along that Heisenberg is Walter White, Hank's brother-in-law.

Toy Story Buzz believes he is an actual Space Ranger. Woody tries to convince Buzz that he is just a toy. We know Woody is right but worry about what will happen to Buzz when he realizes the truth.

Beauty and the Beast We know that the Beast is actually a prince who has been cursed, but Belle has no idea. Beyond creating sympathy for the Beast, there's great suspense: Will Belle discover the secret? Will she fall in love with the Beast?

These relationships leave the audience wondering if and when the truth will be discovered, and what will happen to the characters when it does.

Scenes Based on Dramatic Irony

One of the most famous scenes of all time is based on dramatic irony. In *Romeo and Juliet*, the audience knows that Juliet has taken a sleeping potion. But when Romeo finds her, he believes she has taken poison and that she is dead. He is completely devastated. This creates intense suspense: What will Romeo do? Romeo's choice, to kill himself, leads to even more intense suspense: What will Juliet do when she awakens?

Suspense Within Scenes/Sequences

Writers are always trying to create suspense at every level of the story, whether it comes from the story's premise, a relationship in the film, a sequence of events, or a single scene. Raymond Chandler, one of the great novelists of the twentieth century, famously said that if a scene got boring, he would have a character enter with a gun. That will always crank up the suspense. The questions begin immediately: What do they want? Will they shoot someone? Take prisoners? Now it's not boring.

But you don't need the gun to get the suspense going. Let's take a look at this brilliant little scene from *The Godfather*:

```
                DON CORLEONE
          Barzini will move against you
          first.


                MICHAEL
          How?


                DON CORLEONE
          He will get in touch with you
          through someone you absolutely
          trust. That person will arrange a
          meeting, guarantee your safety...
     He rises, and looks at Michael...


                DON CORLEONE
          ...and at that meeting you will
          be assassinated.
```

There's a reason *The Godfather* is one of the all-time greats. This fantastic scene lights a red-hot fire of suspense. Now the audience will be watching like a hawk. Who is going to try to set up this meeting? A friend? A family member? Will they really try to murder Michael? We are dying to know!

One of the great aspects of *The Godfather* is that Michael, the college kid who didn't want to get mixed up in the mob business, is getting deeply involved in the family business. But since he lacks knowledge and experience, things must be explained to him, which also explains the situations to us, the audience. So, we *experience* situations with Michael. The more we can create the sense of experiencing a story, rather than watching it, the more involving and satisfying the story.

(One note on the formatting: I love how they give Don Corleone a small action line to separate the dialogue so that the key line about being assassinated stands by itself. It's clean, clear, and not buried in the middle of a long section of dialogue. This is a fantastic trick that great screenwriters know: Never bury a key line; make sure it stands out.)

Create Questions in the Audience

Not all stories have murder and guns. In fact, guns are a big no-no in improv because they tend to force a story in one direction. No problem. Suspense is about wondering what characters are going to do, about what is going to happen. No gun necessary.

Often, the key to suspense is information. Don't explain everything. Instead, give some information but not all of it. Parse out enough to engage the audience but without giving too much away. The audience will find themselves hooked as they try to figure out what is going to happen.

Let's take a look at the movie *Locke*: It starts with a phone call that we do not hear. Ivan Locke gets in his car and begins to drive. This will be the entire movie—Ivan in his car on his phone. And the suspense and drama are incredible.

The phone call seems to have had a powerful effect on Ivan and he changes his course. He calls a woman, Bethan, but she doesn't answer, and he leaves a message: He's on his way. He mentions nurses and doctors. This cranks up the suspense. Who is this woman? Why is he driving to her? What has happened? Some sort of medical issue?

Next Ivan has a conversation with Donal, who works for Ivan, and Donal is freaking out. We start to get more of a picture of what is going on. It's a huge job starting early in the morning. Hundreds of trucks and hundreds of tons of concrete. And Ivan, who we learn is the foreman, is not going to be there. What is going on? All Ivan will say is that it is a family matter. Donal tells Ivan he's the best boss he's ever had and then asks him, "What the hell is it that'll make you risk the sack?"

In the next scene, Ivan speaks with Bethan. We learn she is having a baby and Ivan is the father. It's also made clear that she is not his wife. Then Bethan asks, "Have you even told your wife that someone is having your baby?" Asking a question like this is very powerful. It directs the audience's attention toward the future. Ivan is going to have to tell his wife that another woman is having his baby. We can imagine that this will be incredibly difficult. The suspense is intense. When Ivan's phone rings and it says "Home," we know it is finally coming. The scene is every bit as brutal and gut-wrenching as we thought it might be. It is like watching a car accident in slow motion. We know their relationship will never be the same.

This is an amazing story. To watch Ivan, an incredibly hardworking and successful man, lose everything is devastating. He has a wonderful wife and two boys who clearly adore him. He also has a very good job, and it will all be gone. The drama and the suspense are superb. And no guns, no car chases, no "action" of any kind. Just incredible suspense.

Suspense vs. Shock

It's important to note the difference between suspense and *shock*. It was best defined by the master of suspense, Alfred Hitchcock. Shock is when two people are sitting at a table and suddenly, boom! A bomb explodes. Suspense is when you show someone hiding a bomb under the table. Two other people enter the room, sit down at the table but don't notice the bomb. Now the audience is in a state of suspense, wondering what will happen. Will they discover the bomb? Or will it explode? Both suspense and shock can be extremely effective and great movies often use both.

> *Alien,* the great sci-fi horror about the crew of a spacecraft trapped with an incredibly dangerous alien, uses both shock and suspense:
>
> **Shock:** When Kane is investigating the ovoid shapes in the hull of the alien ship, the creature propels itself out at him. In fact, the screenplay states, "With shocking violence, a small creature smashes outward."
>
> **Suspense:** Dallas makes a plan. The alien is using the air shafts to get around the ship. Dallas will go into the air shaft with a flamethrower to "chase" the alien into the airlock and blast it into outer space. The plan sets the suspense into motion. It continues to build with long scenes of Dallas crawling along the dark tunnels with the flamethrower. Lambert is watching her scope and says it's got to be around there. Dallas touches some slime—the alien has been right there. The suspense is intense.

Lambert's scope starts beeping like crazy. "It's moving right toward you!" The suspense is as good as it gets, which is part of the reason *Alien* is an all-time great.

Jaws, Steven Spielberg's epic shark movie dials up the shock and suspense:

Shock: Chief Brody is chumming the water and chatting when the shark comes up out of the water nearly chomping Brody. Stunned by the near-death experience, he utters the famous line, "We're gonna need a bigger boat."

Suspense: The moment we see that fin rise out of the water, the suspense is activated. We see legs kicking in the water and the classic dun-dun rings out on the soundtrack, shifting the suspense into high gear. The whole movie is a setup for the final showdown with the shark and the suspense is epic. We've seen repeatedly how brutal the shark is and how helpless people in the water are. Once the boat begins sinking, the suspense gets about as high as possible.

Suspense and shock are not mutually exclusive. In fact, most great suspense sequences end with a shock. Understanding how to use suspense and shock will make any story more engaging for the audience.

Exercise: Generate Suspense

Go back to a story or scene you have written. Try to add more suspense. Try to create uncertainty about what is going to happen. Maybe you remove some of the information. Or have a character pose a question. Look for ways to get the audience engaged and asking questions.

Eighth Grade (2018).

Finding Nemo (2003).

Minority Report (2002).

Iron Man (2008).

Bridesmaids (2011).

Raising Arizona (1987).

Gattaca (1997).

Silver Linings Playbook (2012).

The Thing (1982).

Alien (1979).

Ataque de Pánico! (Panic Attack!) (2009).

Pigeon: Impossible (2009).

Proof (1980).

16

Set Pieces

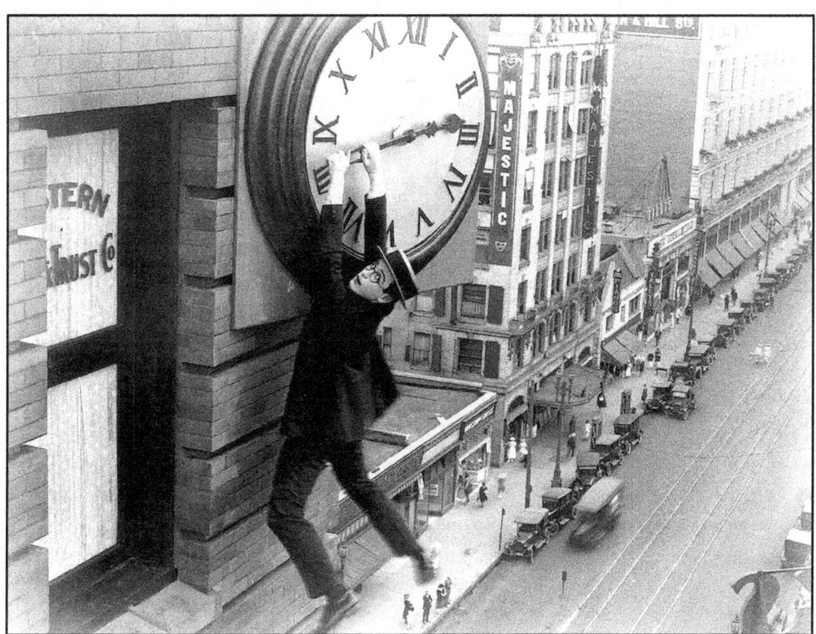
Harold Lloyd in *Safety Last!* (1923).

Make It Bigger!

Early in my career as a professional writer, a producer said to me, "This scene is great, but make it bigger." I said, "Sure. No problem. Bigger." But I instantly began to think, "What the hell does that mean? Make it bigger?" What the producer meant was to elevate the scene into a *set piece*. Set pieces have become one of the most crucial elements of contemporary filmmaking and yet outside of the film industry, they are not well understood.

Creating a set piece means taking a key, suspenseful scene or sequence in your story and making the most of it. That is, making it more dramatic by adding complications, twists, and reversals including the possible addition of a setup scene. In other words, *make it bigger*.

Set pieces basically come in two forms, the *setup* and the *escalating event*. The setup begins with the main character making a plan. This plan builds the audience's expectation, helps emphasize the difficulty of the task, and highlights all the things that might go wrong.

The escalating event (a.k.a. the snowball) tends to skip the setup; instead, a dramatic event happens, then something makes it worse, and then something else happens! The situation keeps building, like a snowball rolling down a hill, getting bigger and picking up momentum. The idea is that once a strong story element is set into motion, the goal for the writer is to find ways to keep it going.

Escalating set pieces and setup set pieces are not mutually exclusive. A setup set piece will escalate, building momentum with dramatic twists and complications. And escalating set pieces may have some form of setup; it's just that there's no specific scene where the characters say, "Here's the plan."

A set piece is *not* a montage. A montage is *never* a set piece. The actions that occur in a set piece take place in (more or less) continuous time. It's possible that there could be a gap between the setup scene and the core action of the set piece, but once it gets going, a set piece is contiguous. A *montage* is a sequence of scenes or shots that jump forward, showing a passage of time. So, a montage and a set piece are basically complete opposites.

 History

From the action sequences of Buster Keaton and Harold Lloyd films to the huge musical numbers of the MGM films, filmmakers have always been looking for ways to "make it bigger." I think where it's evolved more recently is the application of this approach to all genres of film. Even in a coming-of-age drama like *Eighth Grade*, about a thirteen-year-old who makes YouTube videos, the writer, Bo Burnham, set out to include at least three set pieces.

What Does a Set Piece Look Like?

Here's an example: In *Finding Nemo*, Marlin's son, Nemo, is taken by scuba divers and Marlin sets out across the ocean to find his son. Imagine you are writing this story: with a tiny clownfish swimming across the big ocean, there are many dangerous and dramatic situations that Marlin might encounter. One possibility could be a shark. That would definitely lead to some big, dramatic, suspenseful moments. You write a short little scene: Marlin sees a shark. Ah!! He quickly swims away. Check. Shark scene written. But sharks are really dramatic. Seems like you could write a much bigger and better scene.

Let's look at what the brain trust at Pixar came up with:

Marlin is swimming along when suddenly, he is face to face with a huge great white shark. But the shark doesn't attack. It introduces itself as Bruce (the name the film crew gave the mechanical shark in *Jaws*) and invites Marlin and Dory to a little get together. This is an unexpected twist which subverts expectations and extends the sequence, i.e., making it bigger. But the sequence continues with more complications: there's not one but three sharks. There is also a unique location that adds to the challenge: the meeting place for their group has "balloons," which are actually large undersea mines.

The group of sharks have decided not to eat fish, proclaiming that "fish are friends, not food." But we know sharks *do* eat fish. This extends the sequence, while building the dramatic tension. We sense something could go wrong and probably will. Then, there is another unexpected twist: while telling a joke, Marlin spots a scuba mask and it's from one of the divers that took Nemo. As Marlin and Dory wrestle for the mask, it bops her in the nose, and she begins to bleed. Bruce smells the blood and finally his shark instincts kick in. In a complete reversal, Bruce goes full-on shark, chasing Marlin and Dory. The tiny fish manage to escape, swimming into a sunken submarine. Bruce repeatedly rams the sub door. Finally, Bruce flings a torpedo and it explodes, setting off a chain reaction of sea mines exploding, literally making the scene explosive.

If that's not making it "bigger," I don't know what would be! There are many more details to the scene that add complexity, humor, and drama. The entire sequence is over six minutes long. Bottom line, this is a heck of a lot "bigger" than if Marlin simply saw a shark and swam away.

 **Recommendation**

If there are any movies that are referenced in this chapter that you have not seen, you should watch them now. Set pieces are often the most exciting and dynamic sequences in a movie and I will be going into detail about some of the very best ones. If you're like me and you don't like spoilers, then of any chapter in the book, this is the chapter that I urge you to watch these movies first.

What Makes It a Set Piece?

There are several key elements that help build a scene or sequence into a set piece. Let's breakdown the shark sequence from *Finding Nemo* detailed above:

An event sets the sequence in motion. The shark sequence in *Finding Nemo* starts with Marlin encountering Bruce the shark, a villain. (A villain is often the trigger for an escalating set piece.) Having the antagonist disrupt our hero's journey often sets a great confrontational set piece into motion.

Clear stakes. As with any good scene or sequence, the stakes need to be clear. The stakes when encountering a shark are very clear—grave injury or death.

Difficult challenge. Sharks are apex predators so encountering three of them is definitely a difficult challenge. Even though they proclaim that fish are "friends not food," we know what sharks are capable of.

Unique location. The sharks' group meets in an area surrounded by undersea mines, adding to the danger of the situation.

Complications. When the sequence starts, we know that dealing with sharks is difficult, but Dory seems oblivious to the danger, making the situation even more difficult for Marlin.

Twist. A great way to keep an audience in suspense is by using a plot twist. In *Nemo*, we expect a shark to immediately attack but he doesn't, so we're left wondering what is going to happen. This creates tremendous dramatic tension.

Something unexpected. We're always looking for ways to surprise the audience. In *Nemo*, we're focused on the sharks and the undersea mines; that's when Marlin spots the mask from the diver that took Nemo. This surprising element pushes the sequence in a dramatic new direction.

Reversals. In *Nemo*, with the sharks just chatting and the new focus on the diving mask, the audience has maybe let their guard down and forgotten about the danger of the sharks. That's the exact moment that Dory gets bopped in the nose, sending blood into the water, bringing a complete reversal as Bruce switches to full-on shark mode, wildly attacking Marlin and Dory.

Dramatic conclusion. There must be a strong and clear ending to the set piece. In *Nemo*, the wild chase scene ends with huge undersea explosions, a dramatic conclusion that allows Marlin and Dory to continue on their journey.

Set Pieces in Various Genres

Regardless of genre, set pieces tend to be quite active. Things are happening that make life more difficult for the character. Let's look at how set pieces work across different genres.

Action

This is pretty obvious: Action movies are built around thrilling set pieces. Whether it's James Bond, *Mission Impossible*, *Star Wars*, or a superhero movie, they almost all start with a great set piece, have set pieces throughout, and always end with a grand finale set piece.

Minority Report

This movie is loaded with great set pieces. Here is a great example of an escalating set piece:

> Anderton has taken a pre-cog (one of the three clairvoyant people that the pre-crime system is built upon) out of the police headquarters and brought her to a gaming place in a mall to download the minority report about his future that he needs to prove his innocence. But she sees the murder of her mother instead. The set piece kicks off with her saying, "they're inside."
>
> With an elite team of police rushing in, Anderton must escape through the mall with the pre-cog who is barely able to walk. Talk about a challenging task!
>
> "Can you see the umbrella? Take it." Anderton doesn't understand but he grabs the umbrella.

"Man in a blue suit. He drops a briefcase." And a man in a blue suit does indeed drop his briefcase. Now we understand. She is using her power to see the future.

She stops in the middle of the mall. "Wait." But they are totally in the open. We see the police on the floor above rushing in. "Do you see the balloon man?" She continues to repeat, "Wait, wait, wait," but the police are rushing in from both sides. As the police reach the railing on the upper level, they look down directly where Anderton and the pre-cog are standing but just at that moment the balloon man stops to sell a balloon to a little girl. The balloons completely hide Anderton and the pre-cog from the police! The police rush off and our heroes continue.

The pre-cog gasps and grabs a woman, "He knows! Don't go home." The woman looks completely freaked out. A surprising beat that is dramatic and intriguing.

They continue but the police spot them from above. This twist, allowing the villain to close in, increases the dramatic tension that Anderton will be caught.

They exit the mall. The pre-cog makes Anderton drop some money for a homeless man. The man reaches out for the money and the police trip over him.

Outside it's raining. Anderton opens the umbrella (that she had told him to grab) just as police arrive at a balcony and look out. All they see are umbrellas.

Finally free from the police, Anderton spots an image from the crime scene where he is supposed to kill a man. This is the start of another amazing set piece.

One of the things that I love about this set piece is how it uses the main idea of the film—the pre-cogs' ability to see the future. Set pieces should not be disconnected from the story. They should incorporate key story elements and move the story forward.

❓ Steven Spielberg

One of the reasons Mr. Spielberg is one of the all-time great directors is that he is a total master of the set piece. From *Jaws,* to *Raiders of the Lost Ark,* to *Minority Report,* to pretty much any film he has directed, all are built around great set pieces. If you want to really understand set pieces, treat yourself to a Spielberg marathon.

Iron Man

This awesome movie has many great set pieces. Let's look at one that starts with a plan:

> Trapped in a cave by a terrorist army, a location that makes escape nearly impossible, Tony Stark *makes a plan* to build the Iron Man suit so that he and Ho Yinsen can break out.
>
> But the villain, Raza, notices that something is up and sends two guards to check it out. They try to enter to investigate, which triggers a booby trap bomb. This sets a major complication into action and now the clock is really ticking. A ticking clock always adds to a set piece.
>
> Yinsen tries to rush to complete the Iron Man suit, but it is taking too long. This is another big complication.
>
> "We need more time!" claims Yinsen, as he picks up one of the guard's guns and rushes down the cave shooting in the air. It works for a moment, until he rounds a corner and there are a dozen guards pointing guns at him.
>
> But he has bought enough time for the Iron Man system to come online. From this point on, the obstacles and tests continue to build.
>
> In the dark, three guards search for Stark. Suddenly we hear a scuffle and one of them flies backwards. Iron Man emerges and easily defeats the others.
>
> He marches up the cave bashing soldiers as bullets ricochet off his armor.
>
> A group of panicked soldiers seal the iron door, trapping some of their own men in with Iron Man. They scream for a moment, then a couple thumps, then silence. Terrified, a group of soldiers wait behind the iron door as Iron Man begins to punch it. Smash! He breaks through the door.
>
> There's a bit of comedy as he swings his arm, smashing a soldier but also embedding his arm in the cave wall. Seeing Iron Man stuck, a soldier rushes up and point-blank shoots Iron Man in the head, but the bullet ricochets off him and hits the soldier!
>
> Next up, Raza stands with a grenade launcher. He fires at Iron Man, who swings out of the way and fires his built-in grenade launcher back at Raza, taking him out.
>
> Tony lifts his mask and tries to save Yinsen, but Yinsen says his family is dead and he is going to see them now. Tony thanks

Yinsen for saving him and Yinsen tells him, "Don't waste it. Don't waste your life." This is a powerful emotional moment.

Outside, the rest of the army waits for Iron Man, guns trained on the dark cave. We hear pounding footsteps. We see Iron Man's chest lamp and then he emerges. Two dozen men open fire, raining bullets on Iron Man. Not a scratch. Iron Man says, "My turn," and lets loose his built-in flame throwers!

One of the soldiers begins to fire a large caliber machine gun, knocking down and damaging Iron Man. They seem to have Iron Man pinned down. Finally, he launches into the air just as a huge explosion levels everything. Hundreds of feet in the air, the built-in rockets sputter and die! Now Iron Man is falling! Slam! He crashes into the hard sand. Parts are strewn everywhere, but he is alive. There is a clear and dramatic conclusion: Tony Stark is alive and free from the terrorists.

This is a great set piece. It has all the key elements and is the origin of the Iron Man suit. Also, Yinsen's death seems to truly change Tony Stark motivating his character arc from uncaring playboy to superhero.

Comedy

Like a comedian building a big joke and running with it, a comedic set piece starts with a hilarious moment, then does everything to build upon it:

Bridesmaids

The sequence at the fancy gown store is a classic escalating set piece. There's no planning scene but there is a type of setup in that Annie picks a really sketchy restaurant for the bride and bridesmaids' lunch.

The complications begin when they arrive at the exclusive gown store. Annie didn't make reservations and the next opening is in seven weeks! Helen steps up, she knows the woman and they are whisked in.

The moment they get into the classy store, Megan lets a wicked burp fly.

The women all have on the bridesmaids' dresses that they want (all are different) when some of them start to feel discomfort and suddenly, they are all sweating profusely.

Lillian comes out in a wedding gown. The women gush. Megan tries to say something but almost throws up. Helen proclaims that they all got food poisoning from that restaurant. Annie tries to deflect, "You all are fine," when another girl almost hurls! They all start to fart. "I just need to get off this white carpet." Several start to rush for the bathroom.

One woman is throwing up when Megan rushes in. "I need the toilet!" She won't move so Megan clears the sink and sits on it!! The first woman screams, "Megan! No!!"

Annie tries to convince Helen that she's not sick but she's sweating badly.

Another woman throws up on the first woman's head.

Megan screams, "What did we eat? It's coming out of me like lava!"

Meanwhile, Annie is desperate to prove she is not sick (to prove it was not her restaurant that caused this). She's sweating like she's in a sauna but claims she's just hungry. Helen offers her an almond. She struggles mightily to eat the nut.

Lillian comes rushing out. "I need a bathroom." She bolts outside, desperately trying to cross the street to another bathroom. In her huge white wedding dress, she staggers across the street but slows, "It's happening. Oh no. It's happening." She squats down in the middle of the street. "It happened."

This sequence escalates from a beautiful day at a fancy gown store to total scatological mayhem. The main complication is there is only one toilet, and many women are getting violently ill. But as each woman comes into the bathroom, this complication escalates.

Raising Arizona

H. I. (Hi) McDunnough and his wife Edwina (Ed) *make a plan* to break into the Arizona home to steal a baby. Luckily this is a comedy because that sounds like a horrible crime.

> Hi and Ed are miserable since they are unable to conceive a child. That's when they hear about the Arizona Quints. They reason that five babies are more than anyone can handle, so they come up with a plan to take a baby for themselves.
>
> After a humorous intro to the Arizona family, it cuts to Hi upstairs holding one of the babies who is crying. Another baby starts to cry so Hi puts the first down in a chair and grabs the second baby.
>
> A third baby starts crying so Hi sets the second baby on the floor and picks up the third.

He puts the third one back and realizes number one is off the chair and number two is crawling under the crib. He decides to go for number two. He crawls under the crib. Just then another baby flops out of the crib onto Hi's back!

Cut to Mr. and Mrs. Arizona staring at the ceiling with their mouths hanging open.

Back to Hi, it's baby mayhem. All five babies are on the floor and crawling in all directions. A serious complication! Hi manages to grab number two and put them in the crib. Hi turns around and no babies! Where did they go? This is a great twist!

Cut to Mr. Arizona telling his wife to go check on them. She gets up. This is a major complication.

Hi manages to find one in the closet. Just as he gets that one in the crib, he spots one making a break for the hallway. Hi tiptoe scrambles after it, grabbing it just before it gets to the stairs! He spins around and scoops up number five and darts back into the room just as Mrs. Arizona reaches the top of the stairs.

She comes into the room to find all five babies sitting up and looking content.

Cut to Hi returning without a baby to Ed waiting in the car. Ed yells at Hi, "You go right back up there and get me a toddler! I need a baby, Hi; they got more'n they can handle!"

Cut to Mrs. Arizona holding a baby over her shoulder, we see Hi's head rise up in the window.

He returns to Ed with a baby. "I think I got the best one!"

This is a great set piece which sets up the rest of the story.

Drama

Drama seems the least likely candidate for a set piece, but building up and making the most of a crucial sequence can really deliver key emotional moments:

Gattaca

A sci-fi drama with no lightsabers or aliens, *Gattaca* is simply an amazing story about the human spirit. In this future world where only genetically designed (and therefore superior) humans can have good jobs. Vincent has gone to incredible lengths to secure a position in the space agency. But now his brother Anton shows up and threatens to expose Vincent as an "Invalid," a genetically inferior human. In this case, Anton is a villain, and represents a huge obstacle for our main character.

> There is an intense argument with Anton arguing for and representing society's view that genetically engineered humans are, by definition, superior.
>
> Vincent refutes this, he has succeeded despite being "Invalid."
>
> Anton refuses to accept that Vincent is capable of being better. Vincent reminds Anton that he has defeated him before. This motivates them to return to the sea and once again attempt their childhood challenge of who can swim further out to sea.
>
> They stand on the beach staring at the dark raging waters, stripping down.
>
> The two men swim into the breaking waves.
>
> Further and further out to sea they swim.
>
> Anton stops, "Vincent, where's the shore? We're too far out!" Vincent replies, "You wanna quit?" No. And they continue swimming. Beyond exhausted, the challenging test continues.
>
> Further and further, they swim. Finally, desperate, Anton calls out, "How are you doing this Vincent? How have you done any of this?" Vincent replies, "You know how I did it? I never saved anything for the swim back."
>
> Defeated, Anton turns around and begins to swim back.
>
> Exhausted Anton gives up and begins to sink down, and once again Vincent saves his genetically superior brother.

This is a fantastic escalating set piece caused by the villain showing up. This is the biggest obstacle Vincent has had to face. It is a beautiful and moving scene that represents the thematic heart and soul of the story. The secret to success is not superior genes but the willpower of the human spirit.

Silver Linings Playbook

There's a big setup: Pat Sr. has lost everything by betting on the Eagles and he blames Pat for causing the bad luck. Tiffany suggests Pat Sr. get it back by making a big bet on the Eagles to beat the Cowboys. But the bet turns into a parlay: the Eagles must beat the Cowboys *plus* when Pat and Tiffany dance, they must score a five.

> The first complication is that Pat doesn't want to be involved. Pat had agreed to dance with Tiffany as part of another deal. But now

that the dance is part of the big bet and their dance scores matter, it seems to be too much for Pat.

So, Tiffany comes up with a white lie to get Pat to do it: his wife will be there. That leads to a reversal: Pat agrees to do it.

It's the night of the game and the big dance. Once they arrive at the unique location, the hotel, the action is fairly continuous.

The next complication is that the other dancers are amazing.

Then an unexpected twist: Pat's wife actually shows up! This leads to a major complication: Tiffany, who is clearly in love with Pat, completely freaks out! Tiffany starts drinking and flirting with some random guy.

As Pat nervously searches for Tiffany, another complication pops up: the judges' scores are really harsh. Even great dancers are only scoring in the low sevens. And we know that Pat and Tiffany are not at that level. Getting a five will be extremely difficult.

Pat finally finds her. Throughout the story Pat has had almost no self-control, criticizing anything Tiffany does that he disagreed with; but now, he is calm and polite to her as he focuses his anger on the guy. This is an unexpected twist. Tiffany tells Pat you're the worst thing that ever happened to me. And still Pat controls himself.

Meanwhile, the Eagles win, so the whole bet is on Pat and Tiffany. Their names are announced, they are on. Pat drags her out there.

They start. It goes well. They aren't amazing but they are pretty darn good. But then comes the big move. They have practiced it over and over but never really got it down.

Tiffany runs at Pat and jumps; he catches her but it's not good. They struggle and spin. The crowd and the judges see it, it's not good. It seems like they may completely fall but they recover and finish!

The scores are announced: 4.9, 4.8, 4.9, and... 5.4 for an average score of 5.0! Everyone goes crazy! They won the bet!

Finally, there's a great comedic button on the scene when the announcer asks, "Why are they so excited about a five?"

The entire second act builds toward the dance and then the writers add as many complications as possible. Like all great set pieces, it moves the story forward in a dramatic way. After the dance, Pat goes to talk to his wife. We don't hear what they say, but Tiffany sees it and gets very upset. She rushes out. Pat chases her and finally tells her he loves her. We realize he is over his wife and that Pat and Tiffany are going to be together!

Horror

Like the action genre, great horror movies are built on great set pieces. We all know what to expect in horror when a character says, "What's that sound? I better go down to the basement and check it out." This statement will probably be followed by an extended sequence, with several false scares, and then just when we think it's okay: Boom, the character is brutally killed.

The Thing

Kurt Russell holds a flame thrower on the other guys. He *comes up with a plan* to test each man's blood with a burning hot wire. His logic is that "Thing" blood will fight back when "attacked." This leads to one of the greatest set pieces of all time:

> The other men are tied down to chairs and blood is drawn from each. Kurt Russell heats up a thick wire with his blow torch. Everyone watches as he tests the first man's (Windows) blood by putting the hot wire in it: nothing.

> Windows gets a flame thrower and joins Russell.

> He tests his own blood: nothing.

> He tests the blood of the two dead guys: nothing.

> Garry says this is pure nonsense. Kurt Russell accuses him of being a Thing and says we'll do you last. This confrontation is a great misdirection. It gets our guard down.

> Kurt Russell tests Palmer's blood: Boom! A mini creature bursts out of the blood! This is an unexpected twist since we were thinking it would be Garry, not Palmer.

> Russell drops the blood and the puddles of blood rush off across the floor. Okay, this is a complication, now there's more Thing rushing around the floor.

> Russell tries to blast Palmer, but his flame thrower misfires. More complications!

> Palmer, still tied to the chair, begins to violently transform into the Thing. Unfortunately for Garry and Childs, they are still tied to their chairs which are tied to Palmer's chair! Serious complication for those guys!

> The Thing bursts from its chair, flying to the ceiling. Windows tries to blast it but there's a complication: he freezes! The Thing drops down right in front of him and attacks.

> Finally, Russell gets his flame thrower working and blasts the Thing.

It's an amazingly dramatic set piece. Despite what seems like a great plan, just about everything goes wrong.

Alien

Alien has some all-time great set pieces. Let's take a look at one that is an amazing variation on, "I'll go to the basement and check it out."

> Dallas, Kane, and Lambert have discovered that an alien ship is the origin of the distress signal. (The reason their mining ship has landed on the planet.)
>
> Meanwhile back at the Nostromo, we learn that the distress signal may actually be a warning.
>
> Kane connects to a winch that lowers him down a hole in the alien ship (the "basement"). Lower and lower he goes, emerging into a cavernous room.
>
> Kane says the ground is filled with leathery objects, like eggs or something. And there is a layer of mist that reacts when broken.
>
> Kane seems smart enough to avoid entering the mist but he slips and falls into it. Now that he is down there, he begins to examine one of the eggs. When he touches it, there is a zap sound, and Kane recoils.
>
> Kane spots movement in the egg. Life, organic life. The top of the egg opens like a flower. Kane instinctively steps back. But he is drawn forward toward the beating object in the center of the egg/flower.
>
> Then with shocking violence, a creature bursts from the egg, sizzles through Kane's mask, and attaches to his face.
>
> Above, Dallas and Lambert immediately sense something is wrong. They try to contact Kane but get nothing. They switch on the winch and start reeling Kane up.
>
> It seems to take forever. Finally, they see Kane, realize there's something on his face, and that he is totally unconscious.

The set piece starts with a unique location, the lower hold of an alien ship and then escalates as a series of mysteries: the room, the mist, the eggs, the movement. Each is an obstacle for Kane to investigate and try to overcome. It has a clear ending with the creature attached to an unconscious Kane, which will force the crew to make a major decision.

As you can see, set pieces can happen at any time in any genre. The main idea is to build the key sequence by adding complications, twists, reversals, and other surprises in order to maximize the challenges to the character.

Short Films That Play Out as a Single Set Piece

Set pieces are often described as a sequence that could stand alone like a short film. This implies that there must be short films that consist of a single set piece. And in fact, yes, there are some amazing short films that are excellent examples of set pieces. Here are some great ones:

> *Ataque de Pánico! (Panic Attack!)* This excellent short, which I described earlier in this book, plays perfectly as an escalating set piece. Starting with giant robots emerging from the fog, to the start of the robots' attack, to the counter attack of the Uruguayan Air Force jets (they are quickly eliminated), to the dramatic conclusion when the robots gather in a circle, forming a protective barrier around themselves and then unleash a massive explosion which seems to wipe out everything.

> *Pigeon: Impossible* This hilarious short escalates from a pesky pigeon wanting some bagel to launching a nuclear missile toward Russia. That is a serious escalation of action and stakes.

> *Proof* by Kevin Reynolds is a fantastic example of a setup set piece. A group of buddies convince one of their gang to sky-dive and prove his manhood. A short lesson in basics of skydiving from a super sketchy pilot, along with the scariest looking plane you've ever seen, are all part of the setup and buildup. But the complication once their buddy is in the air is one of the all-time greats! I'm not going to reveal it, you just have to watch it!

Exercise: Build a Scene into a Set Piece

Go back to any of the stories you have come up with so far. Is there a key scene that you think could be built into a set piece? Maybe you hope to build your entire short into a set piece?

Could you add a setup scene that increases the audience's expectations and adds dramatic tension?

Or perhaps the main character is trying to achieve their goal when an unexpected obstacle (often the villain) blocks their progress?

However you decide to do it, you want to milk your set piece and make the most of the sequence by adding:

- A unique location that heightens the drama or adds to the complications.

- Complications. What can you add to make it even more challenging?

- Unexpected twists. The main character made a plan, but we didn't see this coming.

- A ticking clock. Less time for our hero means more dramatic tension.

- Clear stakes. What will happen if they fail?

- You also want to make sure there is a clear resolution: the set piece (or short film) must resolve in some way.

- If it is a part of a larger story, you want to make sure that it pushes the story forward. Like all good scenes and sequences, set pieces need to enhance the plot.

- Button. If it's a comedy, it's always great to add a button to the end of the scene.

Spoiler Alert! | Chapter 17

Peluca (2003).

Office Space (1992).

The 400 Blows (1959).

The Alphabet (1969).

Dear Basketball (2017).

Koyaanisqatsi (1982).

17

The Non-Traditional Film

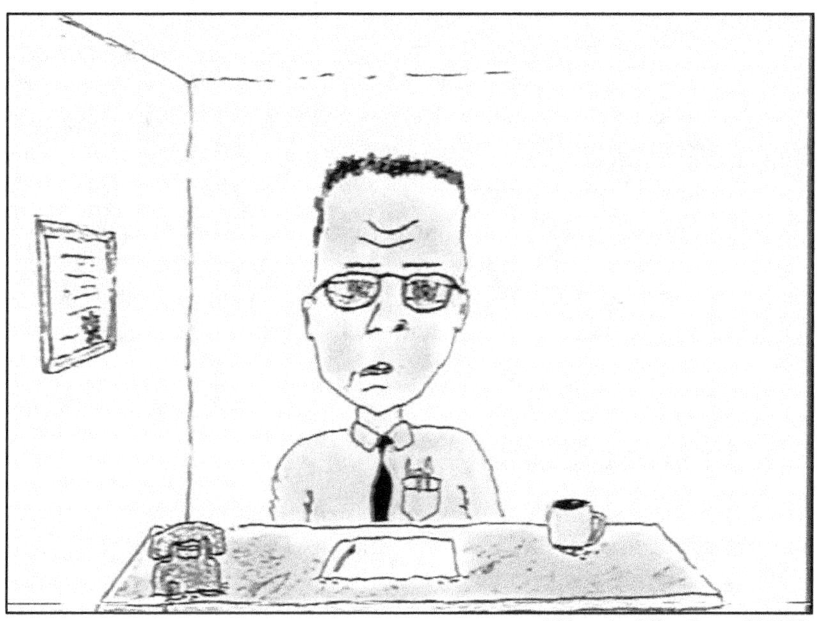

Milton in *Office Space* (1992).

Freedom!

One of the great things about short films is that you can do whatever you want! Some filmmakers have completely embraced this freedom to create very unique short films. These films may not have traditional three-act structure, but they do use many of the techniques we have discussed in this book. A short film can be almost anything, but for the purpose of discussion I'm going to group these unique films into two categories: *the character study* and *the visual poem*. (It is much more rare to find a successful feature film that ventures into these waters, but there are a couple very worthy entries we'll look at.)

> *If you really want to hear about it, the first thing you'll probably want to know is where I was born, and what my lousy childhood was like, and how my parents were occupied and all before they had me, and all that David Copperfield kind of crap, but I don't feel like going into it, if you want to know the truth.*
>
> *—J. D. Salinger, "The Catcher in the Rye"*

The Catcher in the Rye is one of the most beloved novels of the last century. It doesn't have a strong plot or any real structure at all. With J.D. Salinger, it's all about character and style. The basic plot is that a teenage boy gets expelled from high school. He heads home early and hangs out in New York city for a couple days. Try pitching that story in Hollywood!

When you break or disregard a "rule," it can only work when the other elements are that much stronger. These character-based stories are sometimes referred to as *low-density narratives*, which means that there is not much plot or, in other words, not much happens. I think of them as a *character study*.

The Character Study

The character study obviously focuses on character over story. With the lack of traditional story structure, you really need to knock it out of the park with the other elements. Often it is the character's dialogue and unique goals that carry the film.

Peluca

This short by Jared Hess launched the careers of both Hess and lead actor, Jon Heder. It was also turned into a feature film, *Napoleon Dynamite*. (It's interesting that the feature had a more traditional, narrative structure.)

This short consists of several scenes that basically cover a day in the life of Seth. It opens with Seth playing with a small action figure and then getting on a school bus. As he sits down in the back and a younger kid asks, "What are you going to do today, Seth?" As we discussed in Chapter 15, "Suspense," posing a question like this is a great way to involve the audience. Seth's response is distinctive (and so is Jon Heder's delivery), ending with his trademark, "Gosh!" Then Seth ties a string on the action figure and dangles it out the back of the bus. Seth is very pleased with himself. In class, Seth must deal with a bully who is pestering him about his drawings and shakes him. Pedro defends him. Seeing a character treated unfairly really helps to get the audience to care.

In the cafeteria, Pedro asks how Seth's neck is and Seth quickly responds, "It's fine," but then mutters, "It kills." This tough-guy/wimp dichotomy is hilarious. Then Seth comments about Pedro's ninja-like technique and how it's probably illegal. Next, Seth makes a plan to ditch class and go to the thrift store to find a fanny pack. Which is a pretty ridiculous plan, but Pedro goes along with it. That's part of the fun, the ridiculousness of it.

Seth takes a detour to buy an Idaho Lotto ticket, but gets shut down for being a minor. Pedro suggests that his friend Giel looks old enough and sure enough, his little mustache does the trick. At the thrift store Giel and Pedro become obsessed with a wig (a *peluca* in Spanish), since Giel has cut his hair too short.

Seth finds the perfect fanny pack, but its seven-dollar price tag is too steep for him. Giel gets the wig and even though he looks ridiculous, some girl compliments him. Then Seth runs off and ridiculously falls down. On the bus ride home, Seth gives the little kid his action figure. He's a good guy and we like that.

As you can see, not a lot of story; just several random scenes. The short relies on quirky dialogue, unusual behavior, and ridiculous situations. Seth is an unforgettable character who is at once the familiar nerd character and yet heightened and unique due to his passion and wacky dialogue.

Office Space

This animated short by Mike Judge is about as simple as you can get. Milton sits at his desk and expresses his frustration at having his desk moved three times. He tells us how he's supposed to have a stapler, so he took one. He threatens to set the building on fire if he has to move again and picks his nose. About halfway through, Milton's boss enters and tells Milton that he must move his desk again (to make more room for boxes), then the boss spots Milton's stapler and takes it. Milton tries to object but ends up just saying okay. After the boss leaves, Milton picks his nose and says he is going to set the building on fire.

Obviously, not much of a story. What makes it work is the oddly stylish dialogue from Milton and his boss. Using quirky dialogue makes the characters stand out. Also, we know from Chapter 6, "Getting an Audience to Care," that we connect with characters who are treated unfairly. Milton expresses his frustration at this poor treatment and we feel for him. Then his boss comes in and does more of the same. Also, the absurdity of wanting a stapler so badly that he would threaten to burn down the building is pretty hilarious.

The 400 Blows

This amazing film by François Truffaut is one of the few feature-length films to pull off a character study format. It follows a young boy growing up in Paris. Loosely based on the childhood of director François Truffaut, it is a true masterpiece. The fact that we need to look back to 1959 in order to find a great feature-length character study tells you how challenging this unstructured format can be.

The Visual Poem

A *visual poem* film can kind of be anything. Music videos are the most common visual poems with interesting imagery and story fragments that complement the tune. But there are almost unlimited subjects for visual poems:

The Alphabet

Even in film school it was clear that David Lynch was a visionary master whose provocative images disturb pretty much everyone. The first half of the visual poem, *The Alphabet*, plays out like an odd *Sesame Street* animation of the alphabet, with a male singing the letters more or less as they appear. This would seem fairly harmless, if it weren't for Mr. Lynch's use of the *fast start* technique (Chapter 11) to set the tone of the story: a short segment of a woman sleeping and then a strange image of a woman wearing dark sunglasses, half her face obscured in darkness.

After the alphabet, the animation starts to get weirder, which is greatly intensified by a very strange, repetitive, animalistic sound. After about two minutes, an animated woman gasps and blood begins to pour out of her eyes, nose, and mouth. The short plays out like a nightmare version of learning the ABC's with bizarre visuals and freaky sounds.

Dear Basketball

This love letter to basketball, by Kobe Bryant and Glen Keane, is moving and passionate. The visual poem gets going with the *fast start* technique by opening with the clock ticking down and Kobe making the winning shot.

Then the story progresses from six-year-old Kobe up through his retirement as a player.

It could be argued that since it progresses through Kobe's life, it has a chronological structure. That's true, but the focus of the story and the drama does not come from this chronological progression. The drama comes from the expression of passion: Kobe's love for the game. It also works as a character study. As we discussed in Chapter 6, "Getting an Audience to Care," having a passionate character really draws us in. It's hard to imagine anyone more passionate than Kobe Bryant and his love for basketball.

Koyaanisqatsi

This film by Godfrey Reggio is one of the few feature-length visual poems. This masterpiece has no characters (although people appear after twenty-three minutes), no dialogue, and no "story;" just spectacular imagery and a hypnotic, haunting soundtrack by Phillip Glass. The title is a Hopi Indian word meaning "life out of balance," which is our first clue to the meaning of this poem. The film progresses from stunning imagery of nature to images of humanity that grow faster and more chaotic until they conclude with a rocket launch and spectacular explosion.

No Rules

As I stated from the beginning, there are no rules except, "Don't be boring." All the shorts and features discussed in this chapter are anything but boring. As a creator, anything goes but the more you understand successful techniques and incorporate them into your work, the greater your chance for success.

> *I'm a great believer in luck, and I find the harder I work the more I have of it.*
>
> *—Often attributed to Thomas Jefferson but alas, he never said this, but it's good.*

Good Luck!

The remainder of this book contains valuable information for students and teachers, but we have reached the end of our screenwriting journey together. Hopefully, you have enjoyed it and learned a few things along the way. I wish for you that this is just the beginning of a grand journey.

So go out there and create. Pour your heart and soul into it. But passion alone won't get it done. Kobe Bryant was famous for being an incredibly hard worker. He exercised, practiced, and studied relentlessly. So be like Kobe. Be passionate. But be willing to put in the work.

I wish you the best of luck!

18

Film School Applications and Breaking In

Writing Your Way to a Career

The most common question I hear is how do I break in? Writing a truly great screenplay is as close to a golden ticket as you can get. But that's not the only way. There are a million different ways to get started in the business, but for many people going to a great film school is the first step. There are a variety of options when it comes to film schools from traditional universities to for-profit film schools.

Off to College

The most common path to a career in filmmaking involves going to school:

> **Four-year university film programs.** Most top film schools are part of traditional four-year universities, such as USC, UCLA, NYU, and Loyola Marymount University (LMU). There are also standalone art schools, like Art Center College of Design, or Rhode Island School of Design, that offer film degrees. Film schools are highly competitive with some of the lowest acceptance rates of any programs in the country. They are usually very expensive. (Although most four-year colleges are very expensive, no matter your major.)

> **Graduate school film programs**. The same universities that offer undergraduate film degrees usually offer graduate degrees as well. The American Film Institute (AFI) is a graduate school that focuses on filmmaking exclusively. A master's degree in film or screenwriting would be a likely choice if you already have an undergraduate degree in a different (non-film) major.

> **Non-traditional film schools.** These are often referred to as *for-profit schools*. These types of schools may offer a solid education

but be sure to do your research. There are often no application requirements, meaning that, if you can afford the tuition, you can attend the school.

Getting Into a Top Film School

Obviously, there's a reason so many people want to go to the top film schools: they have a proven track record of success. These schools give you the skills and knowledge that help create a clear pathway to jobs in the business.

So, what does it take to get into one of the top film schools? First off, you will need to have excellent grades. It helps to have a portfolio (resumé) of work—projects that are related to the program you would like to apply to. That means short films for directors and creative writing samples for writing programs. If your works have won awards, even better. Also, it helps to have quality extracurricular activities—maybe you worked on the school newspaper or yearbook, or perhaps you were class president.

For writing programs, it will all come down to your writing samples. Writing samples demonstrate your writing skills and separate you from the madding crowd.

Writing Samples

Every film school requires some type of writing sample. And we're not just talking about the writing department. Applications for directing, producing, even animation, will require at least one writing sample. Why? Because all great film and television starts with great writing. Understanding and having at least some writing skill is critical to all major aspects of filmmaking.

> *To make a great film you need three things - the script, the script, and the script.*
>
> *—Alfred Hitchcock*

So, how do you make sure your writing samples knock it out of the park? Read this book and do the exercises! If you bought this book and flipped to this chapter to see if there's some magic bullet, some golden ticket shortcut, sorry, there just isn't any. You need to do the work.

Assuming you're awesome and have read this book, let's take a look at the various types of writing samples that you may encounter in a film school application.

Step One

The most important step for any writing sample is to be sure to follow all the instructions. If the directions call for five pages, don't turn in ten. Don't even turn in six pages. Often the application will call for the story to be in screenplay format. Most require that you deliver the document as a PDF, so don't turn in a Word doc or a Pages doc. Be sure that there are no typos and that it generally looks professional. (Don't forget to review Chapter 9, "Screenplay Format," to ensure that your script follows screenwriting conventions.) These are relatively simple instructions. The assumption is that if you can't follow them, you probably won't be a good student and by extension, you won't be a good professional.

Sample of Your Work

Almost all writing programs will require a sample of your own work. This is not based on a prompt, it could be anything. It will usually be ten to thirty pages. It can be a complete story or part of a larger work (with some context). The work must be original, not based on any existing property. No spec scripts from existing TV shows. No adaptations of novels, or comic books, etc. What the selection committee is looking for is your style and your voice. What do you write when left to your own devices? This sample should be in your preferred genre. You want it to be your strongest work that best demonstrates your abilities. If you have an amazing new idea but the story is not polished, don't send it. The assumption will be that this is the best you can do.

Creative Writing Prompts

Most university writing programs will offer at least two creative writing prompts. These are often simple scenarios that are designed to allow you to show your creativity in a short form.

For any creative exercise, start by following the core foundation of logline (Chapter 3, "Loglines"), major beats (Chapter 4, "Basic Story Structure"), and character worksheet (Chapter 5, "Character"). This will help you have confidence that your story is solid, allowing your writing style to shine.

Something you want to research is if the university changes the prompts every year or if the same prompt has been used for years. If it's the same prompt, then the admissions committee has probably read most of the standard story ideas. USC School of Cinematic Arts (consistently ranked #1) is a school that doesn't change their prompts often, so they have seen all the basic story concepts in response to the standard prompts. The issue when you lean into standard story tropes, according to David Isaacs, the former head of the writing department at USC SCA, is that there's an immediate response, "I know where this is going." As you recall from Chapter 15, "Suspense," the lack of uncertainty raises the bar for everything else. That means your "clever" plot is not going to blow them away. (It's an elevator to Hell. No! It's an elevator to Heaven!) It puts all the weight on your characters, dialogue, and description.

Regardless of whether this is a new or old prompt, you should focus on your strengths. Write in a genre that you love to write. If dialogue is your specialty, then focus less on plot originality and more on creating a scenario that will allow your lingo to fly.

Most good universities are looking for all types of writers. Don't think you have to be a certain "type" e.g., the "serious drama writer," to get in. Be yourself. Write what you love. If they don't want you, then that's probably not the right school for you. (The people who read your application are usually the full-time professors—the people who will be teaching you.) Seriously, you don't want to be at a school that doesn't understand you. You will be frustrated. You want to find a school that connects with you. Maybe it's just one or two professors who think you're great but that may be all you need to rise to the next level.

Most Challenging Moment

I believe this is one of the more critical types of writing sample. Film school is incredibly demanding, and it will challenge you. This exercise will allow you to talk about yourself and how you handled something difficult in your life. It's really a chance for you to tell a story with yourself as the main character. I think it's important to be open and honest. It shows strength to be willing to write about personal flaws or issues.

Whatever the moment, tell it as a story. It should not be a news article. Nor does it have to be melodrama. If you are a comedy writer, have fun with this. Tell a story with style, *your style*. That's the key to all the writing prompts—you want to tell a story. The bottom line is that film schools are looking for storytellers.

Please don't write that you've had an amazing life and have wonderful parents, so you really haven't had any great challenges to overcome. Even if this is true, there has to be something that was difficult.

Autobiographical Character Sketch

This is another chance to tell a story with yourself as main character. This is not a resumé with bullet points. Although, you may want to make one as a starting point. But I believe this exercise is less about being comprehensive, more about creating a portrait of you. You may want to build the sketch around a specific incident or event featuring you, that highlights your best qualities.

Why You Chose This School

This one feels like a request from the administration, "Wouldn't it be great to have stories from the students about why our school is the best?" Yeah, sure. Honestly, don't knock yourself out over this one. But if you can find a way to make it fun or dynamic, that would be amazing.

A little research could go a long way. Who are your icons that attended this school? What aspect of the program seems particularly intriguing?

Why You Want to Be a Writer

This one doesn't seem that critical as well. It seems like it would be tough to come up with something that the admissions committee hasn't heard thousands of times. But, if you can find a way to be inventive with it, maybe you could surprise them.

Seven years of college down the drain.

—John Blutarsky (John Belushi)
in "Animal House"

You Didn't Get in, Now What?

So, you didn't get into your dream school. Or maybe you did but you hate it. Not everybody is meant to go to *the* school. Your second or third or even tenth choice may end up being the right school for you. Many very successful people didn't study at their dream school or didn't even study film or writing:

> **Steven Spielberg** was rejected (three times!) by his dream school USC, so he went to Long Beach State (CSULB). Seemed to work out for him. (Actually, I've taught many classes in the Steven Spielberg Building on the USC campus. So, he eventually got in there.)

> **Christopher Nolan** studied English lit at University College London.

> **Wes Anderson** graduated from the University of Texas with a degree in philosophy.

> **Mike Judge** got a physics degree from University of California San Diego.

> **Paul Thomas Anderson** spent two semesters at Emerson and only two days at New York University.

Some people even started out in completely different fields before switching to film and television:

> **Michael Crichton** went from medical doctor to incredibly successful writer.

> **David E. Kelly** went from practicing lawyer to amazingly successful TV writer.

> **James Cameron** was working as a truck driver prior to becoming an incredibly innovative director.

There are many paths to success. So, if going to a top film school is not in the cards for you, don't sweat it. Hollywood really respects people who have made their own way to success.

Other Options

Even if you badly want to go to a top film school, it may not be the right call. It may not be financially feasible. You may not have the grades. No worries. There are tons of options.

Community College

A year or two at a community college can be extremely beneficial. You could complete your general education requirements for little or even no money! (That could mean cutting in half the student loans you would need for a four-year college.) It's a tremendous opportunity to show that you can get good grades at a college level. Also, many public universities are required to take a certain percentage of community college students. So, community college could be a great pathway to a film school!

Gap Year

Take a gap year or two. Work, travel, join the Peace Corps, create. Mostly, create. Christopher McQuarrie worked at a detective agency and traveled for five years. He didn't even go to college. But his childhood friend, director Bryan Singer went to USC and coaxed McQuarrie into writing.

Skip Film School?

Maybe you don't have the money or the grades for film school. Or maybe you're not really a classroom type, more of a doer.

> **Write**. The Christopher McQuarrie three-dollar film school. Get yourself a pencil, some paper, and write a screenplay. The message here is just do it. The only thing you really need is time and effort. That's the allure of writing. You can create your masterpiece from the comfort of your couch.

> **Shoot**. You can shoot amazing looking video with your phone these days. You can do sophisticated editing on your computer. You can even create stunning special effects or animation with a laptop. It's best to start with a well written story. Again, it's about time and effort.

Breaking In

Whether you have completed film school, are still in it, or are skipping it altogether, you still need to break into the business. Film school doesn't give you a free pass. If you want to work as a creative, you will have to create work that gets you noticed. If you were an athlete, the path would be clear. You would begin competing in high school (or earlier). You would compete against other high school athletes, allowing you to clearly demonstrate your talent and skills. In sports there are clear winners. The most talented athletes get recruited to college or go directly to the pros. For filmmakers, it's not quite so simple. College is an opportunity to hone skills and develop talents to prove you belong in the pros. Unfortunately, it seems that creative work is harder to judge. Some people get noticed right out of film school, thanks to advanced project screenings at their prestigious university. But that's a tiny percentage of students. So what about the rest of us? How do we get noticed? This need to evaluate talent has brought about the rise of screenwriting contests and film festivals.

Contests

Screenwriting contests are a great way to get your work out there and the list of contests seems to grow every year. There are huge contests with thousands of entries and much smaller ones, often with very specific criteria. It's important to do some research. You can spend a fortune if you try to enter every one of them. Pick contests that fit with your work. Many of the contests also provide feedback, which can help you improve.

➡ *I've Got You Covered*

Formal feedback on a screenplay is often referred to as *coverage*. Coverage is an important part of the film industry. If you'd like to know more about coverage and the job of being a script reader, please check out Beverly Neufeld's excellent book, *I've Got You Covered*.

Pitch Fests

This is a hybrid form of contest where you pitch your screenplay to producers, execs, managers, and agents. These seem to take two forms. A kind of speed dating, where you pitch to specific people and companies, or the contest format, where you pitch to judges and a winner is declared. You usually get one to three minutes, so obviously this is all about your logline. Follow up the logline with the most captivating aspects of your story. Also, you want to highlight your characters and their relationships. With only a minute or two, you really just have time for your best stuff, the tip of the iceberg. The key is to hook your audience and convince them that there is an awesome iceberg below. Since pitch fests are live events (either in-person or via video conference) you really want to practice. You may want to write your pitch out and time yourself.

Film Festivals

Festivals love short films. The shorter the better. (Short films are grouped together for screenings. Festival programmers like shorter films because they can group more together.) This is a tremendous way to gain recognition for your short masterpiece.

Film festivals play a critical role at all levels of feature films, from world premieres of big studio films to discovering indie gems. Getting your feature film accepted at one of the major film festivals can catapult your project into worldwide awareness and lead to distribution deals.

There are film festivals all year round and all over the world. Again, you could spend a fortune trying to enter them all. You may want to see if you can get a festival coordinator. They could facilitate your entry into many of the festivals.

Internships

One of the real values of the top film schools is access to high-quality internships. But not all internships are limited to film school students. Studios, production companies, and agencies need lots of ambitious hard-working people. Whether it is the classic working in the mail room, to answering phones, to writing coverage, there is always work to be done. These can be great jobs that give you up-close insight into how the business works and how deals are made. Or they can be boring jobs that lead nowhere. It's often impossible to tell until you are there.

Production Assistant

Film and television sets need a lot of bodies to get the work done. Beyond the highly skilled positions that productions require, there will be lots of grunt work that takes little or no knowledge or experience. If you are willing to work really long hours, often for little or no money, it is a fantastic way to see how the process of making a movie actually works. Los Angeles is still the film capital, but movies and shows are being shot across the country and around the globe. This is generally not a pathway to writing or directing in the business, but it does offer invaluable experience of participating in a professional shoot and possibly the chance to make some contacts.

 **Business Tip**

I have two rules when it comes to the business.

Rule #1. Never send in your work until it is the best you can do. You only get one shot at a first impression. Let's say you bump into a film and television producer or executive. (This is most likely to happen in Los Angeles, but it could happen at a film festival or conference.) The conversation happens to veer toward what you are working on. (Hollywood-speak for, "Pitch me your story.") So, you drop your great logline. The producer nods, smiles, and says, "Wow, that sounds interesting. I'd read that." You get super excited and email your screenplay to said producer, even though you know it needs a bit of work. Big mistake. I'm about 99.9% sure you just killed that relationship. Producers are going to assume that this is the *best* you can do. You need to make sure that it is your best.

Instead, this is what you should do: Send an email, thanking the producer for their interest. Tell them that you have just gotten some notes. You would like to take a week or two to polish the screenplay and then send it to them. They will always want to read the better version of your screenplay. Then call in sick, lock yourself in your room, turn off your phone, and get writing!

There's a meme about levels of friendship in LA:

4. Take you to the airport.

3. Cover for you if you murdered someone.

2. Murder someone for you.

1. Read your screenplay.

You get the idea. It's tough to get people to read your script. So, if a professional in the business offers to read your screenplay, this is not done lightly. Treat the opportunity with respect.

Rule #2. Never sign a deal without a certified agent or an entertainment lawyer looking over it first. Entertainment contracts are very complicated with a lot of unique language. Some people worry that the 10% an agent takes or the 5% an entertainment lawyer takes is too much. This is a Big Mistake. Every deal I've done, my agent or my lawyer has gotten *significantly* more for me in the deal than the percentage they received. And I know I'm signing a solid deal. So, an agent or lawyer will protect you from signing a bad deal and they will always get you more money, sometimes significantly more.

Appendix:

Course Outlines for Teachers or Self-Paced Learners

One Size Does Not Fit All

I've worked at various universities, teaching screenwriting at all levels. Courses range from slow-paced for beginners to fast-paced for advanced students. They can last from six to sixteen weeks. The goal for a screenwriting course could be a single short screenplay, several short screenplays, or a complete feature-length script. Feature film classes are often spread across two semesters (or more).

For Teachers

I've designed three courses to suit various writing goals and time frames. Each course is designed to use the book's step-by-step process to write a screenplay. Lectures are based on specific chapters in this book. The writing goals are designed to jump right in, so that the work is evenly distributed over the length of the course.

Self-Paced Instruction

Maybe you bought this book and would like to use it to write short scripts or even feature screenplays on your own. Using the course outlines can be a great way to set a goal, create a calendar, then work step-by-step to achieve your goal. There are several issues with writing on your own. Often, you set goals that are too ambitious and when you inevitably fall short, you become very discouraged. Or without the step-by-step structured goals of a class, you end up drifting off track and eventually you've given up without even realizing it. Using the course outlines provided in this appendix is a tremendous way to conquer either of these issues. Once you have picked one of the three courses, mark the deadlines in your calendar. Next be sure to pick a specific time to work each week. It's best if you can schedule time every day. Wake up thirty to sixty minutes early each day and write. Don't watch any TV or videos until you've put in at least thirty minutes of writing. Now, thirty minutes of writing may mean staring at a blank page for twenty minutes or more. But eventually, you'll put something down and next thing you know, you've been writing for an hour. It will be different every time. At times it will be difficult. But if you make the time, and follow the course outlines in this appendix, you will make progress.

The Screenwriting Courses

I usually teach a single three-hour class per week. I generally start with a short lecture of thirty to sixty minutes, then spend the remaining class time on students' work. The lectures I give in class are the basis for the chapters in this book, so lecture topics and the corresponding book chapter go hand in hand.

My standard class description goes like this:

There will be weekly lectures covering key concepts of storytelling framed within the context of screenwriting. These lectures are based on the chapters in this book. There will be weekly assignments (mostly screenplay pages); the goal being not just a solid screenplay but also a clear process to writing future screenplays.

This is a workshop class, so the majority of class time will be devoted to going over your work and also that of your classmates. There is only one way to get better at writing and that is to write. And the only way to know if you are making progress is to receive feedback on your pages.

Feedback

Feedback is always a critical part of my classes because it is a critical part of the industry. You must get comfortable giving and receiving feedback. Participation is always at least ten percent and often as much as twenty-five percent of students' grades in my classes, so I encourage everyone to give feedback following classmates' presentations. However, the feedback must be *constructive*. It is imperative that the workshop environment be one where students feel safe to experiment.

How to give feedback:

- I always start with what works, what is good about the pages. (Knowing what is working is every bit as important as knowing what is not working.)

- Then I look at simple issues: formatting errors, description that is too long, too detailed, or in lumped into large blocks, unnecessary dialogue, etc.

- Then I look at the story and character: Is the character acting in an authentic way? Does the story track or is it jumping ahead? Does the story drag, i.e., does it need to move more quickly?

- Finally, what is an area that the writer could improve? What could they focus on to improve the character and/or story?

- It is essential to remember that when you are giving feedback, what you are saying is your opinion, not fact. Writing is personal and can affect people in very different ways.

How to receive feedback:

- It's critical to listen to the feedback. Resist the desire to defend your work. When a writer defends their work, it can stifle the feedback process. It is acceptable to ask questions if you don't understand the issue or are trying to pinpoint what the issue is. But if you start to explain what your scene is doing, then that's not helping anyone.

- Write the feedback down and allow yourself the time to process the issues brought up. You'll be amazed at how many times a "stupid" note will lead to better choices in your story. I know A-list writers whose first reaction to any feedback is, "What the hell are you talking about?" For many of us, it's difficult if not impossible to get over these feelings but we need to learn how to keep them in check.

- When it comes to executing the notes, you are the captain of your ship. It's up to you whether you use the notes you receive or not. If you attempt to do every note, your story could become a jumbled mess. But if you don't take any notes, your work will not improve.

Writing the Short Screenplay: 6-Week Course

Objectives

The course goal is to complete a five- to six-page short screenplay with dramatic characters and a compelling storyline.

Beginning with a story concept, craft a logline and pitch it to the class, including a brief discussion of the story and characters.

Next write a one-page document which covers all the major beats from the status quo, through the act breaks, to the resolution. This brief synopsis is the first glimpse of your movie on the page. We will discuss your synopsis in class.

Now that you have a basic idea of your story, we really want to focus on your characters. Complete the character exercises which will cover the character's defining personality trait, other traits and qualities, as well as their arc, and a backstory. Also, briefly describe the first scene where we meet your character, which is so critical to establishing them.

The rest of the course is spent on writing the screenplay itself.

(Note: The course objective can be shifted to longer screenplays of eight to twelve pages. In that case complete the first half of the screenplay for Week 5 and the remaining pages will be due in Week 6.)

Outcomes

By the end of the course, students will not only have a short screenplay but a clear understanding of the writing process and a solid methodology for writing future screenplays.

Week 1

LECTURE: Loglines (Chapter 3).

- A great logline is a secret weapon for getting your screenplay headed in the right direction.
- Main character, setting, story, stakes.
- Title, genre, and tone. What kind of movie are we talking about?
- Logline variations: trying out the key elements.
- Analysis and examination of loglines.

REQUIRED READING: Chapter 2, "Story and You" and Chapter 3, "Loglines."

OPTIONAL READING: Introduction; Chapter 1, "Why Shorts? Why Features?"

IN-CLASS EXERCISE: Students break into groups of two or three. Choose two or three popular films and work together to write a logline for the films.

Ten to fifteen minutes for students to write the loglines. Twenty-thirty minutes for discussion.

ASSIGNMENT for Week 2: Please write loglines for two or three stories that you are considering writing for this class. Or if you are already sure about the story you want to write, try two or three variations on the logline for your story.

Be prepared to briefly discuss the story and characters.

Week 2

LECTURE: Major beats: The basic elements that every story must have.

- Status quo.
- Inciting incident.
- First act break.
- A set piece.
- Midpoint.
- Second act break.
- Resolution.

IN-CLASS: Students present their loglines. They receive feedback from professor and fellow students.

REQUIRED READING: Chapter 4, "Basic Story Structure."

OPTIONAL READING: Chapter 7, "Character-Based Structure."

ASSIGNMENT for Week 3: One-page brief synopsis of the major beats.

Starting with a revised logline, briefly describe each major beat (two to three sentences). The complete document must be in PDF format, less than one page, with 12-point font, and normal margins.

Week 3

LECTURE: Character (Chapter 5).

- Two parts to creating great characters—defining character and writing in screenplay format.
- Name, defining personality trait, contradiction, big problem, character arc, backstory.
- Writing your character.

- Opening description, clothing, transportation, environment, opening action.
- Read the opening sequences of: *Erin Brockovich*, *Whiplash*, and *Nightcrawler*.

IN-CLASS: Students present their one-page brief synopsis of the major beats. Receive feedback from professor and fellow students.

REQUIRED READING: Chapter 5, "Character" and Chapter 6, "Getting the Audience to Care."

ASSIGNMENT for Week 4: Complete all the questions for both exercises in Chapter 5, "Character." The complete document should be one to two pages. (Note: Completing the character exercises for any significant character can be extremely helpful but we will only be presenting one main character in class.)

Week 4

LECTURE: Scenes (Chapter 10).

- Two things all scenes must have: plot and emotion.
- Types of conflict.
- Three things all scenes should have: character, style, and elements of the future.
- Scene structure.
- Other important aspects of scenes.
- Format: how your script should look.

IN-CLASS: Students present their main character. Receive feedback from professor and fellow students.

REQUIRED READING: Chapter 9, "Screenplay Format" and Chapter 10, "Scenes."

OPTIONAL READING: Chapter 11, "Start Fast" and Chapter 14, "Scene Description."

ASSIGNMENT for Week 5: Begin writing your screenplay! Write in proper screenplay format. Up to six pages. Post as a PDF.

Week 5

LECTURE: Dialogue (Chapters 12 and 13).

- The role of dialogue.

- Information and exposition, reveal conflict, reveal character's relationship, reveal an ongoing relationship, advance the story, build expectations, emotional state of your characters, personality and attitude of your characters, philosophy of your characters.

IN-CLASS: Students present their screenplay pages. Receive feedback from professor and fellow students.

REQUIRED READING: Chapter 12, "The Role of Dialogue" and Chapter 13, "Dialogue Techniques."

ASSIGNMENT for Week 6: Based on the feedback received, students will rewrite their short screenplay. (Or students will write the second half of their screenplay.)

Week 6

LECTURE: Set Pieces (Chapter 16).

- Make it bigger!
- An event: it's challenging, unique location, complications, twists, something unexpected, conclusion.

IN-CLASS: Students present their screenplay pages. Receive feedback from professor and fellow students.

REQUIRED READING: Chapter 15, "Suspense" and Chapter 16, "Set Pieces."

ASSIGNMENT for the future: Continue writing!

Writing the Short Screenplay: 16-Week Course

Objectives

The goal will be to learn to write compelling scenes, create authentic characters, and complete dynamic short screenplays that can be used in film production courses.

We will begin with writing exercises designed to explore the creative process as well as illustrate some of the basics of writing.

Then we will begin the screenwriting process. Starting with a story concept, students will craft a logline and pitch it to the class, including a brief discussion of the story and characters.

Next write a one-page document which covers all the major beats from the status quo, through the act breaks, to the resolution. This brief synopsis is the first glimpse of your movie on the page. We will discuss your synopsis in class.

Now that you have a basic idea of your story, we really want to focus on your characters. Complete the character exercises which will cover the character's defining personality trait, other traits and qualities, as well as their arc, and a backstory. Also, you will briefly describe the scene where we meet your character, which is so critical to establishing your character.

The rest of the course is spent on writing the screenplay itself.

Outcomes

By the end of the course, students will not only have two or three short screenplays but a clear understanding of the writing process and a solid methodology for future screenplays.

Week 1

LECTURE: Being authentic.

- What makes it feel real?
- Details.
- "No surprise for the writer, no surprise for the reader."

REQUIRED READING: Chapter 2, "Story and You."

OPTIONAL READING: Introduction; Chapter 1, "Why Shorts? Why Features?"

IN-CLASS EXERCISE: Getting to School: Start by making a list of the schools you have attended and how you got there. What is your most vivid memory? What are the important details? What were the important aspects of the trip? People, clothes, shoes, food, weather, car, bicycle… Using your memory of the details, create a short story in prose.

- Students take fifteen to twenty minutes.
- Read and discuss the memory.

ASSIGNMENT for Week 2: Pick one (or up to three) of the prompts below, think through your life, and try to come up with a memory. Write out a page recounting the story. Be sure to punctuate the story with key specific details.

- Favorite childhood toy.
- That time at school when…

- Memorable relative.
- Scary night.
- On our family vacation…
- We were really lost...

The key here is recalling specific details about the story. It's fine to write in prose at this point. (Unless you're dying to try out your screenwriting software.) We're not looking for a long list of random details. Pick the specific details that bring a story to life.

Week 2

LECTURE: Scenes (Chapter 10).

- Two things all scenes must have: plot and emotion.
- Types of conflict.
- Three things all scenes should have: character, style, and elements of the future.
- Scene structure.
- Other important aspects of scenes.
- Format: How your script should look.

IN-CLASS: Students present one of their memory prompt stories. Receive feedback from professor and fellow students.

REQUIRED READING: Chapter 9, "Screenplay Format" and Chapter 10, "Scenes."

ASSIGNMENT for Week 3: Write a one-page scene with no dialogue. The single location scene will have two parts: First the character prepares for an event and second, the aftermath of that event. We do *not* see the event, but it should be clear what the event was and the results of the event. As the character prepares, focus on the character's actions, clothes, the location, props, etc. When the character returns, we should see how these objects are different.

Week 3

LECTURE: Loglines (Chapter 3).

- A great logline is a secret weapon for getting your screenplay headed in the right direction.
- Main character, setting, story, stakes.

- Title, genre, and tone. What kind of movie are we talking about?
- Logline variations: Trying out the key elements.
- Analysis and examination of loglines.

REQUIRED READING: Chapter 3, "Loglines."

IN-CLASS: Students present their *preparation and aftermath* scenes. Receive feedback from professor and fellow students.

ASSIGNMENT for Week 4: Please write loglines for two or three stories that you are considering writing for this class. Or if you are sure about the first story you want to write, try two or three variations on the logline for your story.

Be prepared to briefly discuss the story and characters.

Week 4

LECTURE: Major beats: The basic elements that every story must have.

- Status quo.
- Inciting incident.
- First act break.
- A set piece.
- Midpoint.
- Second act break.
- Resolution.

IN-CLASS: Students present their loglines. Receive feedback from professor and fellow students.

REQUIRED READING: Chapter 4, "Basic Story Structure."

ASSIGNMENT for Week 5: One-page brief synopsis of the major beats. Starting with a revised logline, briefly describe each major beat (two-three sentences). The complete document must be in PDF format, less than one page, with 12-point font, and normal margins.

Week 5

LECTURE: Character (Chapter 5).

- Two parts to creating great characters—defining character and writing in screenplay format.

- Name, defining personality trait, contradiction, big problem, character arc, backstory.
- Writing your character.
- Opening description, clothing, transportation, environment, opening action.
- Read the opening sequences of: *Erin Brockovich*, *Whiplash*, and *Nightcrawler*.

IN-CLASS: Students present their one-page brief synopsis of the major beats. Receive feedback from professor and fellow students.

REQUIRED READING: Chapter 5, "Character."

ASSIGNMENT for Week 6: Complete all the questions for both exercises in Chapter 5, "Character." The complete document should be one-two pages. (Note: Completing the character exercises for any significant character can be extremely helpful but we will only be presenting one main character in class.)

Week 6

LECTURE: The Role of Dialogue (Chapter 12).

- Information and exposition, reveal conflict, reveal characters' relationship, reveal an ongoing relationship, advance the story, build expectations, emotional state of your characters, personality and attitude of your characters, philosophy of your characters.

REQUIRED READING: Chapter 12, "The Role of Dialogue."

ASSIGNMENT for Week 7: Begin writing your screenplay! Write in proper screenplay format. Up to six pages.

(Note: Often, students are writing these short screenplays with the intention of shooting them. Film schools have specific rules which need to be adhered to when shooting. I generally require my students write at least one short that conforms to the shooting rules, while the other can be anything: set underwater, car chases, huge cast, etc.)

Week 7

LECTURE: Dialogue Techniques (Chapter 13).

- Less is more, naturalistic dialogue, heightened dialogue, more techniques, test your dialogue.

IN-CLASS: Students present their screenplay pages. Receive feedback from professor and fellow students.

REQUIRED READING: Chapter 13, "Dialogue Techniques."

ASSIGNMENT for Week 8: Finish writing your screenplay. Write in proper screenplay format. Up to six pages.

Week 8

LECTURE: Suspense (Chapter 15).

- Not just for thrillers.
- Start with the concept, bigger isn't better, dramatic irony, suspense within scenes and sequences, suspense vs. shock.

IN-CLASS: Students present their screenplay pages. Receive feedback from professor and fellow students.

REQUIRED READING: Chapter 15, "Suspense."

ASSIGNMENT for Week 9: Based on the feedback received, students will rewrite the first half of their short screenplay.

Week 9

LECTURE: Set Pieces (Chapter 16).

- Make it bigger!
- An event: it's challenging, unique location, complications, twists, something unexpected, conclusion.

IN-CLASS: Students present their screenplay pages. Receive feedback from professor and fellow students.

REQUIRED READING: Chapter 16, "Set Pieces."

ASSIGNMENT for Week 10: Based on the feedback received, students will rewrite the second half of their short screenplay.

Week 10

LECTURE: Getting the Audience to Care (Chapter 6).

- Techniques to engage the audience.
- Passion, humiliate, treat unfairly, underdog, introduced by…, unlikable characters, strong action.

IN-CLASS: Students present their screenplay pages. Receive feedback from professor and fellow students.

REQUIRED READING: Chapter 6, "Getting the Audience to Care."

ASSIGNMENT for Week 11: Begin writing your second screenplay. Write in proper screenplay format. Up to six pages.

Week 11

LECTURE: Start Fast (Chapter 11).

> • Open with the villain, flash forward, mystery, set piece, defining moment, already dead, confession, drop the bomb.

IN-CLASS: Students present their screenplay pages. Receive feedback from professor and fellow students.

REQUIRED READING: Chapter 11, "Start Fast."

ASSIGNMENT for Week 12: Finish writing your second screenplay. Write in proper screenplay format. Up to six pages.

Week 12

LECTURE: Scene Description (Chapter 14).

> • Location, character, action.
> • Fit the genre.

IN-CLASS: Students present their screenplay pages. Receive feedback from professor and fellow students.

REQUIRED READING: Chapter 14, "Scene Description."

ASSIGNMENT for Week 13: Based on the feedback received, students will rewrite the first half of their second screenplay.

Lecture Note: The remaining weeks can be used to go back to the longer chapters and dive deeper, or move onto other topics not covered in this book such as subplots, theme, relationships, subtext, the business, etc.

Week 13

LECTURE: TBD.

IN-CLASS: Students present their screenplay pages. Receive feedback from professor and fellow students.

REQUIRED READING: TBD.

ASSIGNMENT for Week 14: Based on the feedback received, students will rewrite the second half of their short screenplay.

Week 14

LECTURE: TBD.

IN-CLASS: Students present their screenplay pages. Receive feedback from professor and fellow students.

REQUIRED READING: TBD.

ASSIGNMENT for Week 15: Students can use the final two weeks to polish one of the first two short screenplays they wrote or they can try a third short screenplay.

Week 15

LECTURE: TBD.

IN-CLASS: Students present their screenplay pages. Receive feedback from professor and fellow students.

REQUIRED READING: TBD.

ASSIGNMENT for Week 16: Students will finish the polish pass or finish the second half of their third short screenplay.

Week 16

LECTURE: TBD.

IN-CLASS: Students present their screenplay pages. Receive feedback from professor and fellow students.

REQUIRED READING: TBD.

Writing the Feature Screenplay: 16-Week Course

Objectives

The course goal is to write a complete feature screenplay with dramatic characters and compelling storyline. Six weeks on story development, character, and outline. Ten weeks on the screenplay (ten pages per week with the goal being a hundred-page screenplay.)

Going from an idea to a completed first draft of a feature screenplay in sixteen weeks is a major undertaking and will take sustained effort and focus to accomplish. The best way to accomplish this goal is to attend class each week and complete the weekly assignments.

Beginning with a story concept, craft a logline and pitch it to the class, including a brief discussion of the story and characters.

Next write a one-page document which covers all the major beats from the status quo, through the act breaks, to the resolution. This brief synopsis is the first glimpse of your movie on the page. We will discuss your synopsis in class.

Now that you have a basic idea of your story, we really want to focus on your characters. Complete the character exercises which will cover the character's defining personality trait, other traits and qualities, as well as arc, and backstory. Also, briefly describe your character's opening scene which is so critical to establishing your character.

Next take your character study worksheets along with the brief synopsis and expand them into an outline. This document will take you from the opening scene to the resolution of your story. It doesn't include every scene, but you should be able to clearly "see the movie."

The rest of the course is spent on writing the screenplay itself. You will need to write approximately ten pages a week. We will proceed in this fashion until the end of the semester, and you have completed the first draft of your screenplay.

Outcomes

By the end of the course, students will not only have a feature screenplay but a clear understanding of the writing process and a solid methodology for future screenplays.

Week 1

LECTURE: Loglines (Chapter 3).

- A great logline is a secret weapon for getting your screenplay headed in the right direction.
- Main character, setting, story, stakes.
- Title, genre, and tone. What kind of movie are we talking about?
- Logline variations: trying out the various elements.

• Analysis and examination of loglines.

REQUIRED READING: Chapter 2, "Story and You" and Chapter 3, "Loglines."

OPTIONAL READING: Introduction; Chapter 1, "Why Shorts? Why Features?"

IN-CLASS EXERCISE: Students break into groups of two or three. Choose two or three popular films and work together to write a logline for the films. Ten to fifteen minutes for students to write the loglines. Twenty to thirty minutes for discussion.

ASSIGNMENT for Week 2: Please write loglines for two or three stories that you are considering writing for this class. Or if you are sure about the story you want to write, try two or three variations on the logline for your story.

Be prepared to briefly discuss the story and characters.

Week 2

LECTURE: Major beats, the basic elements that every story must have.

> • Status quo.
>
> • Inciting incident.
>
> • First act break.
>
> • A set piece.
>
> • Midpoint.
>
> • Second act break.
>
> • Resolution.

IN-CLASS: Students present their loglines. Receive feedback from professor and fellow students.

REQUIRED READING: Chapter 4, "Basic Story Structure."

OPTIONAL READING: Chapter 7, "Character-Based Structure."

ASSIGNMENT for Week 3: One-page brief synopsis of the major beats.

Starting with a revised logline, briefly describe each major beat (two-three sentences). The complete document must be in PDF format, less than one page, with 12-point font, and normal margins.

Week 3

LECTURE: Character (Chapter 5).

- Two parts to creating great characters—defining character and writing in screenplay format.
- Name, defining personality trait, contradiction, big problem, character arc, backstory.
- Writing your character.
- Opening description, clothing, transportation, environment, opening action.
- Read the opening sequences of: *Erin Brockovich, Whiplash,* and *Nightcrawler.*

IN-CLASS: Students present their one-page brief synopsis of the Major Beats. Receive feedback from professor and fellow students.

REQUIRED READING: Chapter 5, "Character."

ASSIGNMENT for Week 4: Complete all the questions for both exercises in Chapter 5, "Character." The complete document should be one-two pages. (Note: Completing the character exercises for any significant character can be extremely helpful but we will only be presenting one main character in class.)

Week 4

LECTURE: Outline (Chapter 8).

- A road map.
- Outline, beat sheet, step outline, outline with intentions, treatment.

IN-CLASS: Students present their main character. Receive feedback from professor and fellow students.

REQUIRED READING: Chapter 8, "Outline."

OPTIONAL READING: Chapter 7, "Character-Based Structure."

ASSIGNMENT for Week 5: Begin writing your outline. Start by solidifying the major beats of your story. Then flesh out the story, summarizing the beats. (It does not have to have every beat.) Complete the first act and the second act through the midpoint (halfway point of your story).

Week 5

LECTURE: Screenplay Format (Chapter 9).

- Start off right: Use screenwriting software, formatting, other aspects.

IN-CLASS: Students present the first half of their outline. Receive feedback from professor and fellow students.

REQUIRED READING: Chapter 9, "Screenplay Format."

ASSIGNMENT for Week 6: Finish writing your outline. Flesh out the remainder of the story, summarizing the beats. (It does not have to have every beat.) Complete from the midpoint to the conclusion of your story.

Week 6

LECTURE: Scenes (Chapter 10).

- Two things all scenes must have: plot and emotion.
- Types of conflict.
- Three things all scenes should have: character, style, and elements of the future.
- Scene structure.
- Other important aspects of scenes.
- Format: How your script should look.

IN-CLASS: Students present the second half of their outline. Receive feedback from professor and fellow students.

REQUIRED READING: Chapter 10, "Scenes."

ASSIGNMENT for Week 7: Begin writing your screenplay! Write in proper screenplay format. Up to ten pages.

Week 7

LECTURE: Getting an Audience to Care (Chapter 6).

- Techniques to engage the audience.
- Passion, humiliate, treat unfairly, underdog, introduced by…, unlikable characters, strong action.

IN-CLASS: Students present their screenplay pages. Receive feedback from professor and fellow students.

REQUIRED READING: Chapter 6, "Getting the Audience to Care."

ASSIGNMENT for Week 8: Continue writing your screenplay. Write in proper screenplay format. Up to ten pages.

Week 8

LECTURE: Start Fast (Chapter 11).

- Open with the villain, flash forward, mystery, set piece, defining moment, already dead, confession, drop the bomb.

IN-CLASS: Students present their screenplay pages. Receive feedback from professor and fellow students.

REQUIRED READING: Chapter 11, "Start Fast."

ASSIGNMENT for Week 9: Continue writing your screenplay. Write in proper screenplay format. Up to ten pages.

Week 9

LECTURE: The Role of Dialogue (Chapter 12).

- Information and exposition, reveal conflict, reveal characters' relationship, reveal an ongoing relationship, advance the story, build expectations, emotional state of your characters, personality and attitude of your characters, philosophy of your characters.

REQUIRED READING: Chapter 12, "The Role of Dialogue."

ASSIGNMENT for Week 10: Continue writing your screenplay. Write in proper screenplay format. Up to ten pages.

Week 10

LECTURE: Dialogue Techniques (Chapter 13).

- Less is more, naturalistic dialogue, heightened dialogue, more techniques, test your dialogue.

IN-CLASS: Students present their screenplay pages. Receive feedback from professor and fellow students.

REQUIRED READING: Chapter 13, "Dialogue Techniques."

ASSIGNMENT for Week 11: Continue writing your screenplay. Write in proper screenplay format. Up to ten pages.

Week 11

LECTURE: Scene Description (Chapter 14).

- Location, character, action.
- Fit the genre.

IN-CLASS: Students present their screenplay pages. Receive feedback from professor and fellow students.

REQUIRED READING: Chapter 14, "Scene Description."

ASSIGNMENT for Week 12: Continue writing your screenplay. Write in proper screenplay format. Up to ten pages.

Week 12

LECTURE: Suspense (Chapter 15).

- Not just for thrillers.
- Start with the concept, bigger isn't better, dramatic irony, suspense within scenes and sequences, suspense vs. shock.

IN-CLASS: Students present their screenplay pages. Receive feedback from professor and fellow students.

REQUIRED READING: Chapter 15, "Suspense."

ASSIGNMENT for Week 13: Continue writing your screenplay. Write in proper screenplay format. Up to ten pages.

Week 13

LECTURE: Set Pieces (Chapter 16).

- Make it bigger!
- An event: it's challenging, unique location, complications, twists, something unexpected, conclusion.

IN-CLASS: Students present their screenplay pages. Receive feedback from professor and fellow students.

REQUIRED READING: Chapter 16, "Set Pieces."

ASSIGNMENT for Week 14: Continue writing your screenplay. Write in proper screenplay format. Up to ten pages.

Lecture Note: The remaining weeks can be used to go back to the longer chapters and dive deeper, or to move onto other topics not covered in this book such as subplots, theme, relationships, subtext, the business, etc.

Week 14

LECTURE: TBD.

IN-CLASS: Students present their screenplay pages. Receive feedback from professor and fellow students.

REQUIRED READING: TBD.

ASSIGNMENT for Week 15: Continue writing your screenplay. Write in proper screenplay format. Up to ten pages.

Week 15

LECTURE: TBD.

IN-CLASS: Students present their screenplay pages. Receive feedback from professor and fellow students.

REQUIRED READING: TBD.

ASSIGNMENT for Week 16: Continue writing your screenplay. Write in proper screenplay format. Up to ten pages.

Week 16

LECTURE: TBD.

IN-CLASS: Students present their screenplay pages. Receive feedback from professor and fellow students.

REQUIRED READING: TBD.

Final Thoughts

Hopefully these lesson plans will allow you to run a positive, engaging class. Or guide you as you make your own path. I've tried to order the lessons and chapters in a way that makes the most sense but obviously some chapters can be moved around. And I'm sure many of you will move them around. Good luck and happy writing!

Glossary

action See **scene description.**

ally or **sidekick** The protagonist's best friend and trusted confidant.

antagonist The villain of the story.

a-story The main story. A term only used when differentiating from the subplot or b-story.

Asymmetric Information Management (AIM) Technique developed for law enforcement officers to help determine whether someone they are questioning is telling the truth or not.

attachments A pre-production agreement of intent to participate in a film or television project by an actor, director, producer, etc.

backstory A key event or relationship from the character's past.

beat or **story beat** When the character takes action or something happens to the character.

beat sheet or **step outline** A detailed outline that includes most, if not all, scenes, but does not include scene details and dialogue.

big problem The main personal issue that the protagonist must overcome. It is often the issue that is keeping the character from achieving what they want.

billboarding Separating or differentiating an important piece of information on the page, so it is more easily seen by the reader.

biopic A movie about a real person, living or dead.

blocking Production term for how the characters will stand and move within a scene.

b-story A separate story from the main story. Often a romance or family relationship. See also **subplot.**

button or **comedic button** A final joke to end a comedic scene or sequence.

calling card A short film or feature screenplay that demonstrates a high level of skill.

call to adventure A beat from the Hero's Journey which disrupts the main character's life and motivates them into action. Similar to inciting incident.

camera setups A production term for separate camera positions when shooting scenes.

character arc How a character changes over the course of the story.

character study A film that focuses on a unique character, often eschewing traditional structure.

chyron Text that appears on screen. See also **super**.

the complete package A type of story that has not only a dynamic start, but a clear end point.

conflict Occurs when an obstacle is keeping the main character from getting what they want.

consequences Results of action or inaction by a character. Often the consequences are implied by the *stakes*.

contradiction In terms of a character, it is an unexpected character trait that contradicts the defining personality trait, thus keeping the character from becoming too clichéd.

coverage A summary of the story and key elements of a screenplay. Used by film industry professionals to quickly evaluate a script.

creative lie A story based on the main character telling a lie (often by pretending to be someone they are not). These stories have a natural conclusion when the lie is discovered.

Dan Harmon's Story Circle A character-based story structure with eight steps.

the debate After the inciting incident, a consideration of all the character's options.

defining moment A single event that dramatically affects a character for the rest of their life.

defining personality trait The basic idea of who your character is and how they act most of the time.

dialogue Text that is meant to be spoken by the characters.

dramatic irony When the audience knows something before a character does.

drop the bomb A piece of information that changes a situation dramatically.

dual dialogue A screenplay format technique where two characters are speaking simultaneously.

elements of the future Scenes should compel the audience to consider what is going to happen to the main character.

emotional character type A character that acts according to their gut and lets emotions guide their decisions.

emotion (for the audience) The reaction of the audience to what is happening to a character. Can be different from the emotion the character experiences.

escalating event A story beat that immediately elevates the stakes, forcing the character into action.

execution-dependent A story that relies heavily on writing skill since it focuses on character and relationship rather than a dramatic plot.

exposition Dialogue that reveals information about characters, plot, etc.

EXT. An abbreviation for *exterior,* used in sluglines.

false victory A point in a story where it appears that the main character has succeeded, but this "victory" is quickly reversed.

first act break The main character decides how to deal with the problem caused by the inciting incident. This choice will be the goal for the entire second act.

flash forward Placing a dramatic scene from later in the story earlier (out of chronological order).

flashback A dramatic scene from earlier in the story, often from before the story began.

functional logline A logline that focuses on the key elements. Used to develop a story, but can also work as the pitch logline when strong enough.

general meeting An introductory meeting with professionals in the film and television business. Also known as *meet and greets*.

genre The type or category a story falls into. Some common genres include comedy, horror, action, drama, and sci-fi.

get out early Ending a scene quickly.

goal This what the main character desires or is the task the protagonist must complete.

heightened dialogue Larger-than-life dialogue, outside of what we might call normal. The opposite of **naturalistic dialogue**.

heightened genre When a popular genre like horror goes beyond the basic elements, adding layers of intelligence, sophistication, and social commentary. Sometimes referred to as *elevated genre*.

herald A character that delivers the call to adventure or rings the warning bell when there is danger. This is a great character for setting the stakes. Other character types can take on the role of the *herald*.

Hero's Journey A popular, character-based story structure. Often visualized as a circle, or circular, because the main character begins in his home, leaves on the adventure, and eventually returns.

Heroine's Journey A variation on the *Hero's Journey*, with a feminine lens.

high-concept A story with an easy-to-understand concept that is intriguing and naturally dramatic.

hook Starting off the story with a bang, something that will grab the audience's attention, and make them want to read/watch more.

idea file List of story ideas, characters, bits of conversations, or any interesting stuff that might become a story or might be added to a story.

I/E. or INT./EXT. An abbreviation for *interior/exterior*, used in sluglines. Occurs when both the interior and exterior are visible in a scene.

inciting incident A disruptive event, that changes everything for the main character, forcing them into action.

INT. An abbreviation for *interior* used in sluglines.

intellectual conflict When there is an intellectual obstacle that is keeping a character from achieving their goal, i.e. a puzzle to be solved.

intercut between Usually used in all caps after establishing characters in two different locations. Generally used during a phone conversation.

larger-than-life character A character who seems to act and react outside of what we might call normal.

logical character type A character that is the classic rational thinker, who plans things out, coming up with the most logical solution.

logline One or two sentences that summarize a story. Also, should include title, genre, and tone.

low-density narrative Story that has very few plot points, focusing on other elements like character or visuals.

MacGuffin A term coined by Alfred Hitchcock for a plot device that interests or motivates the character to take action.

main character or **protagonist** This is the character that the story centers on. We will venture on a journey with the protagonist.

major beats The key beats in a story.

meet and greet An introductory meeting with professionals in the film and television business. Also known as a **general meeting**.

meet-cute The scene where characters meet—a.k.a. where the romance starts.

mentor A character that guides the main character. They tend to be the conscience of the main character and the embodiment of the theme.

midpoint A key beat around the middle of the second act (also the middle of the story.) The midpoint tends to add a new dimension to the story. It often increases the stakes.

montage A series of short scenes to show the passage of time, usually to indicate a change that occurs across time.

moral conflict When there is a moral obstacle that is keeping a character from achieving their goal.

naturalistic dialogue Dialogue that sounds authentic, the opposite of **heightened dialogue**.

needs See **wants vs. needs**.

obstacle Anything that prevents the main character from achieving their goal.

opening action What your character is doing when we meet them.

ordinary world The main character's situation before the *inciting incident* or *call to adventure* disrupts their life.

O.S. (Off-Screen) Typically used in parentheticals after a character's name to indicate we do not see the character. Similar to **O.C.**, or **Off-Camera**.

outline A functional summary of what happens from the beginning to the end of the story, avoiding detail and dialogue. This is a bare bones document, an x-ray of your story.

outline with intentions This is an outline or beat sheet that includes the reason behind each beat or sequence. It helps you understand not only what's happening but why.

physical conflict When there is a physical obstacle that is keeping a character from achieving their goal.

pitch A verbal or written summary of a story for the purpose of selling that story. Can be a variety of lengths from logline to complete synopsis, depending on the situation.

pitch deck A document to help sell a story concept. It will start with the title and logline. It can also include photos, a short synopsis, main characters, possibly a treatment, a budget, and any attachments like actors.

planting and payoff Planting is the setting up of something important that will come into play later in the story (the payoff.)

plot Action taken by a character. Over the course of a story, the plot is a series of interesting and dynamic actions.

proof of concept A short film that demonstrates a story concept, characters, and world, as well as demonstrating the skill of the filmmaker.

protagonist or **main character** This is the character that the story centers on. We will venture on a journey with the protagonist.

resolution Also called the *end place*. The third act concludes when the main character finds a new way to achieve their goal.

scene description Text that describes the location, the characters, and the action that takes place within a scene.

scene numbers Production screenplays are numbered to help coordinate the production process. Scene numbers are placed to the left and right of each slugline.

screenplay format Generally accepted, unique formatting for a film or television story.

second act break The main character fails to achieve their goal. At the beginning of the second act, the main character decides to go for a goal. The second act ends when they fail to achieve this goal. It's often called the *lowest low*. The main character hits rock bottom, they are defeated.

set piece Taking a key scene or sequence and maximizing it by increasing as many dramatic elements as possible.

setup A scene preparation often before an important action.

shapeshifter or **trickster** A character who could be helpful or could be very dangerous, the hero must decide which.

silent types A character type that has little or no dialogue.

skeptic The devil's advocate. The skeptic can be loyal to the protagonist or not.

slugline A key element of screenplay formatting. A slugline is used to indicate the beginning of a new scene and is always capitalized.

spec script A screenplay written on the speculation that it may sell as opposed to writing it as a (paid) assignment.

stakes That which hangs in the balance. It could be a positive like a reward or negative, a punishment or death.

status quo Introduce the main character in their *ordinary world*.

step outline or **beat sheet** A more detailed outline that includes most, if not all, scenes, but avoids scene details and dialogue.

story This is the goal the main character decides to pursue, usually in response to the inciting incident. It should be something active and challenging.

story beat Any action a character takes or action that happens to a character.

style Screenplays should be stylish and evocative. Every word on the page should not only add to the story but also add to the tone, enhancing the mood.

subplot A separate story from the main story. Often a romance or family relationship. See also **b-story**.

super Short for superimposition, meaning the text appears on screen. See also **chyron**.

suspense Anxiousness regarding the uncertainty of the outcome.

tempter This character tries to stop the protagonist from achieving their goal. Similar to the *antagonist* but not necessarily working with them.

tests Obstacles and challenges to the main character.

theme The moral or message of the story. There can be more than one.

three-act structure A classic story form that was first recognized by the Greeks. The three acts correspond to the beginning, the middle, and the end.

threshold guardian A character or a situation that challenges our hero, a roadblock in our hero's journey.

tone The style of a story. In Hollywood-speak, it often refers to a movie that is similar in style.

treatment A treatment is an outline written with style to capture more of the tone and mood of the story. Treatments are written in prose and should read like a story. They are basically used to pitch a screenplay story.

the visual poem A film that focuses on visuals over story.

V.O. (voice-over) Typically used in parentheses after a character's name to indicate that the character is not physically present either on screen or off. It is often for a narrator but can be used in other situations as well.

voice Your voice just means your style, your personality as a writer.

voice of a generation Dialogue that reflects opinions, thoughts, or emotions that represent a generation.

wants vs. needs The character wants something but tends to lack awareness of what they need. They must figure it out over the course of the story.

wrylies or **parentheticals** Physical direction or direction for the reading of dialogue. Wrylies should always be on their own line appearing after the character name. They may occur before, in the middle of, or after the dialogue.